Lincoln
and the
Politics of
Christian
Love

Lincoln
and the
Politics of
Christian
Love

Grant N. Havers

University of Missouri Press
Columbia and London

Library of Congress Cataloging-in-Publication Data

Havers, Grant N., 1965-
  Lincoln and the politics of Christian love / Grant N. Havers.
     p. cm.
  Includes bibliographical references and index.
  ISBN 978-0-8262-1857-5 (hardcover : alk. paper)
  1. Lincoln, Abraham, 1809-1865—Religion. 2. Lincoln, Abraham, 1809-
1865—Political and social views. 3. Charity—Political aspects—United
States—History—19th century. I. Title.
  E457.2.H38 2009
  973.7092—dc22   2009028216

∞™ This paper meets the requirements of the
American National Standard for Permanence of Paper
for Printed Library Materials, Z39.48, 1984.

Designer: FoleyDesign
Typesetter: BOOKCOMP
Printer and binder: Integrated Book Technology, Inc.
Typeface: Minion

TO THE MEMORY OF MY FATHER,

MURRAY HALL HAVERS (1919–2007),

AND TO MY MOTHER,

WENDY HAVERS

Contents

⌒

Preface

∽

*T*his book is the culmination of my long-standing interest in the implications of biblical religion for politics in the United States. While my primary training is in political philosophy, my interests have always combined the humanities and social sciences. Now that the second Bush presidency has left the stage of world history, having inspired a torrent of mainly critical literature on the effects of faith on politics, it is long overdue for Christian scholars to defend their faith traditions with the tools of political philosophy, history, and theology. The ethic of Christian charity, to which even secular figures often lay claim, is worthy of defense in the political realm and beyond. As a life-long student of the complex legacy of Abraham Lincoln, I have learned to appreciate both the positive effects of faith on politics as well as the misuse of religion for political purposes. Charity, the ethic that promotes humility and moral consistency in all realms of life, can help us understand the difference, as Lincoln taught.

The debate over the religiosity of Lincoln's legacy reminds us that our secular age has never transcended the need for religion. Both religious and secular scholars living in the post-Bush era would do well to critique the idolatrous implications of promoting liberal democracy as the best regime for all human beings, a quasi-religious project that is often falsely attributed to Lincoln's legacy. The elevation of *democracy* to a "god word" dangerously exaggerates the depth of commitment and understanding that *all* human beings are likely to have for this regime. As a result, wars for democracy have made the world a more unsafe place. It was not always charitable for the Bush administration to assume that the rest of the world desires the same mode of statecraft that Americans enjoy. Let us hope that the new Obama administration shows greater realism and prudence.

I have greatly benefited from scholars who have already established themselves as experts in the complex and fascinating field of religion and politics. First and foremost I would like to express my deepest gratitude to Paul Gottfried, whose encyclopedic knowledge of conservative thought has constantly enriched my work. Paul, who read through various drafts of this manuscript, unfailingly showed great patience, encouragement, and wisdom while offering invaluable suggestions for improvement. My former dissertation supervisor, Brayton Polka, must also receive my profound gratitude for being the first scholar in my educational journey to take the Bible seriously as a work, perhaps *the* work, of politics in the Western tradition. Thanks must also go to John von Heyking, Bruce Shelvey, Robynne Healey, and Bruce Frohnen for providing information on research sources and publication. I am also grateful to Trinity Western University for support that made possible a sabbatical leave in the first half of 2007. I remain indebted to Bev Jarrett at the University of Missouri Press for enthusiastically embracing and supporting the work of an unknown academic writing his first book; thanks must also go to her colleague Sara Davis for guiding the process of manuscript preparation. Annette Wenda deserves infinite credit for her meticulous copyediting of this manuscript. The two anonymous reviewers provided valuable insights in pointing out areas in the manuscript where greater clarity was warranted. Last but certainly not least, I thank my fiancée, Theresa Willmer, for showing Job-like patience, wisdom, and support as her husband-to-be strove to finish this work.

This book is dedicated to my mother and father, whose keen sense of history will always inspire in me the Faulknerian recognition that the past is not dead, nor is it even past. I am most fortunate for having been raised by parents whose interest in the world, past and present, militates against any temptation to focus on the parochialism of the moment. Having witnessed the horrors of world war in the twentieth century, my mother and father taught their children to face challenges with wisdom, faith, and charity. As my generation faces a new millennium with its unique dangers of religious terror and economic turbulence, I shall continue to look back to my parents as inspiring examples of strength in the face of adversity.

Lincoln
and the
Politics of
Christian
Love

Introduction

And now faith, hope, and love abide, these three;
and the greatest of these is love.

—1 Cor. 13:13

The symbols and myths become . . . the *first*
order of business for the political scientist.

—Willmoore Kendall and George W. Carey, *The Basic
Symbols of the American Political Tradition*

Our age is obsessed with the rise of belief. Since the terror attacks of September 11, 2001, and the start of the Iraq war in 2003, there has been a flood of literature warning of the growing power of religion around the world. Various opinion makers have uttered ominous warnings about the rise of religious fundamentalism and its threat to long-established civil liberties. Anxiety over the survival of the secular state abounds. The mood among secular intellectuals is Spenglerian, with a deeply felt pessimism over the survival of reason and freedom. A return to the Dark Ages remains a possibility for many voices of secularism. The synthesis of politics and religion, which many thought the triumph of liberal democracy had put to rest at the end of the cold war, now arises once again with a vengeance. The separation of church and state—the greatest achievement of the liberal Enlightenment—is supposedly in jeopardy. The rise of religion in the arena of politics is testing the optimistic creed (echoed since the end of the cold war) that liberal democracy would vanquish its old enemy, as it once defeated the ideologies of Nazism, fascism, and communism.[1]

The purpose of my study is not to add another voice to those who fear that a new age of theocratic tyranny has returned. Rather, my purpose is to explain, and even defend, the political usage of a traditionally religious principle, that of *charity* or Christian love in American politics. Out of all the historically religious credos that have intruded into the American public square, "love thy neighbor as thyself" should be welcomed by believer and unbeliever alike. I shall argue that this ethic of love is deeply political in opposing hypocrisy in all aspects of life (private and public), and in demanding that political leaders place themselves in the position of others whose lives they affect. The empathy that charity requires must enter the realm of politics. The fact that the practice of charity has always affected both the private and the public realms is reflected in the English language. Although the proverbial saying "charity begins at home" reminds us of personal morality, the association of charity with social welfare embodies a collective duty. The golden rule of "doing unto others what we want them to do to us" has always been, as a principle of human dignity for all, at once private and public. If charity is indeed the highest law of ethics, then this law must affect even the most secular aspects of life.

I have chosen the context of the American political tradition to explain the political implications of a historically religious credo, since the United States best illustrates that paradox of a nation that is both deeply religious and secular. There is nothing new in claiming that religion and politics in the United States have always been intertwined; as the American political scientist Willmoore Kendall once quipped, the wall between church and state has always been "porous."[2] However, there is more to the political usage of religion than simply an entwinement of secular and theological themes.

The fact that Jesus closely relates love of God with love of neighbor (Matt. 22:36–40) may well provoke secular anxieties, for these two credos

---

1. Francis Fukuyama is the most famous defender of the "end of history" thesis. See his study *The End of History and the Last Man.* Although Fukuyama has withdrawn his support for the Iraq war, he has not given up the Wilsonian goal of global democracy building. See his *America at the Crossroads: Democracy, Power, and the Neoconservative Legacy.*

2. Kendall, *Willmoore Kendall Contra Mundum,* 342.

are not exactly identical. As Anders Nygren argued in his classic study of Christian love, the love of neighbor can easily fall into a conditional attitude of affection toward one's community: love for love, hate for hate. Love of God, however, is not based on the condition of reciprocity. This imperative demands that one love without expectation of reward or like treatment. The love of God places a demand on the love of neighbor that is the essence of a very strict Christian morality.[3] The "God talk" that is central to the ethic of charity, especially its demanding meaning, seems out of synch with a secular age that once pronounced the end of religious belief as an influence over the modern mind.

Still, anyone who fears the return of religion to Western democracy is betraying tremendous ignorance, particularly of America, for faith never left the public sphere. Those who fear this return make two erroneous assumptions. First, the secular Enlightenment of the seventeenth and eighteenth centuries once successfully removed religion from the political context. Second, the history of modernity is characteristically irreligious. Both of these premises were never true (particularly in America), and their currency today only adds confusion to the debate over the role of religion in modernity. The modern age *never* banished religion successfully, especially since modern ideas possess a religious root. Thus, the fear that religion has returned to the public realm is a colossal misunderstanding, since it never disappeared in the first place. Moreover, there is nothing sinister about the political usage of religion if one properly understands what a religiously based ethic like charity truly means for politics.

As a Christian and a political philosopher, I have always been interested in comprehending the politics of scripture. If it is true, as Jesus famously teaches, that "love thy neighbor as thyself" is akin to love of God, then Christian love must be the guiding imperative for all aspects of life, including politics.[4] Although I do not intend to provide a commentary on the most famous biblical passages that express the priority of charity over all other biblical doctrines, I humbly stand with Jesus and

---

3. Anders Nygren, *Agape and Eros*, 97–99.

4. Whenever necessary or appropriate, I also alternately refer to the principle of agape (from the New Testament Greek) or *caritas* (from the Vulgate), as well as the colloquial "golden rule." I see no benefit from distinguishing between the meaning of *agape* and *caritas*. Although there may be valid reason to do so in a book on theology, there is no equivalent reason in a work on political theology.

Saint Paul on the primacy of this ethic as the highest truth of Christian revelation.

The application of the golden rule to politics, however, has been rare, to say the least. There is a long tradition of resistance to what I call the "politics of charity" in the Western tradition. From Machiavelli onward, many political philosophers have dismissed Christian love as too sentimental and otherworldly for use in the tough-minded and unforgiving realm of statecraft.[5] When the more radical formulation "love thy enemy as thyself" receives consideration, the relation between Christian ethics and politics becomes even less obvious. Why should any self-respecting regime love anyone who is not a citizen? Why is it necessary or even prudent to treat strangers as neighbors, as Jesus commands in the parable of the Good Samaritan (Luke 10) or the Sermon on the Mount (Matt. 5:44)?

For that matter, most Christian thinkers have not understood charity as directly political. Indeed, the few authors who discuss the politics of charity usually conclude that this ethic requires the abandonment of all political loyalties.[6] Apparently, the realm of Caesar truly has nothing to do with that of Christ. (Perhaps for this reason, one of the greatest Christian philosophers of love, Søren Kierkegaard, is silent on political matters in his major treatise on charity, *Works of Love.*)

Nevertheless, a few prominent figures have occasionally acknowledged the close relation between charity and politics. Secular political philosopher Hannah Arendt once wrote that it is impossible to understand "the terrifying question of good and evil" without taking into account the fact that Jesus inspired the "only completely valid, completely convincing experience" that the West has had with "active love of goodness as the inspiring principle of all actions." Moreover, some of the most important figures in American political history have dramatically associated charity with politics. Evangelical populist William Jennings Bryan asserted that Christ gave the American people "a platform more central than any political party has ever written" when he called upon his people to love their neighbors as themselves.[7]

Although I do not intend to provide a study of biblical theology, my purpose is to show that the ethic of Christian charity has often decisively influenced the American tradition of political thought, a reality

---

5. See Machiavelli, *The Prince,* chap. 18.
6. See John Howard Yoder, *The Politics of Jesus.* Yoder is a pacifist.
7. Arendt, *On Revolution,* 81–82; Bryan, "The Prince of Peace," 148–49.

that then makes the separation between religion and politics artificial. My main focus is on the thought and rhetoric of President Abraham Lincoln, who, more than any other leader in his nation's history, boldly articulated a politics of charity. As students of Lincoln well know, this president often invoked charity as the great ethic that condemned the practice of slavery (if no one desires to be a slave, no one can enslave another). Yet Lincoln's use of charity did not stop with the struggle against slavery. By the end of his presidency, it was Lincoln's hope that the imperative of "charity for all" would become the highest political ethic of the nation, a moral force opposed to hypocrisy in the public square as well as an inspiration to heal the conflicts of a divided nation.

Despite my discussion of political philosophy in the pages to follow, I am inclined to classify this work as *political theology*. Most secular academics tend to separate the two fields: political philosophy studies the human understanding of politics, while political theology reflects God's revelation.[8] My contention is that, at least since Lincoln, this separation has never been successful in American political thought, although there have been many procrustean attempts to impose an artificial separation. The fact is that religion and politics have always been mutually dependent in American history, which makes it all the more surprising that the doctrine of charity has received so little attention among political scientists.

The uniqueness of the American use of charity in politics has not received much treatment even in the vast Lincoln literature. A recent study by Matthew Holland of the importance of this subject has gone a long way toward filling this lacuna. What Holland understands as "civic charity" is the ethic of teaching human beings to be "dear" and "affectionate" toward each other in the political realm. The author correctly teaches that Lincoln's great speeches on charity demand far more of Americans than John Winthrop or Thomas Jefferson, who also taught charity as the highest ethic for humanity. In Holland's view, Lincoln's political use of charity demands "compassion over malice, communal attachment over individual isolation and apathy, justice tempered by mercy." The republic has "agapic" obligations that a "timeless" and "pure" political religion of love must embody by adhering to a "transcendent sense of political

---

8. See Leo Strauss, *What Is Political Philosophy? and Other Studies,* 13. I discuss Strauss's ideas as they relate to American political thought in Chapter 5.

justice."[9] Yet it is not clear just what the politics of charity must demand from Americans. The vagueness of Holland's rhetoric on charity does not address the worries of many Americans (and not just in the Old South) that Lincoln's use of charity requires endless social revolution to achieve perfect equality. Specifically, neither Holland's study nor any other known to me addresses questions of great importance to my own research: How far should a politics of charity go in the American context, and how far should it go on a global scale? Is it the mission of Americans, as a "chosen people," to export charity through the promotion of democracy? In plain terms, just how universal is charity? An answer to these questions, which are all too relevant for our time, requires a study of the tension between rhetoric and reality that characterizes debates over charity in the history of American political thought.

CHARITY AND THE QUESTION OF AMERICAN DEMOCRACY

Why, then, is charity so important to the political realm of America? For now, my best preliminary answer reveals my twentieth-century focus. A proper understanding of the distinctively American use of charity in politics can restrain some of the most troubling ideologies of our time. One of these ideologies is the promotion of democracy on a global scale. The post–cold war period has persuaded the most influential American leaders of our time that democracy (American style) is the best regime for all of humanity. Whatever one's choice of appellation for the belief that the entire globe yearns for American democracy (*neoconservatism, natural right, cold war liberalism,* and *democratic universalism* are all worthy terms), this idolization of democracy deserves tremendous scrutiny. I believe that a politics of charity is an appropriate basis for critique of this idolatry.

If the reader is puzzled about my use of charity against the promotion of democracy, I understand. Citizens of Western democracies are so used to the promotion of democracy as the best regime that it is surely incom-

---

9. Holland, *Bonds of Affection: Civic Charity and the Making of America—Winthrop, Jefferson, and Lincoln,* 194, 214, 229–30, 234. Both Holland and I discuss Lincoln's views on charity in great detail. Unlike Holland's study, however, my own focuses on the debate over the political implications of these views for Lincoln's presidency and historic legacy.

prehensible to disassociate charity from a regime dedicated to human rights, liberties, and equality for all. Is it not charitable to build a decent regime like democracy, as every American politician from Ronald Reagan to Barack Obama has declared? My quarrel, however, is not with democracy per se; I personally prefer citizenship in a democracy over any of its rivals. My objection is to the ideological *elevation* of democracy to the status of the best regime for all of humanity, without accounting for the particular religious foundations of the American version of this regime.

In opposing this ideology, the centrality of Lincoln's politics of charity will be apparent throughout this study. If I am correct in arguing that Lincoln taught that charity is the indispensable *precondition* of democracy, then it must follow that the citizens of a potential democracy should embrace a Christian ethic before their efforts on behalf of democracy bear any fruit. Even in a nation where the vast majority of the population was Christian, the universal knowledge of charity did not prevent civil war, although this president in his second inaugural address famously called upon the application of charity to all to heal the nation's wounds. If a nation with Christian roots could not easily practice charity, can nations whose citizenry is not steeped in knowledge of this ethic forge a more successful democracy?

This line of thinking, once again, is out of synch with the political credos of our time. Neoconservatives and liberal democrats alike have argued that the vast majority of human beings desire democracy, regardless of religious faith. In the process, they invoke Lincoln as the prophet of democratic universalism. The fact that America has a Christian history that was essential to the success of its democracy is unimportant to these ideological factions. Ironically, supporters of democracy as the best regime replace one religion (Christianity) with a secular leap of faith in the natural desire of all peoples to become liberal democrats.

The Iraq war has blown this last assumption to smithereens. Yet the unique drama of Iraq is not the exception that proves the rule. If human beings are not used to appreciating love or moral obligation as a call to oppose the hypocritical mistreatment of others (as slavery dramatically illustrated, for Lincoln), democracy simply cannot work. I am not suggesting that Western democracies with Christian roots are necessarily charitable; Lincoln sometimes engaged in actions that violated the spirit of this ethic (as his many critics point out). I am simply suggesting that the historically Christian precondition of charity is a necessary, though insufficient, condition of American democracy. Unless America plans to teach charity to all human beings while it spreads democracy on a global basis, democratic universalism is bound to fail. The universalism of charity is not identical to the universal triumph of democracy.

Still, why should a democracy insist that its citizens be charitable? As Lincoln reminded his fellow Americans, no regime can survive indefinitely if there is little attempt for citizens to put themselves in the position of others. Although "love" comes across as sentimental and unrealistic (as many critics of charity have observed), this ethic requires a great deal of sober intellectual reflection about one's "neighbors" and "enemies." Long before his second inaugural address, Lincoln taught that the eventual victors in the Civil War must place themselves in the position of the vanquished. Even before his presidency, Lincoln called upon Northerners to admit that they were complicit in maintaining the practice of slavery (northern industries greatly profited from southern commodities manufactured by slaves). Although it is sometimes fashionable for theologians to distinguish the Old Testament "love of thy neighbor" from the New Testament "love of thy enemy," the American Civil War completely blurred this distinction. Neighbors became enemies, a tragedy that Lincoln hoped would soon pass after the end of hostilities. (Sadly, it did not.)

In calling upon Northerners to understand the South, Lincoln was obviously not condoning the practice of slavery. He was, however, setting a very high standard for the practice of true democracy. Charity is a two-way street. Democracy loses its moral authority if one faction can oppress the other. The sad reality of our time is that democracies have not lived up to this standard of excellence; even the age of Lincoln did not. Nevertheless, it is hard to imagine how any of us could morally critique political misbehavior in our time without appealing to the ethic of charity, no matter how unrealistic it appears to be. No one respects a hypocrite, although few human beings are willing to admit to their own hypocrisy (as Jesus relentlessly taught).

Complicity in the crimes of one's enemies is particularly hard to accept, although it is a basic imperative of a charity-based ethics. In his second inaugural address, Lincoln insisted that the North refrain from embracing triumphalism, a message that was generally lost on the most radical unionists. In the twentieth century, it was very difficult for supporters of global democracy building to admit that the actions of Western powers, who sought unlimited access to oil reserves in the Middle East, helped spark terrorism.

The recognition of historical truth is an act of charity, not simply an exercise in empiricism. It is also not an exercise in making excuses for one's enemies. If charity is indeed a two-way street, then the victims of terror obviously have every moral right to judge those who prey upon them. Yet charity requires understanding of the causes of evil, without approval of the perpetrators' actions. To love one's "enemy" as the Bible teaches (Luke 6:35) is not to excuse his actions but to comprehend his motives and reasons. Charity is not a politics of surrender. Love of one's enemy necessitates an understanding that, once again, may require some recognition of complicity. The fact that the Allies after World War I had to admit that they shared responsibility both for that conflict and for the rise of Nazism (especially after the punitive Versailles Treaty was imposed on Germany) does not mean that they were also responsible for the actions of the Hitler regime. A true application of charity requires the admission that the West was partly complicit in the rise of totalitarianism in the twentieth century, especially in the aftermath of imperialist wars in the preceding century. Even the fiercest critics of radical Islam have sometimes admitted that Western globalization bears some responsibility for terrorism.[10] (In the parlance of the CIA, "blowback" is a likely reaction to interventions that disrupt fragile regions of the world, perhaps a secular version of "reaping what you sow.") If we are to love our "enemies," perhaps we must recognize that our true enemies are ourselves, when we engage in self-destructive policies.

In short, Lincoln placed moral obligations on the citizens of American democracy that are difficult to fulfill, in America or anywhere else. *Lincoln made it harder, not easier, to build a true democracy, as he understood it.* Without charity as a precondition, democracy cannot work. Moreover, even if a citizenry understands charity in the Christian sense, as Americans certainly did in the age of Lincoln, that may not be sufficient to build democracy. America itself has often resisted charity in dramatic ways. One of the running themes of this study is that charity often clashes with another great biblical credo, the belief in the "chosen people." Supporters of democracy as the best regime have found this biblical myth to be extremely useful, especially in a secularized form (think "chosenness without God"!). Whereas many Americans saw themselves

---

10. See Michael Burleigh, *Sacred Causes: The Clash of Religion and Politics, from the Great War to the War on Terror*, 470–71.

as the "chosen" even before the events of 1776 (John Winthrop's "City on a Hill" was based on this belief), the allegedly secular post–World War II era has witnessed a quasi-religious use of this doctrine. The mission of America, according to the new avatars of chosenness, is to spread democracy to all corners of the world. Since I am not writing a work of theology, I do not intend to examine whether that use of chosenness is an accurate hermeneutic of the Old Testament (although scripture tends to teach that a truly chosen people ought to avoid self-righteous politics lest they face the wrath of God). Still, as a student of political theology, I shall examine the validity of the contemporary view that America, as the land of the chosen people, must export democracy to the rest of the world.

What is particularly troubling about chosenness is the belief that the enemies of the chosen deserve neither understanding nor mercy. Chosen peoples in history have a poor track record for practicing the humility that charity requires, a self-righteousness that Lincoln warned against when he famously called Americans "the almost chosen people." Even benign forms of chosenness, which assume that all human beings deserve decent regimes dedicated to liberty and justice for all, too easily assume that America can duplicate its specific biblical morality across the world.

In defending the politics of charity, then, I do not oppose democracy. Yet, as a believer, I cannot reconcile charity with the idolization of one regime over all others. Believers do not do the true work of God if they simplistically and idolatrously equate his providence with the spread of democracy, especially if we seek to impose it on unwilling peoples. As a political philosopher, I cannot rationally believe that democracy is best for all human beings, particularly if the precondition of charity is absent.

Charity itself entails certain preconditions, as this study will show. Based on my reading of Lincoln's rhetoric and actions, the politics of charity in the American context typically assumes that the people involved are Christians. Lincoln addressed a Christian people of the North as well as the South, a people who reflected on ethics in unmistakably biblical terms. Despite various attempts to universalize the credos of Lincoln's writings, it is hard to avoid the particular preconditions that underpin his most important assumptions:

1. Charity requires a considerably high moral capacity on the part of "We, the People," an intolerance of serious forms of hypocrisy.
2. The American understanding of charity is most understandable to

peoples who herald from a Christian background (and, even then, not perfectly).

3. If charity is the basis of true democracy, one cannot export this regime on a global scale without Christian ethics as a precondition.
4. The humility intrinsic to charity clashes with self-righteous appeals to a "chosen people" whose destiny is to liberate the world.

In short, charity requires of democracy a political ethic that even a powerful nation like the United States cannot easily duplicate on a global scale.

IS CHARITY UNIQUE TO CHRISTIANITY?

In emphasizing the *Christian* nature of charity, I am not advocating a simple Christocentric approach to the overall morality of "love of thy neighbor." Most religious traditions around the world possess some understanding of morality as selfless duty to others. Nor am I claiming that every historical tradition of Christianity has the same understanding of charity; indeed, until the modern era, most of these traditions tolerated slavery as a practice in accord with scripture. I believe, however, that the *American* use of Christian charity since Lincoln makes demands on a population that are specific to the Christian tradition and, therefore, not easily transferable to the rest of the world.

Lincoln always emphasized that the entire American citizenry was responsible to God, who speaks to all of his people on equal terms (since the law is written within every heart). In Lincoln's worldview, the whole people must be participants of covenantal justice, since the law is "within them" and written "upon their hearts" (Jer. 31:33). This understanding of the practice of charity is not easily reconciled with other faith traditions that are laden with hierarchical assumptions about human nature. The lack of a rigid authority structure that separates ruler and ruled in the Christianity of Lincoln's world (the age of the Second Great Awakening) contrasts sharply with revealed religions like Islam and even other traditions within Christianity itself (such as medieval Christianity).[11] Although it is often tempting, for example, to

11. To this day, Islam imposes sharp distinctions between, and applies distinct moral treatment to, believers and infidels (such as Jews and Christians). See Bat Ye-Or, *The Dhimmi: Jews and Christians under Islam.*

compare the Christian golden rule with the Confucian rule of reciprocal duty *(shu)*, there is a vast difference between the two traditions over what properly constitutes the authority to speak on behalf of the divine. Whereas Christianity teaches that a personal deity addresses all human beings directly, "Heaven's Imperative" in Confucianism addresses only the ruler. The people are subject to him alone, who speaks on behalf of heaven. In sharp contrast to the history of American Christianity, there is no attempt in classical Confucianism to place ruler *and* ruled on an equal footing before heaven.[12] The world of Lincoln, by contrast, was full of often violent attempts to question "authorities" who dared to speak on behalf of God, particularly in the debate over the injustice of slavery. Master and slave, unionist and secessionist, all believed that God spoke to them directly; as Lincoln famously observed in his second inaugural address, both sides "prayed to the same God." Americans have made the most of Paul's charitable refusal to see any important difference between master and slave in the eyes of God (Gal. 3:28). The egalitarianism of American charity, particularly its support of universal human dignity, is specific to the historical faith of the republic.[13]

At this point it is advisable to clarify what, if any, difference I presume between Jews and Christians on the question of charity. For my purposes, there is none. As any reader of Lincoln knows, this president could, with equal plausibility, sound like both a Hebrew prophet who warns of the nation's imminent receipt of divine punishment for slavery and a Christian apostle who preaches a universal morality. Ultimately, Lincoln himself made no distinction between Judaism and Christianity, and gave every impression that the Law of Moses was indeed the law of Christ. Whatever the differences between Jew and Gentile, both worshiped the same God.

Nevertheless, there has always been a lively debate over how particularistic Judaism is.[14] The tensions between the practice of charity and the belief in chosenness are important to this study, particularly what I

12. See Wm. Theodore de Bary, *The Trouble with Confucianism*, 93–94; and Francis Fukuyama, *Trust: The Social Virtues and the Creation of Prosperity*, 92–93, 286–87.

13. Even in the antebellum South, the belief in a personal God who related to master and slave on equal terms was often voiced. See Elizabeth Fox-Genovese and Eugene D. Genovese, *The Mind of the Master Class: History and Faith in the Southern Slaveholders' Worldview*, 559.

14. See Nygren, *Agape and Eros*, 61–104.

understand to be Lincoln's subtle attempts to warn against the temptation of his fellow Americans to act as the "chosen" in an aggressive and
arrogant manner, devoid of the spirit of charity toward all. It is well
known, however, that the holy texts of both biblical faiths privilege charity above all other imperatives.

In light of this book's focus, my incomplete answer to the question of
the differences between Judaism and Christianity is that Lincoln believed
that the dogma of chosenness was every bit a temptation to Christians
as it was to Jews. In each case, both peoples can forget charity while
privileging themselves as the favored of God. At the same time, both Jew
and Gentile can be universalistic in their morality. Even a determined
opponent of chosenness like Spinoza taught that scripture *everywhere*
reveals "moral lessons" that follow from a "universal foundation."[15]

Lincoln's belief in an almighty God in no way presupposes the difference between Judaism and Christianity. Lincoln's God is the deity of the
entire Bible, who constantly tests his people (as he tested America) in
their fidelity to his moral commandments. The patriarchal God of *both*
Judaism and Christianity is the God of tough love who demands that his
subjects protect their oppressed brethren (for example, the slaves).[16]

What is important to recognize is that a biblically based tradition,
whether Jewish or Christian, has a different understanding of politics
and ethics from that of an extrabiblical tradition. A biblical ethic of
charity imposes demands on politics that are unthinkable to the pagan
traditions. In this vein I am indebted to two of the greatest political
philosophers of the twentieth century, Eric Voegelin (1901–1985) and
Leo Strauss (1899–1973), both of whom wrote extensively on the differences between revelation and paganism and what this difference meant
for the meaning of Western political thought as a whole. Although neither Voegelin nor Strauss wrote on charity in detail, they studied certain
unique features of scripture that have no parallel in pagan politics. To

15. Benedict Spinoza, *Spinoza's Theologico-Political Treatise,* 153. Most readers of Spinoza miss his perspective that the Old Testament is also universalistic. See Emil L. Fackenheim, *To Mend the World: Foundations of Future Jewish
Thought,* 38–58.

16. I agree with Holland that, at least in Lincoln's mind, there was no difference between the Old and New Testaments on the meaning of charity (*Bonds
of Affection,* 242–43). For a profound elaboration of this understanding of the
God of both Judaism and Christianity, see Leon J. Podles, *The Church Impotent:
The Feminization of Christianity,* chaps. 4–5.

be sure, as Voegelin showed in his famous 1938 essay on political religions, the political usage of religion preceded the rise of Christianity. In his analysis of the sun religion of the Egyptians (which came into being around 1376 BC), what interested Voegelin was not only the tight identification of the regime with the divine and the corresponding absence of any separation between the two that later characterized Western Christendom. It was also significant that the Egyptian gods had no concept of universal love comparable to the God of revelation. No Egyptian deity demanded that his or her people love their neighbors, nor especially their enemies. Moreover, not even the highest gods claimed the role of loving savior of his people.[17]

In a pivotal essay on the differences between Athens and Jerusalem, or classical political philosophy and revelation, Strauss also commented on the absence of a concept of divinely sanctioned love among the Greek pagan traditions. It was not just the Greek gods who were silent on the message of universal love; the greatest Greek philosophers also provided no understanding of the duty to love others, friend and foe. The truly oppressed and downtrodden in the pagan cosmos receive comfort from neither mortal nor immortal. As a result, Strauss concluded that there was something "heartless" about Greek philosophy.[18]

As I shall argue, the politics of charity imposes obligations and demands on politics that are unthinkable to pagan traditions. The moral demands of the God of revelation push politics toward what Voegelin called the "immanentization of the eschaton." Even a secular age still lives with the influence of biblical symbols: the biblical quest for peace on earth, the subordination of the cosmos to one God, and the promised end of history have all had profound consequences on the political realm, especially in the United States. The power of a biblically driven politics seems inescapable in the modern age. As Lincoln well understood, it is also inescapable that a charity-based politics will face the pressure to end practices such as slavery and other forms of hypocrisy. Yet it is my contention that charity must raise questions about the wisdom of assuming that American democracy is the best regime for all human beings, regardless of culture or creed. If the American experiment in democracy has uniquely Christian features, can this model be successfully exported elsewhere?

17. Voegelin, "The Political Religions," 38.
18. Strauss, "Progress or Return? The Contemporary Crisis in Western Civilization," 277.

1

The Demanding Politics of Charity

As I would not be a *slave,* so I would not be a *master.* This expresses my idea of democracy. Whatever differs from this, to the extent of the difference, is no democracy.

—Abraham Lincoln, "Definition of Democracy," August 1, 1858

So it is the policy of the United States to seek and support the growth of democratic movements and institutions in every nation and culture, with the ultimate goal of ending tyranny in our world. . . . Eventually, the call of freedom comes to every mind and soul. . . . The rulers of outlaw regimes can know that we still believe as Abraham Lincoln did: "those who deny freedom to others deserve it not for themselves: and, under the rule of a just God, cannot long retain it."

—President George W. Bush, second inaugural address, 2005

The security and well-being of each and every American depend on the security and well-being of those who live beyond our borders. The mission of the United States is to provide global leadership grounded in the understanding that the world shares a common security and a common humanity.

—Barack Obama, "Renewing American Leadership"

*W*hat does Christian charity demand from politics? How, as Hillary Clinton once remarked in her 2008 campaign for her party's presidential nomination, does the golden rule call on us "to act" in politics? Most religious and secular intellectuals have been skeptical of spying any relation between politics and charity. It has never been obvious that Christian love has had a political impact (even if politicians pay lip service to this ethic). For one thing, it is often fashionable to claim that "love thy neighbor as thyself" is either too utopian or too ambiguous for application in the tough-minded world of politics. If politics is indeed the art of the possible, then this ethic appears to clash with practical matters of statecraft. Although Sigmund Freud lauded the golden rule for being "the strongest defence against human aggressiveness," he also faulted it as a commandment that is "impossible to fulfill," since it forces adherents into an unrealistic "inflation of love."[1] Presumably, charity is an unnaturally demanding way of contending with the all too primal forces that civilization uneasily represses.

Whereas the bias of Freud can be attributed to his hostility to revelation, even Christian theologians have often warned that the "modern" use of charity (as a doctrine of ethics or politics) dangerously strips this great credo of its most profound spiritual foundations.[2] Liberal Protestant theologian Reinhold Niebuhr doubted that a "social ethic" could be derived from a "pure religious ethic." Jesuit scholar James V. Schall warns Christians not to "confuse politics with salvation. States are not saved. Persons are." Presumably, charity is perfectly compatible with *apoliteia*. Catholic political theorist Ernest L. Fortin, for example, summarizes the position of many Christian academics when he confidently claims that the New Testament is indifferent "to problems of a purely political nature"; love (which has nothing to do with justice) is a "fuzzy thing" in the political realm. In short, Christian love provides no lessons on matters of statecraft.[3]

Has charity, however, always been a "fuzzy thing" in the realm of American political thought? The spurious separation of faith from politics that these authors are entertaining was inconceivable to the presi-

---

1. Linda Feldmann, "Candidate Clinton Goes Public with Her Private Faith"; Freud, *Civilization and Its Discontents*, 90.

2. Nygren, *Agape and Eros*, 95.

3. Niebuhr, *An Interpretation of Christian Ethics*, 55; Schall, *Christianity and Politics*, 66–67; Fortin, "Rational Theologians and Irrational Philosophers: A Straussian Perspective," 289.

dent who most forcefully and thoughtfully brought religion and politics together when he insisted that charity become the highest ethic of its citizens. It is well known that Abraham Lincoln did not shy from integrating faith and public duty. In his famous speech to the Young Men's Lyceum in Springfield, Illinois, a twenty-nine-year-old Lincoln called on his countrymen to embrace the rule of law rather than capitulate to the "mobocratic" violence sweeping the land. Lincoln understandably worried that rising bloodshed and lawlessness were making a mockery of the republic's ideals. These ideals had to be not only obeyed but *revered,* and the sheer passage of time since the fiery passions of the Revolution inhibited the necessary rebirth of the creed. Nevertheless, Lincoln was confident that every American should "swear by the blood of the Revolution, never to violate in the least particular, the laws of the country; and never to tolerate their violation by others." Additionally, citizens were enjoined to support the founding documents, and express "reverence for the laws." What Lincoln then called the resultant "political religion" would become, he hoped, the dominant creed of the nation.[4]

Still, what is this demanding "sacrifice" that Americans, according to Lincoln, must make "unceasingly upon its altars"? Should this sacrifice provoke secularist worries about the incursion of faith into politics? The answer to this question is not so easy, in the face of considerable confusion and anxiety over what constitutes the meaning of America's mission in the world.

Numerous scholars have used various terms such as *Americanism, American Creed, civil religion, civil theology, consensus,* or *covenant* to underscore the interdependence of faith and politics in the republic.[5] Yet, to my knowledge, few scholars have investigated even in the American setting what charity means, practically speaking, for the political realm.[6]

---

4. Lincoln, *The Collected Works of Abraham Lincoln,* 1:112.

5. See David Gelernter, *Americanism: The Fourth Great Western Religion;* Samuel Huntington, *Who Are We? The Challenges to America's National Identity;* Richard V. Pierard and Robert D. Linder, *Civil Religion and the Presidency;* Joseph R. Fornieri, *Abraham Lincoln's Political Faith,* 9; John Courtney Murray, *We Hold These Truths: Catholic Reflections on the American Proposition,* 101; and Robert N. Bellah, *The Broken Covenant: American Civil Religion in Time of Trial.*

6. Once again, the one exception is Holland's *Bonds of Affection,* although even this fine work does not discuss the political implications of charity for America's relation with the world.

It has always been easy to acknowledge the persistent force of religion in American politics (there have been at least ten born-again presidents in the nation's history).[7] As Tocqueville famously observed more than 170 years ago, America has always wedded democracy to religious belief. This French aristocrat (whose ideas on charity and politics I shall discuss in Chapter 2) saw no contradiction between fervent faith and passionate republicanism, at least in America. To date, however, the specific demands of a charity-based politics have received very little attention.

This inattention may well be due to the fact that most secular scholars who are sensitive to the demands that religion places on politics understand these demands in solely *negative* terms. From a conventionally European perspective, America has always been that exceptional Western democracy that retains dangerously strong religious roots. Indeed, academics on both sides of the Atlantic are often baffled at the revival of religion in American politics, to which they react with equal doses of horror and surprise. Not only does America presumably challenge the secularism of the West, but it also becomes a harbinger of darkness on the march again. Historian John Lukacs has dismissed American Christianity as "medieval," unworthy of the great Western devotion to enlightenment, since this nation suffers from an "unrestrained spiritualism" that encourages the coexistence of "medieval" as well as "supermodern" notions of faith.[8]

The George W. Bush presidency (2001–2009) also seemed to vindicate the worries of scholars like Lukacs, even among the American intelligentsia. The fact that the president at times referred to God in speeches struck many as dangerously threatening to the separation of church and state in the republic, and therefore out of synch with the best intentions of the founding fathers (who were presumably irreligious). This attitude is a long-running theme among liberal American historians and social scientists. In the 1960s, liberal historian Richard Hofstadter warned of demagogues on the Right who possess "the tendency to secularize a religiously derived view of the world, to deal with political issues in Christian imagery, and to color them with the dark symbology of a certain side of Christian tradition." More recently, journalist Jeff Sharlet fears that the "Religious Right"—that broad coalition of Protestant

7. Pierard and Linder, *Civil Religion*, 239.
8. Lukacs, *A New Republic: A History of the United States in the Twentieth Century*, 186–87.

evangelicals, Catholics, Orthodox Jews, Mormons, and some Muslims—threatens to reinvent and deconstruct the secular foundations of the nation. "Fundamentalism is writing us out of history," asserts Sharlet. Even a few conservatives have contended that Bush's evangelism is the harbinger of something new in American politics. Kevin P. Phillips, once a political adviser to Nixon, declares that the GOP is now the "first religious party in American history." Jeffrey Hart, a former editor of the neoconservative *National Review,* observes that the president's devotion to faith was a novel one in the history of the republic.[9] In short, religion in America threatens to redefine the political as never before.

Despite the fact that these authors ignore the reality that religion is nothing new for American politics, there is more than a grain of truth to their worries, for they correctly sense that biblical credos and symbols do transform the political realm, even though they consider this transformation to be mainly destructive. What they ignore is that the American political usage of religion *at its best,* as Lincoln understood it, is a civil creed based on the practice of "love thy neighbor (and enemy) as thyself." The very essence of democracy lies in this understanding and practice of charity. Certainly, Lincoln's defense of equality is also, I believe, a political application of charity (although there are interesting exceptions to this rule, as I shall argue in Chapter 6). Despite the famous claim of President Eisenhower that it does not matter what religion America has (as long as it has one),[10] it is my contention that what Lincoln considered the highest ethic of the American "political religion" must be based on Christian morality.

Lincoln was not the first leader of stature to articulate the implications of a politics of charity. As I show in the following chapter, Spinoza, Winthrop, Jefferson, and Tocqueville had already drawn a relation between charity and politics. Yet he certainly was the first political leader to insist that a *true* democracy requires charity. Lincoln demanded a moral excellence that no democratic leader had ever come close to insisting upon. Charity, as Lincoln understood it, is the only viable faith

9. Hofstadter, *The Paranoid Style in American Politics, and Other Essays,* xi; Sharlet, "Through a Glass Darkly: How the Christian Right Is Reimagining U.S. History," 43; Phillips, *American Theocracy: The Peril and Politics of Radical Religion, Oil, and Borrowed Money in the Twenty-first Century,* vii; Hart, *The Making of the American Conservative Mind: "National Review" and Its Times,* 349.

10. Pierard and Linder, *Civil Religion,* 200.

for a democracy because it puts an end to egregious double standards (like the inequality of slavery) that make a mockery of self-government. Charity also presupposes knowledge of the Christian commitment to duty, which transcends mere self-interest.

If my discussion so far sounds like a version of the famous "secularization" hypothesis made famous by Max Weber and other prominent twentieth-century minds, it is. It is undeniable that Lincoln secularized charity for political ends (most famously in his attack on slavery as immoral). Yet the secularization of this Christian ethic does not change the fact that a secular democracy can inherit the demands of this ethic. However far reaching the secularization of religious credos is in modernity, the Christian roots of charity do not disappear. This cautionary point is important, since I discuss in Chapters 5 and 6 how many secular intellectuals (including neoconservatives) who make use of biblical credos (like that of the "chosen people") to justify aggressive democracy building forget just how indispensable a Christian foundation for American democracy has been. If it is true, as Lincoln thought, that democracy needs Christian morality, it may be impossible to export this model of democracy to lands that lack a Christian history.

In assuming throughout this study that secularization does not eliminate the religious roots of an idea, I am indebted to political philosophers who recognize just how influential biblical themes have been in the politics of modernity (despite the denials of most secular intellectuals). Once again, I rely on the thought of Eric Voegelin, whose work on the influence of Christian ideas on modern politics is indispensable to any student of the political usage of religion. Voegelin did not share the secular intellectual's confidence (at least before the end of the cold war) that religion had simply given way to the secularization of modernity. To make this claim was tantamount to giving far too much credit to the triumph of reason. In his famous 1938 essay on political religions, Voegelin warns that the "secularization of the soul" may have severed its roots from religion, but all modern polities in some sense remain religious, despite secular denials. A community must "take into account the religious forces inherent in a society and the symbols through which these are expressed" if it is to enjoy a proper self-understanding. To dismiss these forces as "areligious" inhibits this awareness.[11]

11. Voegelin, "The Political Religions," 70.

Voegelin was also one of the few twentieth-century political theorists to understand that the unique *demands* of Christianity forever transformed the politics of the West in ways unimaginable to the pagan religions of Greece and Rome. Moreover, secularization had not eliminated the influence of Christianity. In Eric Voegelin's view, Christianity had accomplished two feats of great importance to politics with impacts felt well into modernity. First, Christianity emptied the cosmos of meaning (a process that he labeled "dedivinization"). Instead of a direct relationship with the gods or nature mediated through rituals and rites, Christianity forced the "uncertainty" of faith onto its adherents. They were now alone in the world, with a completely transcendent (yet loving) God. Second, Christianity to a large extent countered this existential uncertainty with the promise of an "end of history," culminating in the return of Christ. Gone was the pagan belief in cyclical time: true believers could now look forward to the reign of peace for the saved in history. The insecurity that Christianity introduced into the world in the meantime fueled desires for "firmer foundations."[12] It was Lincoln's fondest yet often unrealized hope that charity would become that firm foundation.

Generally, a biblically based politics will be more demanding than a politics with different religious roots, as Voegelin taught. A tradition of politics with Christian roots will make demands that are inconceivable to other faiths. Indeed, a biblically based political religion is far more demanding of humanity than its pagan rivals. As political philosopher Muhsin Mahdi has astutely observed, the revealed religions "raised the sights of their followers too high to remain satisfied with a moderate regime" that seeks the merely "intermediate" (or golden mean) between the virtuous and the ignorant. Charity indeed raises "the sights" in a manner that forcibly associates politics with the ethic of God. Both Voegelin and Mahdi properly warn intellectuals not to understate the lingering influence of the Bible on politics in modernity, or to embrace simplistic separations of one from the other. As if to display this confusion front and center, one author of a recent study on the religious roots of the American enlightenment states that the supporters of 1776 "arrived at that position not by attenuating or secularizing their religion but by spiritualizing politics itself."[13] (How, then, does a spiritualized politics differ from secularized religion?)

12. Voegelin, *The New Science of Politics*, 118–23, 162–63.
13. Mahdi, *Alfarabi and the Foundation of Islamic Political Philosophy*, 168–

One irony about the mainly secular literature that deals with Lincoln in particular and Western political thought as a whole is perhaps an unconscious adherence to biblical credos that irreligious intellectuals integrate into their politics. Most scholars of Lincoln literature devote more attention to what they consider Lincoln's quasi-religious commitment to the promotion of American democracy as the best regime for all of humanity. Secular intellectuals (including liberals and neoconservatives) who are otherwise hostile or indifferent to Christianity nevertheless find it very tempting to believe in a secularized version of the "chosen people" who desire to liberate all peoples of the world from tyranny. As I show in Chapter 3, there is little evidence that Lincoln supported what amounts to a twentieth-century ideology. Indeed, the president always emphasized the primacy of charity over spurious appeals to chosenness that both unionists and Confederates of his age made.

The appeal of chosenness to even secular minds dramatically vindicates Voegelin's suspicions about the premature prediction of the "end" of religious belief in modernity. This appeal also has greater intensity than that of the ethic of charity. As I observed in the Introduction, the practice of charity clashes with another demanding biblical credo, the belief in a "chosen people" whom God commands to launch imperialistic democracy-building crusades, based on the assumption that all the peoples of the world can become democratic, with the encouragement of the United States. It is a popular assumption in the Lincoln literature (both pro and con) that his presidency provides the ultimate rationale for wedding Christianity with the aggressive spread of democracy all over the world.[14] The pivotal question for this study is whether Lincoln understood charity to sanction such an enterprise. This president tried mightily to distinguish chosenness from charity. Although charity is a universalistic ethic, it does not demand the universalization of democracy.

I make this distinction between rival biblical credos to assuage the concerns of secular critics of religion that not every political usage of the Bible is necessarily destructive. Lincoln was no theocrat. The emphasis on charity actually demands only one thing of all citizens,

---

69; Gertrude Himmelfarb, *The Roads to Modernity: The British, French, and American Enlightenments*, 212.

14. Fornieri, *Abraham Lincoln's Political Faith*, 136; Gelernter, *Americanism*, 103–46. See also Chapters 6–7 below.

religious and secular: the end to the most serious and divisive injustices (slavery being the most blatant one). On this basis of charity, Lincoln most famously articulated his understanding of equality. Yet charity also often eschews other elements of a traditional biblical worldview: the belief in "chosenness" is the most potent of these, which can justify the war of one people against another in the name of God's favoritism. For this reason, Lincoln famously referred to the "almost chosen people." A people who are not yet chosen must be humble and charitable enough to avoid inflicting injustices upon others. This is as far as Lincoln went in appealing to Christianity. Any appeal to chosenness or supernatural-ism was either qualified or ignored altogether. This attempt to portray Christianity as mainly a religion of ethics—no more, no less—follows in the footsteps of Spinoza and Jefferson, as I argue in the next chapter. This was the Christianity that Tocqueville discovered in America. A truly literalist faith would have sanctioned slavery, as most Southern preachers never tired of pointing out, just as a truly literalist reading of the Declaration would have had the same result.[15] Lincoln raised the sights by interpreting both texts in the light of charity. Most impor-tant, this is the only Christianity that works politically. The biblical idea of chosenness, in contrast, threatens to derail political usage of *agape.* Indeed, a charity-based ethic itself may be the only moral teaching that saves modern politics from the most frightening forms of secularized religion.

To be sure, the politics of Lincoln itself has radical implications, since, unlike the ancients, the president was able to invoke a "higher law tradi-tion" that subjected the state to a "moral law more authoritative than itself."[16] Unlike ancient (or pagan) religions that lack an understanding of the separation between religion and politics, the biblical foundation of Lincoln's politics must transcend the authority of the regime itself: ruler and ruled must bow down to one God. Any rivals—political or religious—to the worship of this God must be shunned. The paradox of this political faith is that God is above the political, yet he is also involved with it. God cannot be identified with any one regime (not even a democracy), but his authority must command political leaders to practice his morality.

One sacrifice that this "higher law tradition" might demand is the

---

15. See Mark A. Noll, *The Civil War as a Theological Crisis,* 31–50.
16. Bruce P. Frohnen, "Lincoln and the Problem of Political Religion," 377.

abandonment of crusades for democratic universalism in favor of a humble (and charitable) foreign policy that George Bush promised in the 2000 election campaign. The quintessentially American temptation to equate the work of God with the spread of democracy must cease. Whether it is likely that most Americans will abandon the secularized belief in the "chosen people" that has inspired the nation's politics since even before the Revolutionary period is another matter.[17] Still, the subordination of this mythology to the imperative of charity may be the price of survival.

CHARITY VERSUS THE POLITICAL RELIGION OF DEMOCRACY BUILDING

However influential Christian and biblical ideas continue to be in modernity, some practical questions immediately arise: Can any regime—American or other—sustain the demands of biblical credos, charity included? Is a politics of charity akin to a new political creed that threatens to wreak havoc on politics with immoderate demands to create a utopian kingdom? Predictably, these questions arise in current debates over the return of religious fundamentalism. The fear of utopian religious movements is partly justified by the fact that the origins of the term *political religion* tend to be found in the nether regions of Western Christendom. An obscure Dominican friar, Tommaso Campanella (1568–1639), coined the term *political religion*. As the author of the utopian tract *The City of the Sun* (1602), he argued for the establishment of Christianity as a state religion, under Catholic control, naturally. Although Campanella captured the favorable attention of Louis XIII and Cardinal Richelieu (and later the admiration of Lenin), his utopian dreams came to nothing.[18]

Since Campanella's time, scholars have tended to associate political religions with elements on the fringes. Toward the end of World War II, French political philosopher Raymond Aron penned an influential essay on "secular religions." Unsurprisingly, Aron was chiefly concerned with

17. See Kevin P. Phillips, *The Cousins' Wars: Religion, Politics, and the Triumph of Anglo-America*.

18. See Burleigh, *Earthly Powers: The Clash of Religion and Politics in Europe, from the French Revolution to the Great War*, 19–20.

Nazism and communism, the most lethal forces of his age. As a result, he was determined to describe these totalitarian religions as inhabitants of the outposts of civilization, far beyond the decency and moderation of Western democracies. For this reason, his analysis gives the unmistakable impression that the practitioners of political religions are as psychologically disordered as the regimes that they propose. These radicals possess a "Manichaean" view of the universe, whose flaws call for a "savior" to cleanse it. While these religions provoke as much fervent passion as traditional religions, they fanatically and impatiently want to transform the world now. Despite the fact that the war against the Nazi political religion was not over at the time of writing, Aron with cautious optimism concludes that British parliamentary democracy is the best chance of staving off the recurrence of other political religions. Russell Kirk, writing in the 1950s, seems to concur with Aron when he remarks that fanatics who take advantage of mass deprivation tend to create political religions.[19]

The recent literature on political religions since the terror attacks of 2001 has tended to echo the bias of Aron and Kirk that political religions happen only to undemocratic citizenries. In a recent study on radical Islam, Barry Cooper contends that the most extreme variants of Islam have more in common with the ideologies of Nazism and communism (both of which are committed to a bloody reconstruction of reality) than with Islam itself. Yet the attempt to marginalize political religions, perhaps as a supreme act of self-assurance in a zeitgeist of fear and terror, is questionable. In a recent study of political religions, Michael Burleigh invites his readers to confront the mainstream origins of political religions when he reminds them of the necessity of "looking at the Christian world of representations that still informs much of our politics."[20] As an admirer of Voegelin's work, Burleigh is dissatisfied with a shallow understanding of political religions as simply the playthings of parochially minded radicals. If Christianity is the ultimate source of these religions, then it is legitimate to study how Western liberal democracies with *Christian* roots are still prone to fashion political religions.

Does a charity-based politics encourage, then, old-style religious fanaticism in the form of political religion? At the political and ethical

<hr />

19. Aron, "The Secular Religions," 161–242; Kirk, *The American Cause*, 121.

20. Barry Cooper, *New Political Religions; or, An Analysis of Modern Terrorism;* Burleigh, *Earthly Powers*, 9.

level, Lincoln insisted that Americans confront the question of whether even a Christian people who tolerate slavery can truly practice charity. Indeed, can any regime, even a liberal democracy, successfully practice it while avoiding the creation of a political religion? It may be tempting to believe that liberal democrats are best able to suppress religious extremism, since they characteristically portray themselves as the voices of moderation, the reasonable middle between the far Right and Left, the only politicians committed to individual rights and equality. Indeed, all political parties in the West today refer to "liberal" democracy as the best regime. Presumably, liberals moderate the radical tendencies of Christianity, once they incorporate its most ethical dimensions (like charity) into the public square. Yet the historical record suggests that liberalism not only fails to moderate Christianity but may even inspire its most radical expressions in politics (see Chapter 6). As Richard M. Gamble has amply documented, liberal pastors pushed for America's entry into World War I, to spread democracy (which they conflated with the will of God). Lest anyone doubt that liberal democrats portray their own regime as the ideal for all peoples, we may consider the provocative thoughts of two political scientists on the emergence of this creed in the cold war period. In the wry prose of Austin Ranney and Willmoore Kendall, *democracy* by the 1950s was becoming a "god-word" that only an "extreme eccentric" would seriously oppose.[21]

The outcome of this faith in democracy as the best regime for all of humanity is that anyone who questions this type of regime stands accused of heresy or injustice. Either one is for democracy or one is against it. Democracy is simply the opposite of tyranny, a claim that ignores the myriad of other regimes that are neither democratic nor tyrannical (aristocracy, oligarchy, monarchy). At least since World War II, it has become increasingly hard to question democracy without incurring the wrath of its defenders.

It is tempting to invoke the precedent of Lincoln here. Since he invoked this term in a positive sense in his famous Lyceum speech, does he deserve praise (or blame) for creating a political religion of global

21. Gamble, *The War for Righteousness: Progressive Christianity, the Great War, and the Rise of the Messianic Nation;* Ranney and Kendall, *Democracy and the American Party System,* 3. For an insightful discussion of how political religions function in modern liberal democracy, see Paul Edward Gottfried, *The Strange Death of Marxism: The European Left in the New Millennium,* 119–41.

democracy building? Many answer in the affirmative, for did not this president impose liberal values on the American South by destroying the institution of slavery? More than a few critics have associated Lincoln with twentieth-century democratic imperialism.[22] Yet these imperialistic ventures have imposed alien values upon peoples without experience of a Christian worldview. As I shall argue in Chapter 3, however, Lincoln's act of denying the South the right to self-determination was premised on the view that Southerners *already* adhered to biblical values common to the entire nation. The tragedy was that this common adherence to these values did not produce a common understanding. Lincoln, the great universalist who believed that all peoples deserve liberty and equality, nevertheless never taught that all peoples are *equally* cognizant of the burden of democracy. This recognition of particularity, based on religion and other circumstances, is a reality that imperialistic presidents after Lincoln have learned the hard way (particularly in the Philippines, Vietnam, and Iraq). If a Christian nation like America could tear itself apart over how to understand common values like religion and liberty (as Lincoln famously observed in his second inaugural address, both sides "prayed to the same God"), what chance of success is there for America to export these values elsewhere? Unlike many of his self-professed followers, Lincoln's theology of charity eschews the goal of bringing democracy to all corners of the world unless knowledge of Christian charity is already present.

Despite the elaborate attempts of some scholars to portray Lincoln as a "pagan" or Machiavellian statesman with a mainly utilitarian interest in biblical ideas (see Chapter 5), there is no question in my mind that Lincoln's thought is biblical to the core. Of course, the president's use of biblical themes has inspired friend and foe to project various agendas onto his legacy. The name of Lincoln is invoked in order to explain America's democracy-building crusades and other grand adventures in its history. Whether one is neoconservative, paleoconservative, liberal, or leftist, it seems that this most religious of presidents can be either credited or blamed for the most expansionist periods in the nation's history. There is vast consensus across the ideological spectrum that Lincoln—rightly or wrongly—inspired the republic to look outward and create the world in the republic's own image and likeness. Frederick

---

22. See Richard M. Gamble, "The Problem of Lincoln in Babbitt's Thought." See also Chapters 6–7 below for a discussion of Lincoln's legacy.

Jackson Turner praised the president as the first great leader from the frontier who inspired the settlement of the West. Protestant liberal pastors agitated for America's entry into World War I by comparing the war against Southern slavery with the war against German imperialism.[23] Neoconservatives regularly refer to the president's reading of the Declaration of Independence for this purpose.[24] Critics of Lincoln fault him for legitimizing various wars of expansionism against Confederates, Indians, Filipinos, the Vietnamese, and eventually Iraqis.[25] These writers all draw a straight line between Lincoln's presidency and the foreign policy of America in the twentieth century.

Although I believe that Lincoln's understanding of charity as political was a demanding one, it does not require the formation of a new political religion, democratic or otherwise. It was not the purpose of Lincoln's political usage of charity to treat the entire globe as a large-scale version of the American South. The religious and political particularities of America—resting upon a faith common to both Northerner and Southerner—make it impossibly difficult to transport the republic's ideals beyond its borders. These attempts have tended to end in failure because they ignore the precondition of democracy as Lincoln understood it: the already present commitment to Christian charity. In his views of the capacity of secessionists, Native Americans, and newly freed slaves for self-government, Lincoln usually attempted to know the other (which is not to say that he always satisfied the interests of the other).

My purpose is neither to contribute to presidential hagiography nor to write a civics book on the greatness of Lincoln. Very often the supposed defenders of the president have simply provided aid and comfort to his many enemies who fault him for setting America on the course of imperialism. Lincoln was a man, not a "god-like" being, as one effusive admirer puts it, who sought to re-create the world in a democratic image

23. Gamble, *War for Righteousness,* 125, 140–42, 203.

24. Gelernter, *Americanism,* 106–7.

25. See, for example, Dwight G. Anderson, *Abraham Lincoln: The Quest for Immortality,* 224–29. Anderson accuses Lincoln of emancipating American foreign policy, that is, providing the justification for imperialist wars. Joseph Scotchie blames Lincoln for being a "guide for the totalitarian fanatics that defined the twentieth century" (*Revolt from the Heartland. The Struggle for an Authentic Conservatism,* 6). Thomas DiLorenzo has spied a historic connection between Lincoln's legacy and the Iraq war (see *Lincoln Unmasked,* 161–62).

and likeness.²⁶ To be sure, no president wedded charity and democracy as forcibly as Lincoln did. No other president has emphasized universal moral credos as much as he did. His most globalizing followers have thrilled to his declaration that the foundation of America lies "in the love of liberty which God has planted in our bosoms."²⁷ Yet his understanding of charity as the true foundation of democracy does not, despite the polemical claims of friend and foe alike, logically lead to crusades for democracy building. Even if charity is written on the hearts of all human beings, it does not follow that they all *desire* democracy, and it is not up to the United States to impose this desire upon them (or "force them to be free," *pace* Rousseau). Lincoln was addressing a Christian people, steeped in the study of agape. The fact that all Americans possessed this understanding made it somewhat easier for the president to appeal to their conscience (although it did not prevent war, tragically). Moreover, Lincoln regularly emphasized that charity and democracy need each other; there cannot be one without the other. If there is no understanding of charity, democracy cannot succeed. Yet it is not up to America to promote charity through democracy crusades. It is the nation's duty only to provide an example of how charity is supposed to work in its government, as an example to the world. If America fails to set up democracies (as in the case of the Wilson, Johnson, and Bush II presidencies), the nation is vulnerable to the accusation that Lincoln most feared: hypocrisy. It would be bad faith to fault the Europeans, the Vietnamese, or the Iraqis for refusing American democracy if they did not want it in the first place.

A charity-based political faith is a demanding one, although the ethic of charity tends to be a more restraining force on political leaders than a belief in chosenness. Chosenness itself usually receives far more attention as the sheet anchor of America's political creed than charity; one defender of "biblical republicanism" has even proclaimed that Americans are the chosen people, the Declaration is the American Decalogue, and the Fourth of July is the American Passover.²⁸ My view is that Lincoln tried to downplay the chosenness of his people while focus-

---

26. Harry V. Jaffa, *Crisis of the House Divided: An Interpretation of the Issues in the Lincoln-Douglas Debates*, 217, 263–65.

27. Lincoln, *Collected Works*, 3:95. The occasion was his debate with Douglas on September 11, 1858.

28. Fornieri, *Abraham Lincoln's Political Faith*, 133. The neoconservative

ing on charity above all. Still, a charity-based political religion requires a great deal of ethical understanding on the part of Americans.

It is far from obvious that America can always live up to this kind of civil creed. Yet a charity-based politics is indeed a practical one if a utopian politics of global democracy building is abandoned. The fact is that the particularities of a Christian faith may not be universalizable on a political level. Indeed, because the Bible is not a work of political philosophy (although it has deep political implications), we should not look to scripture to justify unconditional democracy building. Evangelical Christians, who typically believe that the Word of God is universally "written" on the hearts of all human beings, are not deterred by the challenge of ethical and cultural diversity. Yet those who practice moral universalism should be cautioned that what is meant to be universal in a religious sense is not universal in a political sense. America's most famous global democrats (Wilson, Bush II) have all learned the limits of universalism and the reality of religious particularity the hard way.

In this study, I am mainly concerned with the implications of charity if there is a sincere commitment to practice it. I am far less concerned with cynical attempts of political regimes to pay lip service to this ethic. Despite their invocations of "Christian love" as the basis of their ideology, the Nazis and their allies in the church clearly restricted the practice of this love to their immediate brethren, the Germans who actually supported the regime.[29] Certainly, "love of thine enemy" had no place under National Socialism! It would be an easy task to identify the gaping cynicism and hypocrisy in the Nazi usage of Christian morality.

It is more challenging to evaluate the realism of charity-based morality if its utopian adherents sincerely conflate democracy building with Christianity. Back in 1965, American leftist theologian Harvey Cox famously declared in his best-selling work *The Secular City* that Christianity, as a religion that forces engagement with the world, cannot help but be involved in secular pursuits like politics. Because revelation teaches that the world is the creation of a personal God, and everything that happened in this world is God revealing himself through history, there can never be a clean separation between religion and a secular

---

supporters of Lincoln have usually emphasized chosenness at the expense of charity. See Chapters 5–6 below.

29. See Richard Steigmann-Gall, *The Holy Reich: Nazi Conceptions of Christianity, 1919–1945*, 44–45.

realm like politics. Cox rejected the view that Christians should stay out of "secularization," which he understood to be the process of acting out the principles of Christ in *all* aspects of his earthly domain (once again, Voegelin's thoughts about secularization are vindicated). Thus, the attempt to create a purely secular state, free of religion, was doomed to failure in America. Although Cox knew that there is still danger in confusing the political with the religious, he was confident that no true separation was even desirable, much less possible. In anticipation of liberation theology, Cox called for a political "revolution" that would spread Christianity around the world while transforming the lives of the oppressed and the poor.[30]

One of the most significant developments in twentieth-century American politics was the rise of movements on the Right who supported their own version of liberation theology. This rightist ideology was not truly conservative, since its avatars tended to minimize the influence of Christianity on American traditions. As a result, the Christian ethic of charity received short shrift in their writings. Whatever terms one wants to use (I alternately refer to natural rightists, neoconservatives, and democratic universalists), this secular rightism has declared that democracy is the best regime for all of humanity. In promoting their ideology, supporters have appropriated the legacy of Lincoln for their own ends. In truly secularizing fashion, this Protestant president who articulated a politics of charity on behalf of a Christian people has been reinvented as a cosmopolitan statesman in charge of a secularized chosen people whose mission was to liberate the entire world from tyranny. Yet a charity-based ethic, based on an accurate understanding of Lincoln's views of Christianity, would more likely discourage than inspire such efforts, as I argue in the last three chapters. The ethic of charity demands a great deal of democracies. If charity requires one to understand the "other," the hard truth may be the discovery that others do not seek, and do not accept the imposition of, democracy as their ideal regime.

I am not the first scholar to question the liberal and neoconservative view that all peoples desire democracy for themselves (and others).[31] Nevertheless, my contribution to this growing debate (especially in light of the Iraq war) is to focus on how the biblically based thought

---

30. Cox, *The Secular City: Secularization and Urbanization in Theological Perspective,* 18–19, 181.

31. See Charles R. Kesler, "Democracy and the Bush Doctrine," 222–32.

of Lincoln presupposes extensive awareness of the other whom one is trying to liberate. Charity requires a profound knowledge of one's opponent (which Lincoln especially had in relation to the South). The supreme act of charity may well be to leave other nations to develop democracy on their own, in full knowledge of who they are as a people. The costly alternative to this prudent morality is to surrender to the temptation of a political religion that Lincoln did not embrace.

2

The Concept of Charity before Lincoln

I am a Christian, in the only sense in which he
[Jesus] wished any one to be; sincerely attached to
his doctrines, in preference to all others; ascribing
to himself every *human* excellence; and believing
he never claimed any other.

—Thomas Jefferson to Benjamin Rush, April 21, 1803

*T*he ethic of Christian charity has often had profound implications for American political thought, even before the age of
Lincoln. Yet its importance and influence have waxed and waned
in the history of the nation. As I argue in the next chapter, Lincoln
assumed that his people already knew the meaning of charity and thus
were compelled to avoid hypocrisies like slavery. Although Lincoln was
not the first American (or modern) to denounce the dangers of such
hypocrisy, he was the first leader to insist that this ethic become the true
practice of a democracy. Still, there were both philosophers and leaders
before Lincoln who also spied a clear connection between a successful
politics and the practice of charity. In order to understand the nature
of Lincoln's forceful inclusion of charity in the public square, we must
understand the thought of those who preceded him in reflecting on the
politics of this ethical teaching.

In situating the president in a long tradition of inquiry into the meaning and practice of charity, we can assess how conservative and radical

Lincoln's own understanding of charity was. Certainly, more than a few scholars have stressed that Lincoln went far beyond any previous American leader in uniting "Christianity to the work of the Fathers" or using the Bible "in a way unimaginable from the nation's earliest presidents."[1] Yet Lincoln himself stressed that he was the true "conservative" for spying the relation between charity and equality. Was Lincoln, then, a defender of tradition or its transforming agent?

The answer to this question lies in understanding this tradition before Lincoln. Certain figures in Western political philosophy stand out. The seventeenth-century Enlightenment philosopher Spinoza in particular first argued for charity *(caritas)* as the foundation of real democracy, although he did not have the opportunity to lead a regime toward the actualization of this relation. Although there have been a few political leaders of stature who reflected on the meaning of charity for politics—especially John Winthrop and Thomas Jefferson—they did not pursue the fundamentally democratic implications of this ethic as far as Lincoln did. The American founders as a whole, who respected the influence of Christianity, nevertheless refrained from grounding all moral principles in charity. A revolutionary like Thomas Paine, who called upon America to spread its nascent values universally, was far more enamored with a belief in "chosenness" (albeit in secular garb) than the ethic of charity. Yet Lincoln benefited from a religious tradition that had at least made some preliminary attempt to relate charity and democracy, a tradition that Tocqueville saw in existence in his famous travels in the early 1830s to America.

John Winthrop: Theocratic Charity

While on board *The Arrabella* in 1630 as it was sailing toward the New World, John Winthrop composed his classic treatise "A Modell of Christian Charity." This document was both revolutionary and conservative in its own right. It was revolutionary because Winthrop was the first Christian leader to undertake a defense of charity as the foundation of a successful regime that he and his fellow Puritans hoped to establish

---

1. Glen E. Thurow, *Abraham Lincoln and the American Political Religion*, 36; Mark A. Noll, "The Contingencies of American Republicanism: An Alternative Account of Protestantism and the American Founding," 243.

in what later became the Massachusetts Bay Colony. Up to this time, various scholastic philosophers in Western Christendom had made use of Aristotelian political philosophy rather than scripture alone to address matters of politics. As an heir to the Reformation, Winthrop could not possibly ground a new regime upon a discredited scholasticism that confused paganism with revelation.[2] As a devotee of *Sola Scriptura,* he had to find the answers to all questions—political or religious—in the Bible rather than a pagan text. Winthrop established the precedent for colonial Americans who sought wisdom in scripture rather than "heathen" philosophical texts. Charity was complete as the moral authority for all matters: "Upon this ground stands all the precepts of the morall lawe, which concernes our dealings with men."[3]

Yet Winthrop was also a seventeenth-century conservative in his understanding of charity. It was not his intention to understand biblical ethic as a justification for building a democracy. To be sure, Winthrop understood the Spirit of God to manifest his truth so that "the riche and mighty should not eate upp the poore, nor the poore and dispised rise upp" against their oppressors. Winthrop sincerely desired the avoidance of class warfare between the rich and the poor in what he later famously described (based on Matt. 5:14) as the "Citty upon a Hill." In opposing social conflict, however, the future governor did not then embrace the gradual disappearance of all inequalities. Indeed, Winthrop began his essay with the message that the Almighty had determined that "in all times" some must be rich while others poor.[4] Justice and mercy, the corollaries of charity, did not require the leveling experiments that a few of his radical brethren had advocated in England. In refusing to associate equality with charity, Winthrop was reflecting his belief that human nature is too base to return to a lost state of nature in which such equality may well have obtained (a view that his fellow preacher Thomas Hooker famously contested).[5] With the Fall, however, it was

---

2. See Holland, *Bonds of Affection,* for a useful discussion of Winthrop's thought, although he does not focus on Winthrop's attempts to distinguish his theology from appeals to "nature," as in the case of pagan thought.

3. Winthrop, "Modell of Christian Charity," 38.

4. Ibid., 37, 40, 37.

5. As Michael P. Zuckert states, "Equality is neither the beginning point nor the end point" in Winthrop's political philosophy ("Natural Rights and Protestant Politics," 31–32). For Hooker's debate with Winthrop, see Clinton

necessary for a system of divinely sanctioned inequality in authority to restrain the sinful passions of his brethren.

It might be tempting to point to the massive differences between Winthrop and Lincoln. Even the attempt to draw the slightest connection between Winthrop and Lincoln offends defenders of the president who see his thought as wholly original. Usually these defenders (who are devoted to "natural right" philosophy, an ideology that I discuss in Chapter 5) insist that the key difference between the two leaders lies in the obvious fact that only Winthrop pays homage to the authority of God, not nature. Presumably, Winthrop is not nearly as universalistic as Lincoln, since he does not believe that natural rights befit all human beings. Winthrop denies exactly what the Declaration of Independence affirms: the naturally mandated *equality* of human beings.[6] At first glance, then, Winthrop has more in common with the slave owners of the South than with republican defenders of natural rights. Therefore, only the Declaration, not scripture, can truly inspire human beings to embrace equality.

This line of thinking is not the most promising way to dissociate Winthrop from the founders or Lincoln.[7] Winthrop did not object to all concepts of equality based on nature. The future governor clearly refers to the *laws of Nature,* in reference to the revealed truth that God bestowed upon his creation before the Fall. Whereas the laws of nature apply to the state of innocence, the laws of the gospel apply to "the estate of regeneracy." In a state of innocence, there was no need to emphasize truths that contend with the conflicted soul of man. In the precovenantal state of nature, there is indeed law that presupposes the goodness of man, his natural love of his brethren. Yet Winthrop then declares that the fall of humanity required God to replace the law of nature with that of the gospel, since the latter presumes the utter sinfulness of man. Although the laws of nature prescribe no rules for dealing with enemies, the gospel commands us to love them.[8] Winthrop essentially makes a distinction between nature's authority (law, right) and the gospel, which

---

Rossiter, *Seedtime of the Republic: The Origin of the American Tradition of Political Liberty,* 172–78.

6. Zuckert, "Natural Rights," 32–33.

7. For a comparison of Winthrop and Lincoln on the Christian basis of universalism, see Fornieri, *Abraham Lincoln's Political Faith,* 24–26.

8. Winthrop, "Modell of Christian Charity," 38.

is not substantively different from the thought of Lincoln. In a state of innocence, it is indeed "natural" to understand and practice charity as love of thy brethren. After the Fall, however, there is only conflict among human beings. What was perhaps self-evident in a state of innocence is no longer so obviously true to a sinful mind. As I argue in my next chapter on Lincoln, the president understood as well as the governor that the most important truths are hardly self-evident to human beings who have a vested interest in twisting the claims of scripture. Sadly, neither charity nor equality is an idea that human beings "naturally" (easily) embrace.

The crucial difference between Winthrop and Lincoln, however, is that the governor of a Puritan theocracy refused to insist that true Christian love requires *reciprocity* in authority. Any notion of a hierarchy (or an elect) governing people with an iron hand is not charitable.[9] The fact that Winthrop saw inequality as a divinely mandated state suggests that he, unlike Lincoln, confused the state of innocence with a postfallen world that tolerates inequality. Lincoln always emphasized that people are capable of knowing by nature that all human beings are equal, yet they forcibly deny this truth, this natural right, to others. The fact that many Americans still tolerated slavery on biblical grounds represented to Lincoln a transparently self-serving distortion of scripture. Yet Winthrop was still quite willing to tolerate a double standard, which would justify authoritarian rule.

Both Winthrop and Lincoln knew that nature alone was no protection against injustice, since an appeal to the purity of nature was simply the illusory desire of returning to a state of innocence that disappeared with the Fall. Yet Lincoln also knew that the traditional usage of charity in America (as represented by Winthrop) did little to address injustices like slavery. Lincoln would have agreed with Winthrop that reason is not sufficient for true morality. It is not enough to say that in the beginning humanity knows the difference between right and wrong. Because the republic does not consist of angels (as *The Federalist* taught), there must be a political ethic that *transcends* the authority of nature. Being the biblical realist he was, Lincoln held out no hope of returning to a lost state of purity, like so many in Christendom. The fact that people are capable of knowing the truth by nature in no way compels them to obey it.

Unlike Winthrop, Lincoln's understanding of love demands from its

---

9. See Holland, *Bonds of Affection*, 193, 245–46.

adherents a greater scrutiny of authority. Both men agreed that they must worship a God who is above nature, who shall deliver them from their fallen state. Moreover, before they attempt to save the world, they must recognize how infinitely fallen they are, beyond the original law of nature. Yet Lincoln alone believed that hierarchy itself is often a reflection of fallenness: this was not the conclusion of Winthrop. Although both men agreed that human nature was frail and self-serving, Winthrop did not draw from this biblical psychology the conclusion that only a democratic regime could restrain the sinful impulses of man.[10] Indeed, the governor was far more convinced than the president that his people were the "chosen," liberated from the English pharaoh. Whereas Lincoln took pains to qualify this belief in chosenness, Winthrop possessed absolute certainty that his followers, who were equal (in sin) among themselves, were nevertheless morally superior to all others (especially the "heathen" Native Americans)[11] as they sought to build the city on the hill. In the words of one historian, Winthrop was the "Nehemiah" who led the new Israelites from Babylon to the Promised Land.[12] In calling upon God to judge the English oppressors, the governor did not admit in the spirit of charity that his own people may become oppressors as well. Despite the later secularization of politics of America, the myth of chosenness would not disappear with the Puritans.

CHARITY AND THE SOCIAL CONTRACT TRADITION

Any discussion of the historical precedents to Lincoln's usage of charity requires an understanding of the social contract tradition whose main avatars also saw in charity the best morality for their political philosophy. I shall discuss mainly Spinoza in this context since he more than any other political philosopher of early modernity wedded democracy to the practice of biblical charity. Spinoza alone is most comparable to the spirit of Lincoln's thought on charity and its relation to democracy. Spinoza's relevance here is twofold: he was the first defender of liberal democracy in the modern West, and he was the first political philoso-

10. See ibid., 193, 207, 245–46.
11. See Richard Drinnon, *Facing West: The Metaphysics of Indian-Hating and Empire Building,* 46–55.
12. Phillips, *Cousins' Wars,* 18.

pher to understand the Bible as the foundation of this regime. Spinoza thus anticipates the success of Lincoln in defending charity as the precondition to democracy. Unlike Winthrop, Spinoza refuses to accept the self-serving teaching that charity is somehow compatible with a divinely sanctioned system of autocracy.

It is certainly true that other social contract theorists like Hobbes and Locke also assumed that charity would be the ultimate foundation of morality in their respective versions of the social contract. Yet Hobbes, as a critic of democracy, believed (like John Winthrop) that a monarchist regime could practice charity well enough by taking care of the physical needs of its citizens. Locke argued that tolerance of religious freedom rested on charity, but he ultimately preferred to judge his ideal regime according to its commitment to economic rationality rather than Christian love. In his *A Letter Concerning Toleration* (1689), Locke asserts, without much argument, that the true tolerance of religious freedom for all human beings (excluding those who subvert the social contract) is utterly compatible with charity. Yet he does not plumb the political depths of Christian morality. In *The Reasonableness of Christianity* (1695), Locke is at one with Spinoza in understanding charity as the true spirit of the gospel, but he does not draw from scripture any teaching of the relation between democracy and biblical morality. (Additionally, Locke places far greater importance than Spinoza in belief in miracles as a fundamental truth of the Bible.)

Only Kant moves closest to Spinoza in elaborating upon the implications of charity (the categorical imperative), yet the message of his political writings (especially *Perpetual Peace*) suggests that his social contract—consisting of a race of rational devils—would function perfectly well without any need for Christian ethics. Rousseau, the last great contractarian, rejected the golden rule and Christianity in favor of a political religion that (*pace* Machiavelli) was more realistic in forging a "General Will" that placed the regime above any Supreme Being.

Spinoza alone emphasized that the health of a true democracy rested entirely on the acceptance and practice of charity among the people.[13] Yet matters are not so simple when we compare the aims of Lincoln to those of Spinoza. In the same work in which he defends the utility

13. For a detailed discussion of the relation between charity and democracy in Spinoza's political philosophy, see Brayton Polka, *Between Philosophy and Religion: Spinoza, the Bible, and Modernity*, 2:143–287.

of charity—his anonymously published *Theologico-Political Tractatus* (1670)—Spinoza also clearly addresses the "Philosopher Reader" as his prime audience. Like Lincoln, Spinoza cautiously hopes that the great mass of people are capable of following either charity or other "dogmas" (mainly tenets of mercy, forgiveness, and belief in God, as he outlines in chapter 14),[14] which he insists upon as the criteria of true citizenship. The egoistic psychology, which Spinoza, Hobbes, and Locke all acknowledge, might lend even more doubt to the sincerity of their view that charity is a solid foundation for a democratically minded people. Spinoza's view of religion as "useful" for the "vulgar" masses has unfortunately persuaded some Lincoln scholars that the philosopher's apparent contempt for the popular wisdom (and faith) puts Spinoza at odds with Lincoln. Presumably, Spinoza used religion merely to accommodate the "cultural prejudices" of a Christian people.[15]

Like Lincoln, however, Spinoza believed that a democracy without the golden rule is no democracy at all. What is necessary for true "obedience" to a democracy is love of one's neighbor, which recognizes that "each is in God . . . and God is in each." It is significant that Spinoza returns to the Hebrew Covenant, not to Periclean Athens, as the foundation for democratic statecraft. This covenant puts all of its human servants on the same level of equality before God. It cannot be otherwise if all human beings already know charity. If all of humanity acts "with God's Spirit on the heart," then it must follow that democracy is the "most natural" regime of all.[16] Democracy requires the practice of charity among its citizens.

Does democracy, then, allow any religion or ideology to have influence, even if the majority demands it? Like Lincoln, Spinoza did not believe that a charity-based democracy can invite *all* ideas or forms of behavior to enjoy perfect freedom. Spinoza is well known for opposing the concept of "chosenness." There cannot be a chosen people in a true democracy, particularly if this body seeks to oppress others in the name of God. As controversial as Spinoza's critique of Judaism (or his

14. Spinoza, *Spinoza's Theologico-Political Treatise,* 164–65.
15. Fornieri, *Abraham Lincoln's Political Faith,* 97. Fornieri, who is one of the very few Lincoln scholars to discuss the relation between Spinoza and the president, uncritically accepts the Straussian view that Spinoza is an avatar of double truth (philosophy for the few, religion for the many). For an alternate reading, see Polka, *Between Philosophy and Religion,* 1:68–134.
16. Spinoza, *Spinoza's Theologico-Political Treatise,* 64, 181, 185, 211.

embrace of Christianity) is, his concept of the social contract foreshadows Lincoln more closely than any other figure. Spinoza's insistence on charity as the most important teaching of scripture above and beyond claims to know the supernatural (usually the source of claims to chosenness) would have been welcome to Lincoln, who often scorned the attempts of pastors to reveal what they took to be their special knowledge of Providence (while ignoring the very knowable injustice of slavery).[17] Despite his reputation as a liberal critic of Judaism,[18] Spinoza in fact is a prudent critic of all attempts to uphold the practice of a chosen people in a regime. Near the end of his discussion of the politics of the Hebrew Covenant, Spinoza not only targets the prophets and Pharisees for hypocritically claiming knowledge of "divine right" that they deny to others. In observing that "this brash license is covered by a show of religion," Spinoza also critiques the English revolutionaries of his time for overthrowing the Stuart monarchy in the name of a Providence that they falsely claim to know. The English Puritans were no wiser than the Israelites in believing that they were doing God's bidding as they slaughtered monarchists without any regard for the bloodshed and instability that left a "worse state" in their wake.[19] Spinoza's preference for democracy does not invite him to support uncharitable (and murderous) revolutions against undemocratic regimes. (His position on revolution is no different from that of Edmund Burke's.)

The fact that Spinoza doubted the ability or willingness of *all* human beings (without doubting their right) to become true citizens of a democracy perhaps relates more to Lincoln's thought than conventional scholars often acknowledge,[20] since both of these "liberal" democrats still insisted on a vital Christian foundation to sustain political stability. Spinoza knew as well as Lincoln that the power of reason is so weak among humanity that obedience to charity is far from guaranteed. As he somberly observed in his last and incomplete work, *The Political Treatise,* the fact that religion teaches every man to love his neighbor as himself is not persuasive enough to undermine the power of selfish passions.[21] Yet it is ultimately more prudent to appeal to charity—which everyone

17. Allen C. Guelzo, *Abraham Lincoln: Redeemer President*, 322.
18. See Leo Strauss, *Spinoza's Critique of Religion.*
19. Spinoza, *Spinoza's Theologico-Political Treatise*, 215–16.
20. See Grant Havers, "Was Spinoza a Liberal?"
21. Spinoza, *"A Theologico-Political Treatise" and "A Political Treatise,"* 289.

expects for themselves while they deny it to others—than exotic claims to know the supernatural.

It has been argued that Spinoza's insistence on a charity-based religion does not fit well with American religiosity. God, as Spinoza understood the deity, lays down moral dicta but offers little else in the way of comfort or consolation. Any attempt to portray God as a being who is personally involved with his creation is pure anthropomorphism that reveals more about humanity's self-serving desires than it does about the Almighty. (This truth about human beings is what the Bible actually *reveals,* according to Spinoza.) For this reason, literary critic Harold Bloom has contended that Spinoza's concept of God has little in common with an "American Religion" that teaches that God personally loves every American.[22] Yet Bloom ignores the emphasis on charity (rather than an anthropomorphized God) among religious denominations that Tocqueville later encountered in his travels. Moreover, Lincoln too had doubts about the wisdom of emphasizing a "personal God," especially when both sides believed that this God was on their side during the Civil War. Although this most religious of presidents faced political pressures unimaginable to Spinoza, he still felt it necessary to coax his people away from the spurious claims to see themselves as "chosen," and toward charity, an ethics that is simple to comprehend and difficult to practice.

Thomas Paine: Chosenness over Charity

Because Thomas Paine often invoked biblical credos in order to justify the liberation of the American colonies from English hegemony, it may be tempting to draw a parallel between his thought and that of Lincoln. Yet the choice of Paine as a philosophic ancestor of Lincoln is controversial for two reasons. First, Paine is well known as a harsh critic of revealed religion, as his work *The Age of Reason* (1794) illustrates. (Teddy Roosevelt called him a "dirty little atheist.") Thus, it seems absurd to suggest that Paine would use any religious themes for political purposes.

22. Bloom, *The American Religion: The Emergence of the Post-Christian Nation,* 16. Bloom perhaps exaggerates the influence that various indigenous denominations have had on American political elites. Noll contends, by contrast, that these elites have been secular to the core since the end of the Civil War (*Civil War,* 159–62).

Second, there is still great debate over the status of Paine and his influence on the American Revolution. Willmoore Kendall dismisses Paine as a figure who disappeared "from American history" during the course of the Revolutionary War. Irving Kristol similarly claims that Paine was "an English radical who never really understood America" and "is worth ignoring." Barry Alan Shain devalues the contribution of Paine in observing that his radical individualism was "atypical of Americans" that lived during the Revolutionary era. Yet Paine also has his supporters. Harry Jaffa contends that Paine's contribution to the intensity of the Revolution was "incalculable," and that his *Common Sense* did for the early stages of the Revolutionary period "what Churchill's speeches did to rally Britain, in the dark days after Dunkirk."[23]

I am inclined to believe that the influence of Paine lies in his rather selective use of scripture. Indeed, the interest of Paine lies solely in the biblical myth of chosenness rather than the ethic of charity. It is well known that *Common Sense,* a best-seller in its time, is an eloquent rallying cry for the defense of "the natural rights of all Mankind" against the depredations of the English monarchy. Yet it is less appreciated just how theological this work is. Paine shows no reluctance in invoking the authority of the Almighty in his defense of natural rights. America, whose ideals are those of the world's, must reject "the hardened, sullen-tempered Pharaoh of England for ever." It is clear in the mind of Paine at least that God is on the side of the American Revolution, not the tyrannical English king. Because the power of this monarch "needs checking," it cannot possibly be from God.[24] (The deity must, then, sanction a system of checks and balances in government.)

Common Sense makes clear that there is nothing in the Bible that supports tyranny. Paine is particularly fond of Gideon and the prophet Samuel for condemning the absolute power of kings. Indeed, God commands all human beings to stand up for their natural rights, since the Almighty planted in Americans "these inextinguishable feelings" for liberty." Paine unmistakably builds on the message of the gospel: people

---

23. Kendall and George W. Carey, *The Basic Symbols of the American Political Tradition,* 16; Kristol, "The American Revolution as a Successful Revolution," 39; Shain, *The Myth of American Individualism: The Protestant Origins of American Political Thought,* 175; Jaffa, *How to Think about the American Revolution: A Bicentennial Celebration,* 72–73.

24. Paine, *Common Sense,* 2, 26, 7.

already know the truth. There is no distinction between the wise few and the ignorant many (an assumption central to pagan thought). The Almighty is the great leveler of all human authority, who is most sympathetic with the lowliest creature on earth than with "all the crowned ruffians that have ever lived."[25] Paine is absolutely certain that God sanctions the American Revolution (while Lincoln emphasizes the mysterious nature of Providence). It is up to Americans to liberate the natural desire for freedom that lurks in the hearts of all peoples.

God is also the first true democrat, who wills "that there should be diversity of religious opinions" among Americans. Despite the fact that the Bible never refers to natural rights, Paine is certain that the new American Revolutionaries must spread these principles all over the world, to exercise "our power to begin the world over again." Lest any reader think that Paine is not referring to biblical concepts of God, he warns of the malevolent attempt to confuse obedience to tyranny with the Christian faith, or to put the "Bigot" in the place of the "Christian."[26]

Perhaps Paine's use of Christian themes is a calculated one, suitable for his readership at the time, or perhaps, as Michael Novak has observed, he was not fully aware of the Christian influence upon his work.[27] Whatever the original intent of Paine in *Common Sense,* it is unwise to overemphasize the "Christian" nature of Paine's thought, when his revolutionary thought has the greatest affinity to chosenness. It would also be premature to exaggerate the family resemblances between his ideas and those of Lincoln, when the president often critiqued the temptations of belief in being "chosen."[28]

Nevertheless, to this day, the legacy of Paine persuades many Americans, both religious and secular, that Providence and politics are completely intertwined. It is reckless to claim, as some scholars do, that the political creed of Paine has nothing in common with a religious faith.[29] There is no tension or separation between the cause of natural rights and the Supreme Being. Paine is the first evangelizing defender

25. Ibid., 33, 17.
26. Ibid., 41, 51, 54.
27. Novak, *On Two Wings: Humble Faith and Common Sense at the American Founding,* 164.
28. For the relation between Paine and Lincoln, see Guelzo, *Abraham Lincoln: Redeemer President,* 314, and Jaffa, *How to Think,* 75.
29. Thomas L. Pangle, *The Spirit of Modern Republicanism: The Moral Vision of the American Founders and the Philosophy of Locke,* 278.

of "natural rights" in America (an ideology that I discuss in Chapter 5). Indeed, Paine was more certain than Lincoln in spreading universal credos of liberty and equality to peoples who were not already schooled in Christian morality.

Paine's critique of English absolutism, we have seen, presupposes his favorable view of chosenness as a doctrinal thorn in the side of tyranny. The fact that Paine ultimately repudiated the ethic of charity (but never ceased to embrace chosenness) separates his thought decisively from that of Lincoln. To be sure, both agreed that Christian morality is necessary for a truly just life. As Paine wrote in *The Age of Reason,* the morality that Jesus taught and lived "was of the most benevolent kind," and "it has not been exceeded" by any other. Yet Paine (like Freud) also believes the Christian command to love thine enemy to be unrealistic and even vague. It is implausible to love a person (as an enemy) because of (or despite) his malevolence: he even goes so far as to condemn it as a doctrine of "the greatest persecutors" who hypocritically expect love without loving in return.[30] Yet Paine's understanding of Christian love confuses its imperatives with a shallow and self-serving sentimentality. Lincoln, who insisted that the people of the South be loved (that is, forgiven) by a wrongly self-righteous North, called on his fellow Americans to avoid the very teaching that Paine promoted, one that equated realism with hatred of the enemy.[31] Unlike Lincoln, Paine did not fully reflect upon the necessity of charity as the indispensable foundation of a republic that must be forgiving and merciful toward its foes. In demanding that Americans see themselves as the chosen, Paine did not insist that they be charitable as well. In calling on Americans to "begin the world over again," Paine was simply silent on the possibility that a chosen people would forge a new beginning without showing charity to peoples who may not share America's new ideals.[32]

Perhaps what ultimately explains the contrast between Paine and Lincoln is simply the fact that Paine did not live to see the effect of the Second Great Awakening in America in the early 1800s. At this time, Christians in America arguably had more influence than the secularism

---

30. Paine, *The Age of Reason: Being an Investigation of True and Fabulous Theology,* 26, 187.

31. See William Lee Miller, "Lincoln's Second Inaugural: The Zenith of Statecraft."

32. Paine, *Common Sense,* 51.

of the founders, since they managed to forge a "national culture" far more theistic than the founders would have liked.[33] One central element of this culture—as Tocqueville discovered—was the belief in Christian charity. Whereas *Common Sense* spoke to the temptations of Americans to believe in chosenness, *The Age of Reason* ridiculed their most fundamental moral beliefs. At least one of Paine's contemporaries prophetically grasped the future of his republic. Samuel Adams warned his boldly irreligious friend Paine that his countrymen "are fast returning to their first love," the love of God.[34] Lincoln, unlike Paine, had to rely on the charitable nature of the American people, not their faith in their destiny as a chosen people. Since both sides in the Civil War believed that they were chosen, it would be insufficient to use the language of Exodus. The "better angels" of their nature would have to triumph over the belief in providential favoritism. Unfortunately, twentieth- and twenty-first-century secularist ideologies in American foreign policy have forgotten this lesson (see Chapters 6 and 7).

CHARITY AND THE AMERICAN FOUNDERS

Perhaps it would not be too much of an overstatement to assert that charity as a basic ethic was central to all of the founders, who grew up in a Christian civilization. Yet recognition of this heritage does not necessarily translate into political support for charity as the basis of a national creed. Hannah Arendt has argued that the American Revolution was the one modern revolution in which compassion played no role, despite the fact that Christian mercy had been influential outside the political realm for centuries.[35] Arendt's claim is perhaps an exaggeration, since the founders certainly worried that their new regime would degenerate into a tyranny that oppressed the weakest of the earth. John Adams worried about the new republic falling into the hands of leaders who teach "the most disconsolate of all creeds that men are but fire flies, and this *all* is without a father [loving God]."[36] Moreover, Adams had no doubt

---

33. Noll, *Civil War,* 25–26.

34. Adam's letter to Paine (November 30, 1802) is included in Paine, *Age of Reason,* 202.

35. Arendt, *On Revolution,* 70 71.

36. Adams, "Discourses on Davila," in *The Political Writings of John Adams: Representative Selections,* 193.

about the only foundation of resistance to murderous politics. Even if the superstition and tyrannical hypocrisy of ecclesiastical authority were to be overthrown, free peoples would still require the ethic of Christian love as their moral compass.[37]

Yet none of Adams's statements suggests that charity should be the primary test of an authentic republican democracy. Indeed, none of the founding documents even mentions charity. It is reasonable to believe that the authors of *The Federalist* shared the views of Adams. It is also likely that they assumed that the majority of Americans shared these views as well. Still, unlike Lincoln, they did not yet feel the need to remind their fellow Americans of the need to practice their charity as good citizens preserving their new republic. Charity was still not yet politicized.

The inattention of the authors of *The Federalist* to charity should not imply that they were cold-blooded rationalists. They are all too aware that reason alone cannot restrain the passions of "factions." One of the key arguments of article 10 against pure democracy is the baseness of human nature. The assumption of a moral sense is just as utopian as one of rationality: if the heat of popular "impulse" coincides with a crisis, then "we well know that neither moral nor religious motives can be relied on as an adequate control." Unlike Lincoln, these authors indeed do not *rely* on charity to foster good citizenship while mitigating selfishness. It took a war of brother against brother and the brilliant rhetorical gifts of an exceptionally eloquent president to elevate charity as the indispensable foundation of American democracy. While Lincoln built upon an already established Christian polity, he knew that the full embodiment of charity as the creed required greater efforts on the part of the president than any of the founders had ever contemplated.

THOMAS JEFFERSON AND THE UNIQUENESS OF CHRISTIAN MORALITY

Thomas Jefferson deserves his own special discussion, since he reflected more seriously on charity than any other founder. Lincoln also appropriated the legacy of Jefferson in asserting the doctrine of equality as the

---

37. Adams, "A Dissertation on the Canon and Feudal Law," in ibid., 3–21.

true founding credo.[38] It may well be tempting, then, to portray Jefferson as the ideological ancestor of Lincoln. Still, there are two obvious difficulties with this argument. First, Jefferson was notoriously hostile to Christian revelation. Second, there is little evidence that he thought *consistently* that slavery was an affront to Christian charity. We can examine both of these objections in turn.

Jefferson was irritated at the suggestion that only Christian revelation could furnish human beings with an understanding of God, if the truth is truly written upon the hearts of all peoples. This man of the Enlightenment was outraged at the suggestion that knowledge of God was restricted to one-sixth of the human race while the other five-sixths lacked a concept of a deity altogether.[39] Yet it would be hard to deny the unique importance that Christian charity enjoyed as a matter of personal morality, in Jefferson's view. As his famous letter to Dr. Benjamin Rush on Christianity indicates, the Christian doctrine of love is the primary doctrine of the faith, whose truth must be preserved from distortions at the hands of modern-day sophists who confuse paganism and revelation. Jefferson—who famously declared that Christianity makes "one half the world fools and the other half hypocrites"[40]—nevertheless celebrated charity when (in his letter to Rush) he distinguished between the "corruptions of Christianity" and the "genuine precepts of Jesus himself." The deist Jefferson was quite willing to praise Christian morality as "the most sublime and benevolent"—and even superior to the ancients—as long as the essence of revelation was understood as the moral teaching of charity. Jefferson genuinely respected the faith, which, as an ethic, applied to all mankind "under the bonds of love, charity, peace, common wants and common aids." This ethic was "more pure and perfect" than anything that the greatest pagan philosophers had ever defended. It is imperative, Jefferson constantly thought, to emulate "the innocent and genuine character of this benevolent Moralist [Jesus]" by rescuing his moral commands from "the heresies of bigotry and fanaticism" that have held back reason.[41]

38. Lincoln, *Collected Works,* 2:249. The occasion is the debate with Senator Douglas on October 16, 1854.

39. Jefferson to John Adams, April 11, 1823, in *The Life and Selected Writings of Thomas Jefferson,* 611.

40. Jefferson, "Notes on Virginia," in ibid., 255–56.

41. Jefferson, *Life and Selected Writings,* 519, 515, 522, 634.

It is significant that Jefferson praised the uniqueness of Christian morality. He never asserted that rival moralities (especially pagan ones) could teach charity. This emphasis on the distinctive nature of Christian charity, which contradicts his other view that Christianity alone does not monopolize the truth, would be welcome to Lincoln's mind.

Nevertheless, did Jefferson understand charity as the essence of democracy, as Lincoln later did? Lincoln himself seems to suggest that Jefferson had charity in mind when, in a debate with Senator Douglas (October 7, 1858), he remarked that there was a clear contradiction between Jefferson's principle of equality and his ownership of slaves. As Lincoln later portrayed him, Jefferson was painfully aware of this double standard. This slave owner still "trembled for his country when he remembered that God was just," Lincoln reminded Senator Douglas.[42]

Still, Jefferson himself did not insist that this doctrine of love become a political creed. Of course, the best evidence that Jefferson did not have this intention lies in the fact that he kept slaves to the end of his life. However, the pressure of this "personal morality" must have played some role in encouraging Jefferson, as president, to end the foreign slave trade and ban slavery in the western territories. As Lincoln astutely observed in a debate with Senator Douglas, Jefferson was indeed a slave owner, *but* he still insisted on ending slavery and thus actualizing the principles of the Declaration.[43] Why else would Jefferson tremble over the justice of God?

As I have noted, it is sometimes suggested that Lincoln's political usage of charity departs from the founders (including Jefferson) by wedding Christianity with political philosophy. Lincoln would most certainly have deplored this interpretation of his actions, since he portrayed himself as the real "conservative" who resisted the "innovation" of teaching natural inequality. Moreover, Jefferson as much as Lincoln knew that it was all too common for people to violate truths that they otherwise knew by "nature." In his first inaugural address (1801), Jefferson understood respect for equal justice and the "love of man" (not just Americans) as "the creed of our political faith." Like Lincoln, Jefferson understood the paradox of human nature: that we know the truth but

---

42. Lincoln, *Collected Works,* 3:320.
43. Ibid., 2:249.

still sin against it. It would not be necessary to make respect for equal rights of minorities into a "sacred principle," as Jefferson admonished, if all human beings understood this truth as self-evident.[44] Democracies could be just as prone to hypocrisy as tyrannies, as Jefferson and Lincoln knew. If human beings do not remain naturally committed to respecting each other, then only a loving yet punitive God—what Jefferson referred to as "overruling Providence"—can redeem them.[45]

Still, Jefferson's opposition to slavery—at least in principle—did not compel him to politicize charity, or to associate politics with Christianity. Indeed, this president did not even follow Thomas Paine in consistently believing that it was the mission of America to liberate the world, especially if many peoples lacked a basic understanding of their "natural rights."[46] Although Jefferson occasionally referred to Americans as the "chosen," he never developed this theme as a staple of his thought; generally, the only "chosen" people in Jefferson's mind were the farmers and planters of Virginia.[47] Even if Jefferson never attempted to create a new Christian-based "political religion," this would not change the fact that a high number of Americans who grew up during the Second Great Awakening were ready for the moral gospel of Jefferson's eventual successor, Abraham Lincoln.[48]

Tocqueville Discovers American Charity

Even before the famous visit of Tocqueville in 1831, there was an abundance of signs illustrating the religious direction of America, since the

44. Ibid., 3:537–38; Jefferson, "First Inaugural Address," 24–27. Holland perhaps overreaches when he claims that Jefferson, given his deistic tendencies, had little use for a biblical God who must underpin morality (*Bonds of Affection*, 244). Jefferson was often contradictory in his understanding of God.

45. Jefferson, "First Inaugural Address," 26.

46. Jefferson advised that the French should show caution in calling for universal rights, and even declared that the Russians could not take care of themselves, despite the best efforts of the czar in spreading "a sense of natural rights" throughout the nation. For a discussion of Jefferson's "ethnocentrism," see Charles A. Miller, *Jefferson and Nature: An Interpretation*, 257.

47. Jefferson, "Notes on Virginia," in *Life and Selected Writings*, 259.

48. Jefferson was unprepared—like most founders—to accept the rise of mass religious belief at the end of his life. See Gordon S. Wood, *The Radicalism of the American Revolution*, 330–31, 366–67.

Second Great Awakening had already left its mark. The fact that most denominations framed their faith in terms of the moral teachings of Jesus rather than belief in the supernatural was not lost on Tocqueville. Perhaps Jefferson had not been as out of synch with the mainstream of American faith as many scholars portray him to be, when he identified real Christianity with the practice of morality. As Tocqueville observed in his famous journey throughout the republic in the early 1830s, the avoidance of strife and conflict among the various denominations of America was directly attributable both to a love of liberty of worship *and* to an emphasis on the ethics of Christianity. This morality was the one thing that all of these believers could agree upon. Every sect was part of a greater unity of Christendom, since Tocqueville discovered that "Christian morality is everywhere the same" in the republic.[49]

The America that Tocqueville investigated—the republic in which Lincoln came of age—was admirable because of its focus on the ethics of Christianity alone. As a student of Europe's religious wars, Tocqueville could only welcome the avoidance of debilitating doctrinal disputes in favor of a simple focus on charity for all of humanity. In pointed contrast to Islam, Tocqueville admired Christianity for dealing "only with the general relations" between humanity and God, not political maxims in support of theocracy. Beyond the moral teachings of Christ, the Gospels "teach nothing and do not oblige people to believe anything."[50] For this reason, Tocqueville predicted that Christianity would survive and even enrich the age of democracy.

Yet Tocqueville also concluded that Christianity is the source of political change in America. Slavery was doomed to extinction with the advent of this faith, since this faith "destroyed slavery" with the insistence that slaves too had natural rights.[51] This statement of fact, as Tocqueville understood the faith, underscored his belief that the morality of Christianity—especially its basic egalitarianism—had far more power in America than any other tenet of the faith. Like Lincoln, however, this feeling might have been more hope than fact, in light of the American belief in chosenness and claims to know Providence.

Tocqueville arrived at the conclusion that American democracy certainly needed charity, and Christianity as a whole. Indeed, Tocqueville

49. Alexis de Tocqueville, *Democracy in America*, 290–91.
50. Ibid., 445.
51. Ibid., 348.

had prophetically warned, as had John Adams, that this morality rested on faith in the biblical God. Belief in liberty among the people would not survive unless that people was "subject to God."[52] Unlike Paine, Tocqueville had not subordinated charity to the enticing charms of chosenness. Unlike Jefferson, Tocqueville believed that a democracy required a vital belief in charity. The stability of the American regime did not encourage this European aristocrat to embrace the theocracy of Winthrop. Yet Tocqueville perhaps overestimated the strength of charity as a belief that competed with the rising influence of chosenness among the soon to be divided American populace.

TOWARD LINCOLN

Still, how long would it take for Americans to draw the relation between Christian mores and equality? Lincoln knew (as early as his Lyceum speech of 1838) that the principles of the Revolution had been withering on the vine. Lincoln realized as well as Tocqueville that rational self-interest alone could not save the republic from self-destruction. Apparently, the principles of natural right had not become the objects of reverence among the nation, torn apart by the "mobocratic" violence to which he referred in his Lyceum speech. Whereas Jefferson and the other founders had hoped that the truth of the Declaration would be self-evident to all rational individuals, Lincoln soberly recognized that the Declaration must be invested with a religious authority, not merely a rational one. After all, it was possible to deny the supposedly self-evident truth of equality. Lincoln knew, even before the Civil War, that only a "just God," rather than the force of logic or reason, could force Americans back to a full embrace of the founding principles.[53]

Lincoln truly was revolutionary, not in calling attention to the importance of charity but in insisting on its full inclusion in the public square. Charity had to be the precondition for democracy. Only Spinoza understood the implications of this task before Lincoln. As we have seen, Winthrop believed that this ethic could function well in an authoritarian regime. The main difference between Lincoln and his predecessors (Paine, Jefferson, and the founders) is that charity for

52. Ibid., 294.
53. Lincoln, *Collected Works*, 3:375–76.

him (and, he hoped, for all Americans) would no longer be separated from *politics.* Jefferson saw charity largely in terms of a private morality (which his slave owning directly contradicted). Tocqueville certainly spied a relation between Christian mores and politics, and even worried at times about the survival of this synthesis. Nevertheless, he seemed to doubt that charity should necessarily become a civil faith. Paine scorned Christianity and even dismissed the charitable love of one's enemies as vague and unrealistic, a criticism that he did not level against his own use of the Exodus narrative. Moreover, Paine, unlike Lincoln, was hopeful that a new politics could be based on deism rather than Christianity. (Ironically, both the theocrat Winthrop and the democrat Paine were more enamored with chosenness than with charity.) The apparent disjunction between religious morality and politics would have to cease: this was Lincoln's hope. No longer would Americans preach charity in the church halls *while* they practiced injustice in politics.

To varying degrees, however, all of these figures attributed a certain importance to charity. Spinoza returns to the biblical covenant, not to classical Athens, to find the ethic that grounds his concept of modern democracy. The believing Winthrop and the secular-minded Paine and Jefferson agree that Christianity alone is the source of the best morality available to humanity (although the latter do not accept other tenets of Christianity). Tocqueville cannot imagine an America without Christian morality. Although Lincoln the conservative would heartily concur with his philosophical ancestors on the importance of charity, Lincoln the revolutionary would urge his nation to full adoption of this ethic as the highest democratic creed. Only then would America quit the hypocrisy of defending slavery because of the illusory belief that it is a matter of politics rather than religion or morality.

3

"With Charity for All":
Lincoln Raises the Sights

> But, say you, it is a question of *interest;* and, if you can make it your interest, you have the right to enslave another. Very well. And if he can make it his *interest,* he has the right to enslave you.

—Abraham Lincoln, "Fragment on Slavery," July 1, 1854

> With malice toward none, with charity for all; with firmness in the right, as God gives us to see the right, let us strive on to finish the work we are in; to bind up the nation's wounds; to care for him who shall have borne the battle, and for his widow, and his orphan—to do all which may achieve and cherish a just, and a lasting peace, among ourselves, and with all nations.

—Abraham Lincoln, second inaugural address, 1865

O ne of the enduring side effects of the Civil War is the conflict over the meaning of Lincoln's legacy for American political thought. What exactly did he intend to be the moral message of his presidency? Since America's rise to superpower status in the post World War II era, friend and foe alike have claimed that the president set the stage for an ambitiously secular campaign of global democracy building.

Lincoln was allegedly the American Moses who led both Americans and the world into the promised land of democracy. It is no surprise, then, that the president's allusions to chosenness, qualified as they are, have inspired modern elites to justify the spread of democracy (see Chapter 6). Chosenness receives the lion's share of attention in most discussions of Lincoln's legacy.

It would be inaccurate to claim that the president's many statements on charity have encountered a complete lack of interest. No one would dispute the fact that Lincoln emphasized, from his earliest speeches to his last inaugural address, that it was unnatural for northerners and southerners to see each other as strangers and enemies; Lincoln called on both sides to practice the charity that they preached. Even among those scholars who doubt the sincerity of Lincoln's religious faith, there is no doubt that charity possesses importance at the rhetorical level. What has not received sufficient attention or study, in my judgment, is one big question related to Lincoln's usage of charity. Can a nation's use of charity, which rests on a particular religion's understanding of moral duty, realistically encourage both its own citizens *and* people all over the world to practice this ethic? The ideal of acting "with charity for all" presupposes that a people already understands justice and mercy, but what if people understand the meaning of these credos in different ways?

Most scholars who study Lincoln have not appreciated the implications of the president's insistence that the American people act in a charitable spirit. Was it simply a matter of rhetoric on his part, or was he demanding a new kind of politics altogether? Every Lincoln scholar is familiar with the perhaps apocryphal story told by Henry Champion Deming (a member of the Connecticut Congress) in which the president allegedly informed Deming that he would become a member of any church that inscribed "over its altar as its sole qualification for membership" the commitment to love thy neighbor as thyself.[1] To my knowledge, however, few scholars have bothered to mine the implications of this commitment for American politics, and Allen Guelzo, one of the president's ablest biographers, has faulted Deming for reading too much into Lincoln's words here; Matthew Holland does not exaggerate when he laments the lack of scholarly attention to Lincoln's thoughts on charity.[2]

---

1. William E. Barton, *The Soul of Abraham Lincoln,* 94.
2. Guelzo, *Abraham Lincoln: Redeemer President,* 446; Holland, *Bonds of Affection,* 5, 14.

Defenders of Lincoln, who typically see his thought as the ideal rationale for universalizing the credos of liberty and equality throughout the world, do not investigate the implications of Lincoln's association of democracy with charity. Nor do they examine the broad implications of Lincoln's appeal to his people to act "with charity for all" on the eve of the North's triumph over the South: was he addressing a particular people or all of mankind? The fact that Lincoln dramatically raises the sights in insisting that *true* democracy in America must be charitable does not invite much discussion among contemporary admirers of Lincoln.[3] It is simply de rigueur to accept the relation between egalitarian democracy and charity without question, as if all human beings must embrace this relation regardless of creed or culture. Harry V. Jaffa treats as an obvious truth that the Declaration of Independence "flows" from the golden rule. Lucas E. Morel states unequivocally that the equality principle is no different from charity. Joseph R. Fornieri asserts that the golden rule and the republican principle of equal consent are "correlative."[4]

Surprisingly, even scholars who have studied the religious nature of Lincoln's thought have written little about his use of charity.[5] Additionally, those who knew Lincoln on a personal basis have commented on his use of biblical morality without providing a thorough analysis. William H. Herndon, his law partner and biographer, rightly points to the centrality of Christian ethics in Lincoln's thought (in contrast to his suspicion of miracles and other theistic claims) as a matter of course without plumbing the depths of Lincoln's belief in charity. As Herndon puts it, Lincoln "loved the *broad* Christian philosophy, maxims, sayings, and moral of Christianity" as the primary truths for human beings, yet Herndon is silent on the political implications of these beliefs for Lincoln's thought.[6]

---

3. See Holland, *Bonds of Affection,* for a rare discussion of Lincoln's thought on charity. This discussion does not raise questions about the twentieth-century understanding of Lincoln.

4. Jaffa, *A New Birth of Freedom: Abraham Lincoln and the Coming of the Civil War,* 353; Morel, *Lincoln's Sacred Effort: Defining Religion's Role in American Self-Government,* 208; Fornieri, *Abraham Lincoln's Political Faith,* 43.

5. Noll cites pastors of the Civil War era who invoked charity but lacked an understanding of Lincoln's own complex usage of this ethic (*Civil War,* 66, 134–35).

6. Emanuel Hertz, *The Hidden Lincoln: From the Letters and Papers of William H. Herndon,* 44 (emphasis in the original).

In the few studies that make mention of Lincoln's commitment to biblical morality, some simply refer to it as a fixture of his faith in Providence, with no real impact on his politics.[7] Others see this rhetoric as a cynical ploy intended to placate the masses. Yet as early as his Lyceum speech, the only time in which he invoked the idea of a "political religion," Lincoln referred to the need for Americans to embrace a "sound morality" alongside "reverence" for the nation's ideals and institutions.[8] It is not a stretch to interpret this morality as the biblical ethic of charity, the only morality to which Lincoln alluded throughout his life. Yet the full implications of reliance on charity as the political creed of the nation have received little critical examination.

Throughout his political career, Lincoln attacked the hypocrisy of his enemies, and even his people, on the basis of charity. It was hypocritical to defend slavery on the grounds that ethics and politics are disconnected. As Lincoln declared in a speech of 1860, it is absurd that "we must not call it [slavery] wrong in politics because that is bringing morality into politics, and we must not call it wrong in the pulpit because that is bringing politics into religion." A truly just nation cannot survive the toleration of hypocrisy any more than it can tolerate the cynical separation of religious morality from politics. "We were proclaiming ourselves political hypocrites before the world, by thus fostering Human Slavery and proclaiming ourselves, at the same time, the sole friends of Human Freedom." As one admiring reader has declared, Lincoln had to fight a *"nation of hypocrites."*[9]

Long before his "House Divided" speech and his attack on slavery, Lincoln was preoccupied with hypocrisy in other political contexts. During the controversial Mexican War in 1848, Lincoln sternly admonished Baptist minister John Peck to reconcile his biblical mores with his support for an imperialist war: "Would you venture to so consider them [these acts of aggression], had they been committed by any nation on earth, against the humblest of our people? I know you would not. Then I ask, is the precept 'Whatsoever ye would that men should do to you, do ye even so to them' obsolete—of no force?—of no application?" America was supposed to be morally superior to other nations because of its historic

7. Guelzo, *Abraham Lincoln: Redeemer President,* 120.
8. Lincoln, *Collected Works,* 1:115.
9. Ibid., 4:21, 2:242; Gelernter, *Americanism,* 107 (emphasis in the original). See also Fornieri, *Abraham Lincoln's Political Faith,* 170.

commitment to one morality for all human beings. To make exceptions of some people at the expense of others is to violate basic morality, an act worthy only of a tyranny. Fearing the eventual acceptance of slavery in America, Lincoln wrote to Joshua Speed in 1855: "When it comes to this I should prefer emigrating to some country where they make no pretence of loving liberty—to Russia, for instance, where despotism can be taken pure, and without the base alloy of hypocracy [*sic*]."[10]

Of course, the paradox of Lincoln is that he often felt compelled to violate his own value system, as both friend and foe have noted. In a debate with Lincoln in October 1858, Senator Douglas pointedly commented: "I assert . . . that he [Lincoln] holds one set of principles in the abolition counties, and a different and contradictory set in the other counties."[11] The fact that Lincoln could be vulnerable to charges of hypocrisy underscores the difficulty of the American political use of charity, which judges all according to their moral consistency. Lincoln was not the first American politician of stature to spy a glaring contradiction between the principles of the founding and the toleration of slavery. After all, Jefferson famously "trembled" for his nation in awareness of God's justice, as Lincoln liked to observe. Yet he was the first to make the resolution of this contradiction into a matter of survival. Lincoln forever *raised the sights* of American politics. If the nation cannot exist "half-slave, half-free," can it indulge in policies that promote egregious double standards among peoples? Can it honestly claim to be a Christian people? The ultimate test of a true democracy lies in its commitment to charity. Lincoln may not have been certain about the providence of God or the chosenness of Americans, as I argue in this chapter. Yet he was certain that a commitment to charity must translate into a politics of true democratic governance. Charity is not simply the basis for the equality of all human beings, as most scholars who study Lincoln argue. It is the imperative to relate fairly and justly to friend and foe alike, as he insisted in his second inaugural address. It is the foundation of true order: without charity, there is no true rule of law (a concern of Lincoln's since his 1838 Lyceum speech).

Still, what kind of sacrifice does charity require of the American people, including its leadership? Specifically, does it call upon the republic to re-create the world in its own image and likeness, unlocking the capacity

10. Lincoln, *Collected Works,* 1:473, 2:323.
11. Ibid., 3:264.

for charity that is the lodestone for a successful democracy? There is a vast consensus on the position that Lincoln demanded the true universalization of the American creed, which the Declaration first embodied. The principles of liberty and equality are for all of humanity, not simply Americans. The "last, best hope on earth" could not possibly express anything other than an absolutist commitment to truths applicable to all peoples. All of humanity could become American, and indeed the republic had an obligation to throw open its doors to anyone who desired to escape from the yoke of tyranny. As he said of newly arrived German immigrants in 1861, "They are all of the great family of men, and if there is one shackle upon any of them, it would be far better to lift the load from them than to pile additional loads upon them."[12] That the American regime, before or since Lincoln, has failed to live up to these moral ideals has not appreciably discouraged scholars on the Right and Left from demanding that the republic fulfill its ultimate mission. Yet what exactly does a political commitment to charity entail? Based on the following analysis of Lincoln's thought, this creed demands the following:

> An avoidance of hypocrisy in the practice of both religion and politics; both leaders and citizens must be charitable by making a considerable attempt to empathize with one's enemy, to understand his grievances from his perspective
> A suspicion of claims to know the supernatural providence of God, including claims of "chosenness," which encourage self-righteousness instead of charity
> The presence of an already established Christian culture, which is willing to privilege charity over other credos (like chosenness)
> A commitment to realistic goals in politics

All of these preconditions, which I shall discuss in turn, make steep demands on both the faith and the political communities of the United States. The implications of each of these are vast.

THE AVOIDANCE OF HYPOCRISY

Lincoln was sensitive to the charge of hypocrisy, at least as it was applied

12. Ibid., 5:537, 4:203.

to his own nation's ideals. Perhaps one of the least-surprising effects of his legacy is that it allows his numerous critics to charge him with hypocrisy when the president saw fit to violate his own adherence to the moral consistency that charity requires. Critics across the ideological spectrum have invoked the morality of Lincoln against Lincoln's acts. On the Right, many fault Lincoln for not extending charity toward the South when he ordered his generals to practice total war against both soldier and civilian. Indeed, he did not invoke the force of charity as he sought to preserve the Union after the Confederates fired on Fort Sumter; charity became important to his presidency only during the Civil War (although it was important to his thought in his early political career at times). On the Left, revisionist historians since the 1960s blame the president for ignoring the legitimate concerns of Native Americans while fighting for equality for the slaves. Moreover, both rightists and leftists have also faulted Lincoln for supporting the colonization—or deportation—of newly freed slaves to Africa or Central America, when he conversely supported the natural rights of all human beings to become Americans.

I am not suggesting that Lincoln's thoughts and policies were always charitable. I simply point to the irony that his many critics are using the terms of *his* discourse to critique Lincoln's deviations. This fact may testify to the influence of charity upon the politics of charity, as Lincoln articulated it. Perhaps it is not surprising that his critics, who are still under the influence of a Christian morality in the United States, assess the legacy of Lincoln in terms of the gap between his words and deeds. Yet they are also living in an America that, after Lincoln, could not wisely forget that charity and politics are inseparable. Even if Lincoln did not always live up to this imperative, he certainly insisted upon it. This insistence is novel. As I argued in Chapter 2, no other political figure in American history before Lincoln had made such a demand. Indeed, with the exception of the small number of abolitionists in the North (who were not very charitable toward the South anyway, when they demanded its complete destruction, come hell or high water), most Christians did not see an obvious relation between politics and religion. As Barry Alan Shain has shown, the earliest Americans were far more concerned with their Christian faith than any political question.[13] Lincoln changed all that.

13. See Shain, *Myth of American Individualism.*

Charity requires tremendous self-critique, as Lincoln well knew. As we have seen, he even went so far as to praise Jefferson, a slave owner, for critiquing slavery, and thus implied that the principles of the founding contradicted the practice of slavery. Nevertheless, it is sometimes suggested (notably by his law partner, William Herndon) that Lincoln thought of Jefferson as a hypocrite, despite his public affirmations of praise for this founder.[14] Certainly in his public rhetoric, Lincoln asserted that Jefferson was just as determined to make hypocrisy into an issue of politics as one of religion, even though privately he may have doubted Jefferson's sincerity. Still, were most Americans any better than Jefferson, since they either owned slaves or purchased goods from the South, while they too trembled with thoughts of God's justice? In the Douglas debates as well as in his presidency Lincoln emphasized the complicity of *all* (himself included) in the toleration of slavery. In his debate of October 16, 1854, he declared, "Before proceeding, let me say I think I have no prejudice against the Southern people. They are just what we would be in their situation. If slavery did not now exist amongst them, they would not introduce it." Toward the end of his second year as president, he reiterated this charitable sentiment: "It is no less true for having been often said, that the people of the south are not more responsible for the original introduction of this property, than are the people of the north; and when it is remembered how unhesitatingly *we all* use cotton and sugar, and share the profits of dealing in them, it may not be quite safe to say, that the south has been more responsible than the north for its continuance." Lincoln's politics of charity, then, relentlessly demanded that all Americans live up to a political faith that even Jefferson did not portray as the leitmotif of democracy. Lincoln demanded charity of the North as well as the South. The fact that he recognized the immoral complicity of Yankees with slavery likely explains why, in his first inaugural address, he was willing to reinforce the fugitive slave law and even support a constitutional amendment in protection of existing slavery. These prudential measures were not acts of hypocrisy on Lincoln's part, as one unkind critic has argued.[15] Rather, Lincoln

14. See Guelzo's discussion in *Abraham Lincoln: Redeemer President,* 3–9.

15. For Lincoln's efforts to empathize with the South, see *Collected Works,* 2:255, 5:531–32 (emphasis added). For a critique of these efforts, see Thomas J. DiLorenzo, *The Real Lincoln: A New Look at Abraham Lincoln, His Agenda, and an Unnecessary War,* 13.

recognized that the outright abolition of slavery at the beginning of the secession conflict would have been a supreme act of hypocrisy on the part of a North that had materially benefited from slavery.

Lincoln taught that hypocrisy is the great scourge that destroys a republic based on universal principles. Even if Lincoln himself did not always adhere to charity (and in fact many have accused him of hypocrisy or insincere faith), it does not change the fact that he gave his full support to a morality that must apply to *all,* including the president. Since its basic morality calls upon Americans to rebel against any hypocrisy, Christianity cannot be a Platonic "noble fiction," as many of Lincoln's defenders argue.[16] Charity raises the sights.

Debates over the precise historic origin of Lincoln's political use of biblical faith often reflect the even larger debate over the status of the Bible in American political symbolism. There are scholars who believe that scripture has little to do with Lincoln's motivations or beliefs, and then there are those who believe that the president's use of the Bible perfectly coincides with the principles of the founding. What is clear in this often unclear debate is that Lincoln knew that biblical revelation puts enormous pressure on believers, and he used this fact to justify his struggle against slavery. Of course, no one denies that Lincoln's Christian background influenced his thoughts on politics. Still, Lincoln politicized charity as no one ever had before. As Michael P. Zuckert states, Lincoln's synthesis of the religious and the political represents an "immanentization of the other-worldly spirit of Christianity."[17] The president's famous appeal to "charity for all" in his second inaugural address is famous enough to dissuade anyone from ignoring the influence of his faith.

The sheer power of Lincoln's biblical hermeneutic constitutes a paradox: His politicization of charity is indeed a new beginning for America (no other president before him saw politics in such evangelical terms) that already rested on the foundations of American Protestantism. What is new is not Lincoln's simultaneous invocation of biblical faith and ethics, but his determination to demonstrate what Willmoore Kendall called the "porous" relation between church and state by elevating charity to the level of a political creed. Charity is both religious *and* secular. After Lincoln, Americans (both believers and unbelievers) increasingly

16. I shall discuss the views of Harry Jaffa and others below.
17. Zuckert, "Lincoln and the Problem of Civil Religion," 359.

framed their political actions in biblical terms (as they had before his presidency), but now they faced, as never before, the pressure to ground the politics of their government upon charity and thus avoid accusations of hypocrisy in the process. He raised the sights of the American regime by committing its people to the fulfillment of biblical charity.

Still, was Lincoln himself hypocritical in his use of biblical credos? Many readers, friend and foe alike, portray Lincoln's use of religion as a mere political ploy. Even admirers of the president have doubted that he sincerely believed in what they call Christian "orthodoxy."[18] The fact that Lincoln invoked biblical themes toward the end of his presidency in no way convinces even sympathetic historians that he authentically supported the most basic scriptural claims. Indeed, as I discuss later in this chapter, Lincoln cautioned against easy claims to knowledge of Providence or the supernatural, especially since both sides in the Civil War had practiced this self-serving theology. Perhaps even privately Lincoln was as dismissive of Christianity as Paine had been publicly: it was rumored that, as a young man, he had penned a sarcastic treatise mocking the credos of this faith. When he was running for Congress in 1846, he had to face his opponent's accusations of deism and scoffing at Christianity. Moreover, Lincoln had never been baptized, never joined a church, and, until late in his presidency, never even regularly attended a place of worship. In the words of even a sympathetic biographer, "no better example" of a politician who invoked religious themes in public while lacking piety in private existed than Abraham Lincoln.[19]

The possibility that Lincoln may have been insincere in his appeals to faith is less important than the attempt to understand the meaning and effect of these appeals. After all, he was speaking a language of piety to an overwhelmingly believing audience, and, therefore, demonstrating how well he understood the American people. Certainly, the founders neglected to do this, and were therefore unprepared for the impact of the Second Great Awakening. By that time, evangelicals had created an American "national culture" that shaped the politician, not the reverse.[20] Lincoln responded to this world, but then he raised its sights. As Harry Jaffa has argued, Lincoln substantively broadened Jefferson's insistence

---

18. See Guelzo, *Abraham Lincoln: Redeemer President*, 151–58; and Noll, *Civil War*, 31–50, 74.

19. Guelzo, *Abraham Lincoln: Redeemer President*, 413.

20. Noll, *Civil War*, 25.

that all human beings respect the rights of others (as taught by John Locke) with the biblical teaching that all human beings are commanded to practice justice toward each other.[21] Whatever his intentions, the president demanded (as none of his predecessors had) that all Americans (himself included) live up to the ideal of charity in politics. If this were a "noble fiction" in the Platonic sense, it was one that required a great deal more of its citizens than obedience to mere ritual.

Even sympathetic readers of Lincoln understate the influence of revelation on the president, since he so often violated the tough morality that Christian ethics requires. Certainly, Lincoln felt great pressure to be uncharitable to his enemies at times. In July 1863, Lincoln signed an order that threatened to execute any Southern prisoner of war in retaliation for an execution of a Union prisoner. The possibility that Lincoln may have been insincere in his use of scripture does not change the fact that he still made great demands on the American people. What Barry Alan Shain says about the founders (who were not classic theists) could easily apply to Lincoln himself. Even if they used faith instrumentally, they did not dispute the need "for Christian-based corporate oversight of the lives of individuals to effect it."[22] Whatever the motives of the president, his appeal to charity resonated with a truly believing people, who then felt the demand that the nation live up to its historic faith and morality. Indeed, his critics have every right to judge him (and their nation) according to this moral standard.

The issue at stake here is not so much the sincerity of Lincoln as the *difficulty* of fulfilling the demands of this political use of charity. This civil faith calls for an end to all serious double standards enshrined in the body politic. The division between religious and secular spheres of influence is not the issue. Religious and secular authority alike are subject to charity. Moreover, the very foundations of the American regime must be measured and scrutinized according to this faith. Charity is the constant demand to put oneself in the position of the other, to avoid committing injustice to others that one would not tolerate against oneself. I believe that Lincoln, particularly in his crusade against slavery, elevated this principle of charity to the status of a political creed (although Chapter 6 discusses the limits that charity imposes on equality as a goal). The founders were no strangers to the use of charity, since they built upon a

21. Jaffa, *Crisis of the House Divided,* 327.
22. Shain, *Myth of American Individualism,* 214.

social contract tradition that appreciated the role of charity. Moreover, the predominantly Christian people of America had learned the virtue of charity from the pulpit since the Mayflower Compact. Nevertheless, charity was not the dominant principle of the American founding, nor was it presented as one worthy of political application.

CHARITY AND GOD'S PROVIDENCE

Even in his most rousing speeches, the president used caution in expressing biblical credos that, he knew, would be divisive for Americans because of the infinite variety of ways to interpret them. Lincoln never invoked the person of Christ, or even preferred Christianity to any other religion. In the words of Jaffa, "By belonging to none, he belonged to all."[23] In reminding his fellow Americans in his second inaugural address that the "Almighty has his own purposes," Lincoln never claimed to have special *knowledge* of the divine, but retained the cautious hope that in the spirit of God the North and the South would be reconciled. Still, the potency of his rhetoric has encouraged a variety of radical interpretations.

If any student of American political history desires to gauge the distance between the founders and Lincoln, I offer an elegant (if time-consuming test). Read *The Federalist* through and then read the major speeches of Lincoln's presidency (especially the Gettysburg and second inaugural addresses). It is impossible to miss the difference in content and tone. Whereas Jay, Hamilton, and Madison are describing the meaning and process of government in profoundly secular terms (they rarely mention Christianity), Lincoln's speeches resonate with theological themes. Whereas *The Federalist* presents a new "science of politics," Lincoln offers a political theology. *The Federalist* never discusses Christianity, either among the people or in government. A rare place where this great founding document makes reference to religion is the famous warning of Madison (in article 10) that sectarian conflict over religious opinions discourages citizens from "cooperating for their common good" and inclines them "to vex and oppress each other."

The fact that Lincoln transcended at least the language of the founding has encouraged even sympathetic readers to understand the president as a revolutionary. It is generally taught that the founders (as deists)

---

23. Jaffa, *New Birth,* 352.

were mainly committed to "nature's God," not the God of scripture who teaches universal love.[24] Although no one would deny that belief in charity has always had force in America since Winthrop arrived on the shores of Massachusetts, it is not obvious to everyone that charity has been central to the *secular* thought of America's political leaders since the Revolution. Although students of American political thought are willing to admit that social contract theorists like Locke placed great importance on charity, it does not necessarily follow that the founders attributed to charity the importance that they gave to liberty and self-government.[25]

As Glen Thurow has argued, Lincoln believed that only a political use of religion could rescue the work of the founders from the mob violence that he so eloquently described in his Lyceum speech. Only a creed could improve upon the rather staid rationalism of the founders, since reason alone does not deter the rule of the mob. Although Lincoln respected their work, he felt compelled to "improve" upon it with the addition of a "new political religion that unites Christianity" to the founding documents.[26]

Still, how far was Lincoln prepared to go in rendering the work of the founders more compatible with the demands of charity? Lincoln's use of religion has encouraged some of his admirers to argue that he was completely certain that Americans were the "chosen people" marching under the protective banner of God's providence.[27] Whereas the founders were far more reticent in making such claims, Lincoln presumably advanced the cause of chosenness and theological certainty about the designs of the Almighty.

This interpretation of Lincoln does an injustice to both the Bible and the president's own thought. As Spinoza relentlessly argues in his *Theologico-Political Tractatus*, the Israelites suffered tremendous punishment when they arrogantly and self-righteously claimed to be chosen. Chosenness can be as much an invitation to punishment as it is to favoritism. The fact that various chosen peoples in history have lost their empires due to the sin of pride (which the Old Testament proph-

---

24. Zuckert, "Natural Rights," 26–33.

25. Thomas G. West, "The Transformation of Protestant Theology as a Condition of the American Revolution," 207.

26. Thurow, *Abraham Lincoln*, 36.

27. See Jaffa, *Crisis of the House Divided,* 220–21; and Bellah, *Broken Covenant,* 52–55.

esied, according to Spinoza) reveals the utter folly of claiming with any certainty that one people can be the chosen indefinitely.[28] If they do not act in charity, they are not the true chosen.

Much has been written about Lincoln's famous sole reference to the "almost chosen people," which he made in a speech of 1861. This brief utterance has inspired many readers to believe that America is indeed the chosen nation, without any sense of the cautionary nuance in Lincoln's phrase.[29] The use of *almost* would suggest that neither Americans nor anyone else can be the chosen since the claim to this status presupposes a knowledge of God that no human being can truly possess. Lincoln usually emphasized that no side in the Civil War could claim such knowledge with credibility. As he famously put it in his second inaugural address, "Both read the same Bible, and pray to the same God; and each invokes His aid against the other. It may seem strange that any men should dare to ask a just God's assistance in wringing their bread from the sweat of other men's faces; but let us judge not that we be not judged. The prayers of both could not be answered; that of neither has been answered fully. The Almighty has His own purposes."[30] If any text is a condemnation of easy claims to know the providence of God, and to build an ideology of chosenness upon the Bible, it is surely this one. In the same passage, Lincoln's admonition to "let us judge not that we be not judged" should be a reminder that charity is the true imperative of God, not divisive theologies of favoritism. His famous ending declaration, "With malice toward none; with charity for all," should reveal the supreme importance that Lincoln placed in the authority of love (forgiveness, mercy, and so on) over chosenness.

Some readers of Lincoln have claimed that the president truly believed in the supernatural (especially the power of prayer), while others have claimed that he believed this realm to be completely mysterious and even impersonal.[31] Yet prayer itself was often suspect, because the

---

28. See Clifford Longley, *Chosen People: The Big Idea That Shapes England and America,* 147.

29. Lincoln, *Collected Works,* 4:236. Certainly, authors like Gelernter, Bellah, and Jaffa interpret Lincoln's language to mean that Americans are, unambiguously, the chosen.

30. Ibid., 8:333.

31. See Fornieri, *Abraham Lincoln's Political Faith,* 64; and Guelzo, *Abraham Lincoln: Redeemer President,* 153–54, 318–20. See too Morel, who also rightly

president recognized that it can be just as self-serving as any biblical credo. The fact that unionist and secessionist could pray to the same God reveals the utterly self-serving character of prayer. Indeed, Lincoln knew all too well that prayer is more often a denial of God's law of charity than an affirmation of it. In a White House meeting with the Baptist Home Mission Society in 1864, he distinguished between prayer and charity:

> When, a year or two ago, those professedly holy men of the South, met in the semblance of prayer and devotion, and, in the name of Him who said "As ye would all men should do unto you, do ye even so unto them" appealed to the Christian world to aid them in doing to a whole race of men, as they would have no man do unto themselves, to my thinking, they contemned [*sic*] and insulted God and His church, far more than did Satan when he tempted the Saviour with the Kingdoms of the earth.[32]

Lincoln knew that prayer too often evades the importance of charity; it becomes the great excuse for man's inhumanity against man. To be sure, both sides in the Civil War prayed and even claimed to be charitable. Yet neither side's prayers were as important as the imperative to practice charity (an imperative that both sides often evaded).

Lincoln's public skepticism about the power of prayer reflected his private thoughts about the supernatural, which he expressed to a delegation of Christian ministers from Chicago in late 1862. In response to their claims to know with certainty that the will of God demanded the immediate emancipation of the slaves in the South, Lincoln replied:

> I hope it will not be irreverent of me to say that if it is probable that God would reveal his will to others, on a point so connected with my duty, it might be supposed he would reveal it directly to me; for unless I am more deceived in myself than I often am, it is my earnest desire to know the will of Providence in this matter. *And if I can learn what it is I will do it!* These are not, however, the days of miracles, and I suppose it will be granted that I am not to expect a direct revelation.[33]

---

claims that Lincoln was careful not to "declare" a knowledge of God (*Lincoln's Sacred Effort*, 197–99).

32. Lincoln, *Collected Works,* 7:368.

33. Ibid., 5:420 (emphasis in the original). Nine days later, Lincoln issued

Lincoln clearly condemns Christians who place their belief upon a spurious foundation of knowing God's will, through miracles or other "direct" revelations. Ultimately, all that Lincoln could claim about God is that he demanded charity, which all human beings fall short of practicing (including this president).

Lincoln's critique of using the supernatural as a threat to punish sinners rests largely upon his belief in the primacy of charity. As early as his Temperance Address of 1842, Lincoln objected to the morality of threatening punishment in the afterlife for misbehavior (like excessive drinking) in this vale of tears. Lincoln called on all reformers to seek out the best impulses of human nature to reform the character of fallen beings (in this case alcoholics). It was neither moral nor prudent to judge drunkards from on high, or to threaten them with the dangers of hellfire. These techniques (characteristic of the old temperance movement) were not true acts of love. "If you would win a man to your cause, *first* convince him that you are his sincere friend. Therein is a drop of honey that catches his heart, which, say what he will, is the great high road to his reason, and which, when once gained, you will find but little trouble in convincing his judgment of the justice of your cause, if indeed that cause really be a just one." The alternative method of self-righteous moralizing would have no impact: "On the contrary, assume to dictate to his judgment, or to command his action, or to mark him as one to be shunned and despised, and he will retreat within himself, close all the avenues to his head and heart." Lincoln then ridiculed the consequentialist morality of promising reward and threatening punishment to motivate ethical acts. Surely, a virtuous people are capable of ethics in a more inspired manner, as Lincoln intimates in his scathing prose: "There is something so ludicrous in the *promises* of good, or *threats* of evil, a great way off, as to render the whole subject with which they are connected, easily turned into ridicule. 'Better lay down that spade you're stealing, Paddy,—if you don't you'll pay for it at the last day of judgment. By the powers, if you'll credit me so long, I'll take another, just.'" Significantly, Lincoln builds on a long-standing critique of pharisaical morality from a biblical perspective. Yet he also

---

the first Emancipation Proclamation (September 13, 1862). This decision was based on the strategy of weakening the Southern economy (which fueled the war effort), and was not merely a response to the Chicago pastors.

partly builds on the social contract tradition that predates the founding. Spinoza as much as Lincoln scorned the use of threats in order to motivate moral behavior. This crude technique of fostering "dread" as the basis of morality perversely fosters immoral behavior and resentment of authority.[34] If knowledge of charity is truly knowable to all human beings (who at least have been exposed to biblical influences), then this technique is neither beneficial nor moral. Although a politics of charity may not totally exclude the use of a threat in a time of grave peril (like the Civil War), the ethic of charity cannot be primarily based on such fearmongering. (This belief of his may explain why Lincoln was willing to placate the South on the issue of enforcing the fugitive slave law as well as supporting a constitutional amendment that protected existing slavery, as he indicated in his first inaugural address.)

Admittedly, this politicized charity, stripped of the supernatural (and perhaps comparable to Jefferson's attempt to read miracles out of scripture), coexists very uneasily with the latent religious zeal of many Americans. Lincoln expected charity *alone* to be the primary foundation of a new political theology. Yet Christianity in America has rarely been about charity alone. If Harold Bloom is correct, Americans have always been far more concerned with a mystical yet self-indulgent understanding of their relation to an extremely personable and private God.[35] The dour tone of the second inaugural address (in contrast to the ambitious language of the Gettysburg Address) seems to demand an extremely humble population, while it promises little comforting reassurance of America's superiority or chosen status as a nation.[36]

As I argue in the next chapter, the humility that Lincoln demanded of his people has gradually diminished among the most radical devotees of his "political religion." Unfortunately, Lincoln's most zealous defenders sometimes express less charity than their hero. President Woodrow Wilson, a great admirer of Lincoln, treated Wilhelmian Germany as "a Thing without conscience or honor or capacity for covenanted peace" that deserved annihilation, just as many Protestant liberal pastors urged America to fight this wickedly "pagan nation."[37] Harry Jaffa has com-

---

34. Ibid., 1:273, 275–76 (emphases in the original); Spinoza, *Spinoza's Theologico-Political Treatise*, 59.

35. Bloom, *American Religion.*

36. Thurow, *Abraham Lincoln*, 87.

37. For the sharp contrast between Lincoln's and Wilson's views of the en-

pared the American South to Nazi Germany and has compared even critics of Lincoln to Nazis with an American flavor for simply defending the principle of majority-rule democracy that Lincoln himself upheld.[38] Such charges are hard to reconcile with the legacy of Lincoln, who attempted to empathize with the South, even to the point of admitting Northern complicity for slavery, offering compensation to slave owners, and proposing a constitutional amendment that would protect existing slavery. My point is that this politicized charity poses no threat to the American system of government *if* the majority of Americans accept this charity-driven version of Christianity, over and against the belief in chosenness and the claim to know providential will. Yet this is perhaps an unrealistic assumption (certainly, the founders would have thought it unrealistic, since men are not "angels"), especially if the president's so-called defenders are not charitable.

CAN CHARITY EXIST WITHOUT CHRISTIANITY?

Defenders of Lincoln, who believe in a largely secular view of the founding, contend that Christianity is too exclusivist to live up to the truly universalistic ideals of Lincoln. It is not necessary to embrace the Christian creed in order to understand the universal values of liberty and equality: if these values are truly written on the hearts of all human beings (Rom. 2:15), then even the Bible is not necessary. In its most extreme expression, God himself is unnecessary. Most devotees of "natural rights," who defend them as the ultimate credo of America's political faith, understandably portray Lincoln as the paragon defender of natural rights while downplaying the religious particularity of his own thought. Their typical argument is that the president's allusions to natural rights require no knowledge of revelation, or even sympathy with it. After all, it was a universal moral law that Lincoln affirmed when he declared that no man has the natural right to enslave another. All of humanity by nature is equal. "What *natural* right requires Kansas and Nebraska to be opened to Slavery? Is not slavery universally granted to

---

emy, see W. Miller, "Lincoln's Second Inaugural," 336. For the Protestant liberal hatred of "pagan" Germany, see Gamble, *War for Righteousness,* 170–71. I discuss the relation between Lincoln's and Wilson's thought in Chapter 6.

38. See Jaffa, *New Birth,* 73, 76.

be, in the abstract, a gross outrage on the law of nature?" Presumably, this appeal to natural right has nothing to do with Christianity, since there is no concept of such a right in the whole of scripture. Michael P. Zuckert, for example, has contrasted Luther and Locke on precisely this point. Whereas Luther based his politics on the particular faith of Christianity, Locke based his social contract model on principles applicable to all of humanity. For this reason, Zuckert credits Locke and the Enlightenment rather than Luther and the Reformation for the emergence of a modern universal morality. Indeed, Christianity is far too restrictive to be the foundation of a true universal politics. In the words of Thomas West, self-evident truths cannot be exclusively Christian, because all human beings can "discover" these principles, Christian or not.[39]

Would Lincoln believe that Christianity is unnecessary to democracy, especially since it teaches the importance of charity? The very language of "self-evident" truths of liberty and equality in the Declaration would suggest that acceptance of this kind of truth should be immediately intelligible to all, Christian or non-Christian. Lincoln himself, however, called for a politics of charity precisely because the truths of the Declaration were *not* self-evident to all (just like Spinoza, who believed that all human beings possess the "natural light" of reason yet need the Bible—the only source of ethics that he supports—in order to learn the lessons of morality). Even if human reason were universal, it would not be enough to encourage the practice of self-evident truths. As Lincoln famously put it, "One would start with confidence that he could convince any sane child that the simpler propositions of Euclid are true; but, nevertheless, he would fail, utterly, with one who should deny the definitions and axioms. The principles of Jefferson are the definitions and axioms of free society. And yet they are denied, and evaded, with no small show of success. One dashingly calls them 'glittering generalities'; another bluntly calls them 'self-evident lies'; and still others insidiously argue that they apply only to 'superior races.'"[40] Lincoln is clearly suggesting that a denial of mathematical truth is of a different order from

39. Lincoln, *Collected Works*, 2:245 (emphasis in the original); Zuckert, "Natural Rights and Protestant Politics: A Restatement," 258, 273; West, "Transformation of Protestant Theology," 188–89.

40. Lincoln, *Collected Works*, 3:375. See also Thurow, *Abraham Lincoln*, 62, 74–78.

a denial of human equality. It would be irrational, although not insidious, to deny Euclidean axioms. It is no reflection on the character of a human being to deny them. Yet one can morally judge the character of those who deny equality. For this sad reason, it is a much greater struggle to teach the truth of the Declaration rather than the truth of geometry. Why?

Lincoln's explanation for the persistent denial of equality rests on the biblical concept of *sin*. Sin is the deliberate violation of the moral law of charity. It is deliberate because the agent of sin knows the good yet still chooses evil. Indeed, he convinces himself that the good is the evil, while he knows that this act is still a willful denial of the good. (As Kierkegaard once observed, we always "will the good" in our own minds, even when we will the bad.) It has been said that Lincoln admired the people's judgment more than the founders did.[41] If that is true, it is also true that he *demanded more* of the people than the founders did (who were generally Lockean rationalists). The entire people of America— North and South—knew better than what they merely professed about the injustice of slavery. Because they were both Christian peoples—they worshiped and prayed to the same God—they differed over slavery only because one side denied the truth that it already knew. The paradox of choosing evil over good when one knows the good was apparent to Lincoln as early as his debates with Douglas. When the senator declared that the choice of popular sovereignty (the freedom to choose slavery) is consistent with biblical freedom, Lincoln replied, "In seriousness, then, the facts of this proposition are not true as stated. God did not place good and evil before man, telling him to make his choice. On the contrary, he did tell him there was one tree, of the fruit of which, he should not eat, upon pain of certain death."[42] Lincoln understood, as Douglas (deliberately) did not, that there is no true choice between good and evil. For this reason, a great number of his countrymen had to rationalize to themselves and others that they were choosing the good (indeed, performing God's work) while they oppressed their countrymen. The presumed "orthodoxy" of the South rested on the self-serving hermeneutic that scripture sanctioned slavery. Obviously, Lincoln was addressing an audience (Douglas included) who not only knew the Genesis narrative

41. Thurow, *Abraham Lincoln*, 119.
42. Lincoln, *Collected Works*, 2:278.

but also understood the falsity of the "choice" between good and evil (even if they still willed the choice in order to justify slavery). In short, he was addressing a Christian audience.

I am not suggesting that Lincoln's reading of theology is the only possible one. He knew all too well that the Bible is contradictory: scripture often sanctions slavery even while it celebrates the liberation of slaves from Egyptian tyranny. Yet the golden rule itself is more demanding than any other biblical truth, and, as Spinoza taught, calls on readers to grasp what the Bible reveals: the human propensity to be hypocritically defiant of this rule. Scripture reveals how the people of God violate the moral law of God (the Israelite slaves of Egypt can end up enslaving other peoples), yet this behavior does not challenge the fact that charity is the highest ethic of the Bible.

On a less theological note, Lincoln's ideas are most comprehensible to a people already steeped in knowledge of the Bible. Lincoln honestly believed that people of the North and South were capable of understanding the injustice of slavery, although such an understanding rested on the Bible rather than mathematical reason. Even as the president of a divided nation, Lincoln assumed that the people of the South were good, and would eventually overthrow their usurping regime on their own; unfortunately, this did not happen.[43] This sentiment was not a utopian one on his part. Lincoln *had* to appeal to the conscience of Southerners, to force them to recognize their own humanity, in order to persuade them to end slavery. As Lincoln pointedly asked in Peoria in 1854, if the South had not recognized the evil of slavery, why did they join in the abolition of the foreign slave trade more than thirty years before?[44] Still, if they refused to follow their own biblical principles of justice, they were sinning against God and their brethren. Lincoln put relentless pressure on Southerners to justify the double standard of slavery: his efforts presupposed that they already opposed hypocrisy (after all, they would not want to be slaves themselves).

Lincoln was under no illusion that Christians of the North and South felt little reluctance to justify even sin in the name of charity. Southern slave owners typically believed that they loved their slaves sincerely, perhaps more than the Northern capitalists loved their workers. It is no secret that charity can be invoked even to rationalize imperialism. (In

43. See Guelzo, *Abraham Lincoln: Redeemer President*, 254.
44. Lincoln, *Collected Works*, 2:264.

1842, John Quincy Adams declared that China's policy of denying foreign nations access to its vast markets violated the Christian command of "love thy neighbor.")[45] For this reason, Americans had to practice charity with a pure heart—reflective of the "better angels" of their nature—instead of concealing their self-interest beneath the halo of faith.

The denial of the injustice of slavery, then, was based on a deliberate denial of charity itself. If that were true, could opposition to slavery be a universal truth, waiting to be unlocked in the sinful hearts of all human beings? Lincoln often sounds as if this opposition is so universal that only a fool would ignore it, as he claimed in his famous Peoria speech of 1854: "Now, whether this view is right or wrong, it is very certain that the great mass of mankind take a totally different view. They consider slavery a great moral wrong; and their feelings against it, is [*sic*] not evanescent, but eternal. It lies at the very foundation of their sense of justice; and it cannot be trifled with. It is a great and durable element of popular action, and, I think, no statesman can safely disregard it." Yet earlier in the same speech Lincoln recognized that the denial of equality to Negros was also a "universal feeling" that no politician could ignore.[46] In short, all human beings—in North and South—failed to live up to the better angels of their nature. It would take more than the gentle persuasion of reason to remind them of their hypocrisy. A firmly established Christian culture is the indispensable precondition for grand appeals to moral conscience.

So far I have described Lincoln's dependence on human sinfulness as an explanation for the tolerance of slavery. The fact that a Christian nation could still be stiff-necked in its denial of Christian principles was all too obvious to him. Yet the very awareness of sin in all Americans provided Lincoln with the cautious hope that slavery would be recognized for the injustice that it is. Thus, his universalism was tempered with a biblical realism about humanity's frailties.

The fact is that only a biblically grounded nation like America could tear itself apart over slavery, as a few scholars have grasped.[47] Biblical revelation demands the practice of charity. No extrabiblical society ever debated the merits of slavery so dramatically, or even abolished it (as the British did in the 1830s). Yet those defenders of Lincoln who insist

45. Drinnon, *Facing West*, 271.
46. Lincoln, *Collected Works*, 2:281–82, 256.
47. See Noll, *Civil War;* and Fox-Genovese and Genovese, *Master Class*, chap. 20.

on the universalism of his credos must by necessity claim that peoples *beyond* the biblical tradition are just as capable as anyone of grasping self-evident truths (with enough persuasion, supposedly).[48] Because they are self-evident, they must be eternal; they must be recognizable to all traditions and religions. Moreover, the Bible is not the only means by which to grasp these truths. As Harry Jaffa argues in the context of comparing the Mosaic narrative to Plato's *Meno,* both Jerusalem and Athens teach that the truth cannot depend simply on scripture alone if all human beings by their very nature are capable of comprehending the truth, whether they are exposed to the force of revelation or not.[49]

Jaffa is not simply dethroning the Bible from its status as the ultimate truth. He is also declaring that this truth is equally known to all of humanity. In referring to Plato's *Meno* (particularly his paradoxical teaching that one cannot recognize something of which one is altogether ignorant), Jaffa is asserting that even the pagan mind (untouched by God's revelation) is capable of grasping these truths. There cannot be literal ignorance of the truth if, as Paul declares in Romans (2:15), the law of God is written on all human hearts. Yet Jaffa does not explain why there are massive differences between the pagan and biblical traditions on justice, morality, and oppression. When the *Meno* teaches that one can never recognize the truth unless one already knows it, this message is no different from the most central teaching of Socrates: that one knows only that one knows not. The pagan mind does not "know" the other in a charitable sense. To know the other is put oneself, charitably, in the place of the other. Yet pagan hierarchy discourages the very idea of gods empathizing with mortals, or masters with slaves. (For this reason, there were no debates over the injustice of slavery in the pagan world, nor was there any equivalent to the modern abolitionist movement.)

The very concept of empathy is absent in the pagan world. It is not that the pagan mind denies this truth, like the slave owners of the South. As Lincoln teaches, no one can deny a truth unless one is already aware of it. Rather, there is a complete absence of the assumption that the humanity of the slave is on the same level as that of the master, since nature has determined this unequal status. The fact that Socrates

48. Even neoconservatives occasionally admitted that President Bush addressed all of humanity in a manner quite different from Lincoln's focus on Americans alone. See Gelernter, *Americanism,* 202.

49. Jaffa, *Original Intent and the Framers of the Constitution,* 352.

never appeals to the higher love of agape in Plato's many dialogues is significant.

Despite the overwhelmingly biblical nature of Lincoln's thought, there have been some ambitious attempts to understate his reliance on Christianity, in order to portray his thought as genuinely universalistic. Gary Wills has argued that Lincoln, under the influence of his speechwriter (and classical scholar), Edward Everett, based his Gettysburg Address on the funeral oration of Pericles, which Thucydides included in his history of the Peloponnesian War. Harry Jaffa and George Anastaplo have argued that Plato and Aristotle are the true mentors of Lincoln's ideas on virtue and the good. Joseph Fornieri contends that Lincoln cunningly combined pagan nobility with Christian humility.[50] These authors assure us, then, that Lincoln could not possibly believe that Christianity *alone* is the source of morality as he understood it.

It does not seem to occur to these authors that Lincoln's hope for a truly free nation—which he eloquently expressed in both the Gettysburg Address and his second inaugural address—lacks an equivalent in the great pagan texts. The ambitious attempts of scholars to Hellenize Lincoln utterly fail to locate the idea of a "new beginning" or a "new birth of freedom" in the Greek tradition. Certainly, Pericles, Plato, and Aristotle did not speak of historically starting again. The Greeks—like all pagan peoples—thought of history as cyclical, without beginning or end. The cycle of misfortune and fortune is inevitable, because humanity cannot alter or challenge the movement of time. There is no hope for real change that can break the cycle of tragedy. Oedipus Rex cannot overcome his fate. Plato equally shows no doubt in the *Republic* that the best regime of the aristocratic few will eventually degenerate into tyranny (once it devolves into lower regimes that make the triumph of tyranny inevitable). There is indeed history, but not history as creation, or the story of the personal relation between God and humanity. No pagan god allows human beings to create history: they are playthings subject to fate alone (Lucretius later asserted in his *De rerum natura* that even the gods are subject to fate). Hence, there is no reason to hope for change if the destiny of humanity is already decided.

50. Wills, *Lincoln at Gettysburg: The Words That Remade America,* 41–62; Jaffa, *Crisis of the House Divided,* 345–46; Anastaplo, *Abraham Lincoln: A Constitutional Biography,* 257–62, 348; Fornieri, *Abraham Lincoln's Political Faith,* 107.

It is tempting to believe that this cosmology is no different from biblical teachings on history. Does the Bible not teach that humanity is totally subject to the authority of God? Yet, as Karl Löwith, Mircea Eliade, Fustel de Coulanges, and other distinguished historians of ideas have argued, this God of creation allows *freedom*.[51] Human beings relate to this God; they are not simply his slaves. (Indeed, this God can be murdered at the hands of his servants—a revelation inconceivable to the pagan mind.) It is well known that the Bible offers a concept of time that encourages hope for real change. God and humanity can defy the cycles of nature through miracles, good works, changes of heart, and apocalypse. Both God and humanity are *above* nature. The anthropocentrism of the Bible is obvious: God in history creates and re-creates the world ex nihilo so that he can allow his creation to begin again, to hope for a new world liberated from sin.

Very few Americans have ever believed in cyclical time, except for the Amerindians who were resigned to the twists of fate that reflected life under an indifferent cosmos. Yet even pagan peoples who embrace Christianity must first give up their fatalistic resignation to a system of "natural" inequality that subordinates slaves to masters. As Tzvetan Todorov has argued, the pagan belief in the natural or intrinsic inferiority of the slave to the master presupposes that the slave can never acquire the means to liberate himself from slavery, whereas Christianity nowhere teaches that hierarchy is "irreducible" or impervious to change at the hands of God's justice.[52]

Todorov is describing the fatalism of the pagan Amerindians, who were unprepared for the values of European Christianity. The case of the American South is obviously different, since its people had been ostensibly Christian for as long as their brethren in the North had been. Many Southern slave owners were tempted to see slavery as a fact of nature that no social convention could successfully challenge. It was simply destiny that one should rule over another. Yet these same Southerners felt compelled—long before the Civil War—to justify slavery in biblical terms. It was not enough to appeal to pagan thought, which was alien to their traditions anyway. They had to justify it in the name of the Bible,

51. See Grant Havers, "The Meaning of 'Neo-Paganism': Rethinking the Relation between Nature and Freedom."
52. Todorov, *The Conquest of America: The Question of the Other*, 161.

even though they were under pressure to reconcile slavery with God's love for all of humanity.[53]

Despite these difficulties, those who argue for the marginal impact of the Bible on Lincoln usually contend that the Greeks were most important as an influence on the president. Lincoln presumably opted for Athens over Jerusalem. George Anastaplo and other students of Leo Strauss have chosen Plato and Aristotle as the most important influences on Lincoln, despite their philosophical defense of slavery by nature. Lincoln's understanding of the true statesmen (as mediated through his love of Shakespeare) is decidedly Greek. Anastaplo, unlike Wills, at least attempts to reconcile Lincoln's use of scriptural themes with his overall politics. Still, in insisting that Lincoln is a successor to Plato and Aristotle (whose works, unlike the Bible, were probably not even read by the president), Anastaplo suggests that Lincoln was likely insincere in his public profession of faith. Anastaplo's Lincoln had "private reservations" about issues like revelation, and probably saw biblical imagery in terms of mere "political usefulness."[54] In other words, Lincoln only *appeared* to be a devoted avatar of Jerusalem; he was in fact a sincere (although secretive) admirer of Athens.

Other Lincoln scholars acknowledge the biblical nature of Lincoln's thought, but then they attempt to reconcile it with the political philosophy of classical Athens. Harry Jaffa argues that the president was sincere in his use of the Bible *and* successfully provided a lasting synthesis of the political philosophy of Athens with the revealed religion of Jerusalem. Unlike the Lincoln portrayed by Anastaplo and Wills, Jaffa's version of the president does not force the reader to choose between the two great competing traditions of the West. One can have it both ways. Because he is confident that the traditions of both Athens and Jerusalem call upon America to spread its values globally, Jaffa must enlist Aristotle—a defender of slavery by nature—in the cause of Lincoln. This Greek philosopher is presumably in agreement with Jefferson and Lincoln on the odious nature of tyrannies that do not have "as their natural ends the safety and happiness of their citizenries."[55] Still, Jaffa never provides any textual evidence that the classical political philosophy of Athens contains

53. See Fox-Genovese and Genovese, *Master Class,* 473–504.
54. Anastaplo, *Abraham Lincoln,* 341, 347.
55. Jaffa, *New Birth,* 81; Jaffa, *Crisis of the House Divided,* 343–45.

any equivalent concept of *a new birth of freedom, a chosen people, or an evangelical intent to liberate the world.* In short, where is the Exodus narrative in Platonic or Aristotelian terms? Most important, where is biblical morality in the pagan cosmos?

Perhaps the most bizarre upshot of attempts to "paganize" Lincoln is to portray him as a cynic who used religion in order to control the ignorant masses (akin to the noble fiction described by Plato in the *Republic*). As we have seen, the questioning of the sincerity of Lincoln's faith is nothing new. Back in the late 1940s, Richard Hofstadter spied a contradiction between the president's religious beliefs and his devotion to material success. Yet even the president's most zealous defenders have had doubts as well. Michael Zuckert associates Lincoln with Machiavelli in their common aim of articulating a political ethic that would yield the "practical results" of keeping a people faithful to their regime. Even Harry Jaffa, who tends to give the impression that Lincoln actually liked Christianity, argues that the president knew there was nothing rational about the biblical basis of this new political religion: "reverence for the laws" could not depend on the intellect; it is the task of the statesman to strengthen this conviction at all times, even if that act requires less than rational appeals to the passions. In his long-awaited sequel to *Crisis of the House Divided,* Jaffa makes clear that there is nothing wrong with using myth to justify an unjust regime. In paraphrasing Pascal's view that rule by the stronger may eventually become rule by reason, he counsels that it is necessary to "conceal by myths" the true historic origins of these regimes if they happen to be unjust.[56]

The running theme in these authors' appreciation of Lincoln is that myth, religious or otherwise, is at best a useful means to stabilize a regime. Even Jaffa, who celebrates the role of Christianity in the founding, ultimately agrees with the most secularist devotees of "natural right" that principles of liberty and equality require no support from revelation, since they "are independent of the validity of any particular religious beliefs."[57] Yet revelation at least retains the utility of teach-

56. Hofstadter, *The American Political Tradition and the Men Who Made It,* 123; Zuckert, "Problem of Civil Religion," 359; Jaffa, *Crisis of the House Divided,* 229–30, 242; Jaffa, *New Birth,* 103. Jaffa also asserts that Lincoln never deferred to American "prejudices" against equality, even if he gave that impression in public (*New Birth,* xii).

57. Jaffa, *How to Think,* 42. I discuss Jaffa's ideas in more detail in Chapter 5.

ing morality to the masses. Oddly, these admirers of Lincoln seem to side with critics who accuse "our first Puritan president" of using the Bible to conceal "within the Trojan horse of his gasconade and moral superiority" an agenda that would ordinarily have met only opposition.[58] Yet Lincoln himself, who was not shy about asserting the beneficial relation between Christianity and "moral training," knew that a politicized charity based on Christianity could not indefinitely function as a *double truth*.[59] If Christianity teaches the evil of hypocrisy, then a Christian statesman stands guilty of the gravest sin when he is a hypocrite. Indeed, a Christian people could not possibly tolerate what Jaffa positively describes as a statesman who acts as a "god" or with "god-like virtue."[60] The blasphemous implications of this praise are lost on Jaffa. Additionally, the idolization of Lincoln is out of synch with the president's own view that he himself is not above the only law of the only God, that of charity. If he is serving the people charitably, then he cannot be above them.

Although these sympathetic authors understand that the use of revelation can lead to profoundly destabilizing effects upon a regime, they seem to believe that a masterful statesman—who privately knows that religion is nonsense—can astutely navigate through these effects. Still, the president understood that a political creed inspired by revelation can never inspire people to be virtuous if it is simply a *lie*. Recalling his Temperance Address, Lincoln's dismissal of a consequentialist morality (hell for the damned, heaven for the saved) in politics is also a repudiation of the cynical usage of religion simply as a means of political control. Christianity's demands on the political make it ill-suited for a politics merely devoted to stability. Indeed, a Christian-based political religion shall encourage its citizens to question the regime if it is not committed to far-flung ideals. Even if Lincoln had "private reservations" about the truth of revelation (which many an admirer has suspected), it would not have changed a fact that had been well known since the Puritans landed in America: the vast majority of Americans were still fervent believers in revelation. Nor would it have altered the fact that the

58. M. E. Bradford, "The Lincoln Legacy: A Long View," 162.

59. He made this observation in his annual message to Congress in December 1863 (Lincoln, *Collected Works*, 7:48).

60. Jaffa, *Crisis of the House Divided*, 217, 263–65.

Christian love of truth—and disdain for double standards—is deeply incompatible with a hypocritical use of religion for political purposes.

The ambitious meaning of Christianity is simply too powerful for a "wise" elite to manipulate as a way of controlling the passions of the "ignorant" masses. Although Jaffa can certainly appreciate the force of charity, he does not consider this ethic to be sufficient as the foundation of a political faith. For this reason, he portrays Lincoln as an inheritor of the Platonic-Aristotelian approach to religion. This classical Greek teaching, which never taught that all human beings deserve the same rights or possess the same duties, nevertheless recognizes that religion is a useful "moral restraint" upon masses who are insufficiently rational to grasp the truth of moral equality, even if that truth is "self-evident" to the rational few.[61] Yet it is far from obvious that Lincoln saw the religiously motivated idea of charity as *merely* a "moral restraint" fitted for irrational people. To be sure, as far back as his Lyceum speech of 1838 he demanded that people restrain their violent passions by revering the rule of law. Yet charity itself is as much an incitement to revolution as it is a restraint upon action. The imperative of Christian morality calls for an end, as Lincoln understood it, to a practice that the ancients happily tolerated.

Ultimately, these readers of Lincoln view him as an ostensibly Christian politician with secretly held *pagan* views on religion. As we have seen, a pagan perspective on religion is based solely on the utility of serving the regime. Although Lincoln obviously desired that religion should be useful, it is simplistic to leave it at that. In appealing to "charity for all," the president is decidedly not a pagan. Scholars who either fault or celebrate Lincoln for fostering equality as the creed often forget just how Christian this goal, and how akin it is to agape. Lincoln never supported the idea of justice for the few as distinct from justice for the many. Moreover, ruler as well as ruled, victor and vanquished, must equally live by charity. Lincoln's opposition to double standards will forever contribute to tensions within the American regime. Lincoln's concept of charity is hardly a suitable candidate for controlling the "masses." Unlike paganism, Christian charity brings new features and challenges to the art of statecraft.

61. Ibid., 345.

A Realistic Politics?

Still, is a Christian-based politics ever realistic? Can it ever be compatible with the harsh demands of politics? (These were the concerns, after all, of Machiavelli and Rousseau.) Lincoln obviously thought about this in terms of building this kind of politics among an already established Christian people. It has often been suggested that Lincoln's reading of the Declaration called for America to universalize its principles on a global scale. Yet Lincoln was primarily addressing a Christian people (and a predominantly Protestant one at that). His words could resonate so powerfully among Americans—Northern and Southern—because they believed in the same God. In the spirit of article 2 of *The Federalist*, Lincoln counted on the fact that his people possessed one religion—Christianity. The black slaves could just as easily appreciate his words as free white Americans because all were Christian. Although Lincoln was not a cultural relativist who simply shaped his words according to his audience, he gave every impression of believing that only a Christian people were capable of overcoming sins like slavery. Only Christians could be cajoled into fighting wars over social injustice because their faith compelled them. Only a Christian president could expect a Christian people to begin again under the guidance of God's providence, and to practice charity to all in the aftermath of the Civil War. Only Christians would make an issue of *sin* toward humanity, and seek to address this malady. Lincoln continued the traditional Christian emphasis on caring for the people's *souls* (moving toward eternity) in the political realm, which has no equivalent in Greek philosophy.

Still, is not American Christianity inherently universalistic? It is particularly difficult to dissuade Americans from spreading republican principles with an evangelical spirit, since even a deist like Thomas Paine famously declared in *Common Sense* that this spirit truly characterized the new nation of the United States. Moreover, Lincoln himself blended particularity with universality when he praised the Declaration as an American document that calls for the "progressive improvement in the condition of all men everywhere." Rebellion against tyranny is a "sacred right" that must eventually "liberate the world." This sentiment likely reflected a historic paradox of Christianity: that it is rooted in a particular soil but must never cease to spread its message all over the world. Lincoln's politicized charity, then, is a very demanding one. Whereas pagan religions demand mere lip service to rituals and rites,

Christianity demands that the virtue of believers be constantly actualized in all realms of life, including the political. This faith cannot help but have implications for all of humanity, since it is meant to be universalized. As Harry Jaffa has written, it is the "role and fate of the United States" to be the means for lifting the entire world out of the "Original Sin" of inequality, or to conflate political salvation with the salvation of souls.[62] Yet this universalism—which has no equivalent within pagan civilizations—still possesses a particular foundation. Neither Plato nor Aristotle called for the "lifting" of the oppressed from their enslavement. Indeed, no pagan slave would have possessed such a desire, until he converted to Christianity.

The burden that Lincoln imposed on American Christians is to take their particular faith into the political realm and universalize it. As a result, the devotees of politicized charity are incessantly open to judgment at all times, especially if its practitioners do not practice what they preach. A Christian politics cannot abide hypocrisy or double truth indefinitely.[63] Indeed, the selective application of this political religion will always leave it vulnerable to charges of inconsistency. In defiance of a tradition of political philosophy dating back to Machiavelli, Lincoln believed that "deviations" from high principles not only are costly and likely to happen but utterly destabilize a nation rooted in Christian values. Contrary to his fiercest critics, Lincoln's political theology is least likely to be Machiavellian, since it condemns double standards from the beginning. Charity requires universal consistency—"let us judge not that we be not judged"—and is perhaps harshest on those who appear to be its most fervent supporters. As Lincoln famously suggested in his second inaugural address, the temptation of the victorious North to take vengeance on the South would completely violate the ethic of charity and discredit the war effort. The failure to fulfill charity, which sadly characterized the history of Reconstruction, led to ruin in the context of Southern politics.

Ultimately, Lincoln shared with the founders the assumption that the American people—North and South—are virtuous, are capable of

---

62. Lincoln, *Collected Works*, 2:407; Jaffa, *American Conservatism and the American Founding*, 252.

63. For a systematic discussion of the difference between Christian and pagan views of double truth, see Willmoore Kendall and Frederick D. Wilhelmsen, "Cicero and the Politics of Public Orthodoxy," 25–59.

"deliberate sense."[64] Although they are not angels—the Civil War demonstrated this in ghastly fashion—they know the difference between right and wrong. They are not condemned to the cycles of fortune and misfortune. They can and must learn from this most terrible of conflicts. In the spirit of Genesis, the people possess knowledge of good *and* evil. (This assumption is absent within the pagan tradition, where evil is tantamount to ignorance of the good.) If one assumes the contrary—that the American people are lacking in virtue—then the only option left is tyranny, as *The Federalist no. 55* warns. If the Civil War merely demonstrated that might is right, then nothing has been learned from the conflict.

There is, then, a major difficulty in disseminating American values without the leavening effects of a Christian religion. Charity is unique to a biblical worldview. (Pagan traditions generally lack an understanding of charity, as I discuss in greater detail in the next chapter.) Moreover, those who consider themselves Christian may not find a focus on charity to be particularly appealing. Lincoln cautiously hoped for the triumph of a minimal charity-based religion, free of a supernaturalistic theology of chosenness and certainty about Providence. On a global level, it may be impossibly hard to export a politics with a particular religious basis. Yet the supernaturalistic pretensions of many Americans (including secularists who yearn to spread democracy globally) make this a seductive utopian hope. Charity may not be enough for a universalistic people with global ambitions. It may not be sufficient for a people who are used to identifying God as a supernatural protector of chosen peoples as well. Lincoln never gave the impression that he or anyone knew what God's providence *exactly* was; otherwise, the Almighty would have answered the prayers of both sides in the Civil War clearly (as he remarked in his second inaugural address).[65] God was always a mystery to Lincoln. He gave every reason to believe that he simply hoped that Christians would follow the clearest doctrine of the Bible—charity—even if that meant abandonment of supernaturalistic beliefs. Because no one has "seen" God (John 1:18), it is best to practice charity alone if one is to serve this mysterious deity.

64. *The Federalist no. 55*, 71.
65. Lincoln's refusal to claim knowledge of Providence was also out of synch with the most evangelical factions of his age. See Noll, *Civil War*, 88–90, 94.

If America were to universalize this minimal creed, then a radical program of moral education on a global scale would be the only means. Yet it is far from obvious that either the founders or Lincoln would have unconditionally supported such an ambition. The historical record also shows that global democrats, who see the "chosen people" as enemies of tyranny, often simply identify charity with the spread of democracy, instead of insisting that charity be the precondition for democracy. Most important, both religious and secular factions usually want more than just charity, if they desire this ethic at all. Yet one thing is clear after Lincoln: it became part and parcel of the American creed to worry about hypocrisy, an anxiety that is probably not transferable to cultures that refuse to agonize over the injustice of slavery. The universal religion that Lincoln articulated still has very particular roots.

4

Charity and "We, the People"

〰

They said, some men are too ignorant, and
vicious, to share in government. Possibly so, said
we; and, by your system, you would always keep
them ignorant and vicious.

—Abraham Lincoln, "Fragment on Slavery," July 1, 1854

Lincoln's trust in the judgment of the American people presupposed a stern condition: "We, the People" must act charitably.
The presence of Christian mores was essential in keeping the
people virtuous, lest they fall back into the "mobocratic" spirit of which
he famously warned in his Lyceum speech of 1838. Although other
American leaders had recognized the importance of charity, they had
not required it as a moral test of citizenship. The institutions of democracy alone do not guarantee a charitable people.

The president's thoughts about the capacity of Americans to be charitable are so emblematic of the typically populist rhetoric of a democrat
that it is tempting to forget just how debatable they truly are. Even conservatives in American history who are sympathetic with Christianity
do not insist, like Lincoln, that charity is required for the American
people to be truly worthy citizens. Even liberal admirers of the president
often prefer to insist that enlightened self-interest may be sufficient in
fostering good citizenship. Lincoln, more than any other leader up to
his time (and perhaps for all time), posed this question: can Christian
charity keep the people virtuous?

Lincoln's trust in the capacity of the people to be charitable is controversial, to say the least. This basic trust in the capacity has never been easy or straightforward for Americans of all political stripes, before or after Lincoln. There is little evidence that the founders, liberals, aristocratic conservatives, or even populists have demanded as much virtue from the people as Lincoln did. Trust in the moral strength of the American people has fallen on hard times in the twentieth and twenty-first centuries, perhaps in response to exhausting ideological use of the "chosen people" mythology as a rationale for democracy building at home and abroad. The famous report of the Trilateral Commission of the 1970s warned that democracy was becoming "ungovernable" because the American people were demanding far too much in entitlements.[1] Perhaps the Old Right aristocrats of the ancien régime had been correct, after all, about the people. Perhaps the "mobocratic" spirit of which Lincoln had warned had finally triumphed over American democracy.

A crisis of the people's spirit is ultimately a crisis of an understanding of its traditions, as any conservative from Russell Kirk to Willmoore Kendall would agree. Indeed, American conservatism has always been a paradox. This republic began in revolution against a traditional European conservatism that did not put trust in the "people." Americans—Lincoln included—look forward to a future that is different from (and superior to) the past. What, then, is the nation supposed to conserve? Which traditions do conservatives "conserve" in an age of flux? Should conservatives be populist or elitist, democratic or aristocratic? Today's divisions among American conservatives (usually divided between "neoconservatives" and "paleoconservatives") have forced a return to pivotal concerns: Can the American people be trusted to preserve their nation? Are they "conservative" anymore?

It would be unfair to suggest that *only* Americans must contend with these questions. Conservatism has always been a modern doctrine, protesting against modern movements on modern grounds. Yet American conservatism has generally been more populist than its European counterparts. The republic embraced two dynamics that have had no traditional equivalent across the Atlantic: a faith in the virtue of the people and an embrace of the free practice of Protestant Christianity. To be

---

1. Michael Crozier, Samuel P. Huntington, and Joji Watanuki, *The Crisis of Democracy: Report on the Governability of Democracies to the Trilateral Commission.*

sure, the status of the "people" has not always been clear. As the scholarship of Barry Alan Shain has documented, even in the early decades of the new republic there was a growing division between the Protestant agrarian majority and the secular urbanized minority, a conflict that was bound to have implications for the survival of Christianity as a political influence. The presidency of Abraham Lincoln built upon the Christian ethic of the old Protestant majority, even though the Civil War might have markedly reduced its influence.[2]

Nevertheless, Lincoln was convinced that Christian morality is indispensable. Still, in elevating charity to the status of an indispensable political faith, did Lincoln perhaps demand more of the people than the founders did? Some sympathetic readers of Lincoln have answered in the affirmative.[3] Just how far should Americans trust themselves to be charitable?

THE FOUNDERS AND THE PEOPLE

The Federalist provides a famously influential answer to this question of the people's moral compass. This work, the third most important document of the founding, taught that America represented a new regime because of its dedication to the people. Despite the claim of Russell Kirk, that the American Revolution was simply "a conservative restoration of colonial prerogatives," the founders understood the Revolution to be a *new* kind of politics altogether. In the words of Willmoore Kendall, this conservatism "adjourned *sine die* its quarrel with democracy," and especially with "We, the People."[4] Still, did the authors of *The Federalist* count on the people's unending commitment to Christian conceptions of virtue?

Certainly, *The Federalist* taught that the American people possessed some virtue. They were not a rabble who had to be controlled by a wise elite. They were a people who were trustworthy in their deliberations about politics. The classic statement of American popular sovereignty can be found in *The Federalist no. 55*, where "Publius" warns against an

2. Shain, *Myth of American Individualism*, 55, 146. See also Noll, *Civil War*, 161–62.

3. Thurow, *Abraham Lincoln*, 119; Pierard and Linder, *Civil Religion*, 100.

4. Kirk, *The Conservative Mind: From Burke to Eliot*, 72; Kendall, *Willmoore Kendall Contra Mundum*, 72.

overemphasis on the "depravity of mankind" lest it lead to the despairing conclusion that "there is not sufficient virtue among men for self-government." It is well known that *The Federalist* warns against undue optimism in the popular will, which "factions" or demagogues can always manipulate. There is no guarantee that a republic can abolish factions or even that the majority is immune to them, as *Federalist no. 10* observes. There is also no guarantee that the people will be "angels" in their deliberations, as articles 49 and 51 famously warn. A few scholars have noted that "Publius" has nothing to say about the eternal need to educate the people in virtue.[5] Yet it may not be advisable for "human prudence" to devise a government that seeks to eradicate the capricious passions of humanity (article 57).

Tyranny itself is never a solution to the fallibility or depravity of the people, as *Federalist no. 55* warns, for there is no guarantee that any elite is free of vices. The republic is not meant to be "a nation of philosophers" (article 49). Indeed, this nation will never produce on a regular basis "enlightened statesmen" who will be at the helm (article 10). Just as it is unrealistic to expect a ruling elite to be regularly prudent, so it is unfair to deny that the people possess "prudence and firmness" (article 31). Without these qualities, the people cannot restrain the vices of their representatives. Both the people and their representatives have an equal measure of reason and passion, and it is ultimately up to the public to possess the reason that ought to "control and regulate the government" (article 49). This prudence specifically never calls for the utter suppression of the people, based on the fear that their collective fallibility will lead to a new Terror. As Willmoore Kendall used to say, who would dare say "nay" to the People?

For this reason, "We, the People," for the first time in history, could be trusted to make decisions about a political regime. A community that understands the "constitutional morality" of *The Federalist* would decide to elect the most virtuous person to office: although this act paradoxically combined aristocratic leadership with democratic will, the final authority lay with the people to decide which leaders were truly virtuous.[6] Indeed, the majority of the population could be trusted to be prudent and reasonable in their deliberations (unless ideologues

5. Kendall and Carey, *Basic Symbols*, 39; Kendall, *Willmoore Kendall Contra Mundum*, 400.

6. Kendall, *Willmoore Kendall Contra Mundum*, 222.

and factions derailed the system). The fatal choice between tyranny and anarchy (which the French Revolution so tragically embodied) was not inevitable. In the new and "extended" republic of the United States, "a coalition of a majority of the whole society" would not be possible without a popular knowledge of justice (article 52). The people would not only understand justice but even practice it. Lest anyone think that "Publius" alone believes in the capacity of the people to be prudent, we can consult that other great document in which Jefferson declares to his readership that the new republic presupposes this moderation. The people can be trusted to possess the virtue to retain and abolish government as they see fit, without the whimsicality of radical passions: "Prudence, indeed, will dictate that Governments long established should not be changed for light and transient Causes; and accordingly all Experience hath shewn, that Mankind are more disposed to suffer, while Evils are sufferable, than to right themselves by abolishing the Forms to which they are accustomed." Neither Jefferson nor "Publius" promises that the people will always be prudent or virtuous. However, if they lack these capacities altogether, then the alternative statecraft must be one of tyranny. If the people are truly a rabble, neither an aristocracy nor "enlightened statesmen" nor a philosophic elite will teach the people anything about virtue. Still, what do the people consider prudent or virtuous at any given time? Are there any enduring principles that the people must obey in order to remain virtuous or prudent? (Even a stalwart defender of the founding like Kendall admitted that the "missing" section of *The Federalist* provoked the question: what keeps the people virtuous?)[7]

One popular answer to this question of maintaining virtue among the populace is that unswerving support of natural rights for all of humanity would be proof positive that Americans are still a virtuous people. Rights to liberty and equality are the highest goods. Defenders of this school are confident that both the Declaration and *The Federalist* speak with one voice on the issue of natural right, and not simply for the necessity of the people to have prudence. Indeed, there is no point in being prudent unless the people are equally committed to these natural rights. The people must demonstrate their virtue in committing to the natural rights enshrined in the Declaration. Just as typical is their belief that Americans are becoming less virtuous as they stray from the creed of

7. Ibid., 400.

natural right.[8] In short, the morality of the founding allegedly rests upon natural right philosophy (and not anything particularly Christian).

What does *The Federalist* actually claim about rights? Certainly, there are rights by nature, but the most important natural right of all is the right to *survive*. This a republic can accomplish only if the people are prudent in their deliberations over other rights. Prudence here means the awareness of survival as the right that trumps all other rights. When Madison refers to the authority of "nature" in *Federalist no. 43,* he has in mind the longevity of the republic (particularly in regard to the necessity of individual states to ratify the Constitution with unanimity). Both the "transcendent law of nature" and "Nature's God" declare the supremacy of the safety and happiness of the people as the great goals of all institutions.

Nowhere in Madison's article is there the premise that natural rights are so absolute that debates over them are more important than the "great principle of self-preservation." The safety and happiness of society are possible only if the people decide under which circumstances these debates are to occur. Therefore, the prudence of the people is assumed once more. Nature's "God" (to which Madison refers in order to avoid the fear of theocracy that a direct appeal to the God of revelation might provoke) does not sanction individual rights at the expense of the republic's equally important goods of order and tranquillity. If there is a natural right, it is the right of the people to decide their form of government, not the right of minorities or individuals to question that right.[9] In fine, the people decide the importance of natural rights.

The Federalist also assumes that the representatives of the people will reflect the "deliberate sense" (or prudence) of the people in resisting the temptation to embrace "every sudden breeze of passion" (article 71) that serves the interests of factions rather than the people as a whole. Only through calm discussion of the issues do the representatives serve the common good. If the representatives listen to demagogues (even those supported by the popular will), it will be left to the virtuous people to lament and condemn these leaders (article 63).

---

8. Leo Strauss, *Natural Right and History,* chap. 1; Jaffa, *New Birth,* 84; Jaffa, *How to Think,* 18. I shall assess the claims of the natural right school in the next chapter, particularly their attempt to write Christianity out of the American political tradition.

9. See Shain, *Myth of American Individualism.*

Despite the emphasis of the founders on the people's virtue, it is impossible to find one reference to the necessity of Christian charity in *The Federalist*, the Declaration of Independence, or the Constitution. The people's "deliberate sense" undoubtedly presupposes a moral sense, or at least a distrust of ideologically divisive factions. Yet the founders did not insist that every important decision that the people call upon its representatives to make be one based on charity. That demand entered American political thought only with Abraham Lincoln.

TOCQUEVILLE AND THE "PEOPLE"

As I shall argue in a later section of this chapter, various American political thinkers—liberal, conservative, and populist—have refrained from presupposing that the American people either can be or need be charitable, as Lincoln did. This skepticism over the virtue of the people has even encouraged both liberals and Old Right conservatives to enlist the support of Alexis de Tocqueville to vindicate their doubts. Liberals like Louis Hartz and Thomas Pangle are confident that this French aristocrat was fully sympathetic to the fulfillment of liberty and equality for all human beings. Conservative aristocrats like Russell Kirk and Peter Viereck are certain that Tocqueville much preferred the rule of an elite to that of the people. Historian John Lukacs, who seems to straddle both the liberal and the aristocratic positions, believes that Tocqueville appreciated both liberty and traditional order (but not the popular will) as the true foundation of the American republic.

It is undoubtedly true that Tocqueville saw and even respected the American commitment to liberty, and hoped that the best of America's traditions would survive the relentless love of progress among the people of the republic. Yet liberals and "aristocratic conservatives" selectively ignore another essential finding of Tocqueville in his famous visit to America in the early 1830s. This European aristocrat displayed a cautious admiration for the doctrine of *popular sovereignty* at the heart of the American experiment. Although he dismissed as an "impious and detestable maxim" the belief that the majority can do whatever it pleases in a political order, Tocqueville also believed that this majority is committed to justice in America.[10] Although he doubted that any regime, republican

10. Tocqueville, *Democracy in America*, 250.

or aristocratic, could prevent tyranny, Tocqueville also doubted that majority rule in the United States would inevitably lead to despotism. In his words, true republicanism means "the tranquil reign of the majority." This majority encouraged the formation of a "conciliatory government" in which resolutions of the day would be discussed "with deliberation and executed only when mature." Moreover, Tocqueville continues, "Humanity, justice, and reason stand above" the process of government. Even a popular figure like Andrew Jackson, president at the time of Tocqueville's visit, would not be permitted (nor would he be tempted) to impose dictatorship, according to Tocqueville. He even candidly admitted that his fellow Europeans, who thought of "power to the people" in despotic terms, could not understand the American experiment well.[11]

The fact that this French Catholic aristocrat saw much to admire in the overwhelmingly Protestant majority in America has not been well appreciated even among his admirers. Despite the skepticism that later observers of American politics have expressed toward the virtue of the people, Tocqueville entertained no such doubts. Tocqueville saw no serious contradiction between majority-rule democracy and respect for individual rights. Yet he also could not imagine one without the other. Liberal scholars since his time have often placed emphasis on the most individualistic themes of the founding, at the expense of appreciating the Protestant majority that Tocqueville admired. To understand the historic importance of this majority might, as Shain trenchantly observes, relieve these scholars "from having to describe so much of American history as pathological or mysteriously anomalous."[12] Moreover, Tocqueville could not imagine an America that would *prudently* abandon its commitment to Christian mores. The fact that a later president would have to remind Americans of the implications of these mores was inconceivable even to this wise aristocratic admirer of the republic.

LINCOLN AND THE VIRTUOUS PEOPLE

Since I have already argued in the last chapter that Lincoln always assumed that the American people possessed (even if they did not always

---

11. Ibid., 395, 396.

12. Shain, *Myth of American Individualism*, 327. I shall discuss these authors later in this chapter.

practice) a sense of charity, my analysis of the president's thought will be the briefest section in this chapter. Lincoln's trust in the people was a synthesis of his faith in goodwill and prudent statecraft on his part. Without a sense of collective goodwill, the republic indeed would perish. In this important respect, Lincoln was following in the footsteps of the founders (although some writers, we have seen, argue that Lincoln loved the people more). As the president declared in his first inaugural address: "Why should there not be a patient confidence in the ultimate justice of the people? Is there any better, or equal hope, in the world? In our present differences, is either party without faith of being in the right? If the Almighty ruler of nations, with his eternal truth and justice, be on your side of the North, or on yours of the South, that truth, and that justice, will surely prevail, by the judgment of this great tribunal, the American people." The president continues: "While the people retain their virtue, and vigilance, no administration, by any extreme of wickedness or folly, can very seriously injure the government, in the short space of four years."[13] It is undeniable that Lincoln showed caution in his praise of the people's wisdom. "While" they retain their virtue, the republic is safe, but there are no guarantees. Nevertheless, a true democrat can put his faith only in God and the people's judgment. The people as a whole are to be trusted, as long as they are obedient to God. The "Almighty ruler" alone will decide of what this trust or wisdom consists—since both sides claimed God as their own in the upcoming conflict—but ultimately the people, united or divided, will decide, and God will judge. Lincoln would have happily echoed the sentiment of Walt Whitman, in his introduction to the 1855 edition of *Leaves of Grass*, that the genius of America lays "most in the common people," provided that this people obeys God.

Like the founders, Lincoln worried about the dangers of factions (the slave-owning minority of the South rather than Southerners as a whole were the real enemy in his mind)[14] in the form of a minority imposing its will on a larger number of the American people, particularly after *Dred Scott* opened the door to the toleration of slavery nationwide. Ultimately, the majority must decide. As he observed earlier in the same address, "Unanimity is impossible; the rule of a minority, as a permanent arrangement, is wholly inadmissible; so that, rejecting the majority

13. Lincoln, *Collected Works*, 4:270.
14. See Morel, *Lincoln's Sacred Effort*, 172–74.

principle, anarchy, or despotism in some form, is all that is left."[15] The fact that Lincoln presupposed goodwill among Southerners—which even led him to believe (perhaps with some naïveté) that the planters' aristocracy had manipulated the good Southern folk into war with the North[16]—did not deter him from his belief that the majority must triumph in the end.

Still, was the majority truly virtuous? It was, as long as the majority understood that freedom for all meant freedom for slaves, not just freedom for the majority (or minority).[17] Lincoln was willing to defend majority-rule democracy as enthusiastically as the authors of *The Federalist* and Tocqueville, as long as the majority tried to be morally consistent. What makes Lincoln's political usage of charity difficult is the twofold demand that the majority and minority must be just (charitable) toward each other. Can any leader—even one as talented as Lincoln—please the majority *and* the minority at the same time? Conservative opponents of Lincoln often target the president with two accusations. In deciding to invade the South, Lincoln uncharitably imposed majority rule on Southerners. Moreover, Lincoln upheld the rights of minorities (slaves) at the expense of the Southern minority. In short, Lincoln may well have been charitable to one group of Americans but was not so inclined toward another. Allowing for the exigencies of war, one could still make a case that Lincoln indeed was not always charitable. Yet these critics are invoking the same moral principle as Lincoln did against the slave owners of the South. It is ironic that these foes of the president tend to oppose Lincoln on the basis of the president's *own terms,* since Lincoln is the defender at once of majority-rule democracy and of the rights of minorities in America.[18] Yet critics like Willmoore Kendall, who faulted Lincoln for imposing tyranny on Southerners in the name of "natural rights," sounded just like the president when he later opposed the attempts of minorities (during the civil rights era of the 1960s) to hijack the political process or refuse to take no for an answer: this was exactly Lincoln's position on Southern secession.[19]

15. Lincoln, *Collected Works,* 4:268.
16. See Guelzo, *Abraham Lincoln: Redeemer President,* 330.
17. Lincoln, *Collected Works,* 5:537.
18. I have in mind Willmoore Kendall, Mel Bradford, Thomas DiLorenzo, and George Carey.
19. Kendall, *The Conservative Affirmation in America,* 252; Kendall, *Willmoore Kendall Contra Mundum,* 362–85.

Perhaps the most significant effect of Lincoln's insistence on charity as a political principle is that his opponents can readily use it against the president (just as his defenders can invoke its authority against his critics). This fact reveals the persistent influence of his legacy: after Lincoln, Americans must judge each other at the political level on their practice of hypocrisy. Charity is no longer a private morality, since the "virtuous" people, in the rhetoric of Willmoore Kendall, must act as the judge and practitioner of charity in the political arena.

Are the People Still Trusted?
Liberals and Aristocrats on the People

The influence of Lincoln's politicization of charity has not deterred many distinguished American political theorists from doubting the likelihood that Americans can be as morally consistent as Lincoln insisted they should be. Two of the most important political traditions in the twentieth century challenged the traditional American trust in the people, or at least questioned the wisdom of majority rule. Both considered their readings to reflect the true "conservatism" of the republic.

I shall call the first school the *liberal* interpretation of the American founding. The main thesis of this school is simple enough. America's traditions are liberal to the core because its founders were liberals in the classical sense. Since, unlike their European counterparts, the Americans lacked an established church and a landed aristocracy at the dawn of their regime, they began as a nation of free individuals dedicated to the principles of liberty and equality. The most famous exponent of this school, Louis Hartz, claims that "atomistic social freedom" is the "master assumption" of the American political tradition. On the far left side of this liberal tradition, Andrew Levine (whose work is indebted to the American liberal theorist John Rawls) dismisses as "Rousseauian" any attempt to trust the people unless the people understand rights for minorities as the primary good.[20] Ultimately, the foundation of the liberal hermeneutic is the assumption that Americans act according to enlightened self-interest, not charity.

---

20. Hartz, *The Liberal Tradition in America: An Interpretation of American Political Thought since the Revolution*, 62; Levine, *The American Ideology: A Critique*.

The influence of Hartz on academics studying the American founding is extensive. It has virtually become a credo to assume that what the founders understood as liberty and equality is indeed a liberal one. In the tradition of Hartz, Canadian Tory philosopher George Grant agrees that the only heritage that Americans conserve is the old liberal individualism of John Locke.[21] Despite the mass of textual evidence that suggests that Locke was a defender of majority-rule democracy, most scholars dedicated to the "natural right" school have praised Hartz for what they take to be the enduring accuracy of his reading of the founding.[22] Thomas Pangle concurs with Hartz that the division between the European ancien régime and American individualism has existed from the founding of the republic onward. There is no other tradition indigenous to America.[23] Thomas G. West has claimed that the American founders were as liberal as their twentieth-century counterparts in their egalitarian assumptions about slaves, women, and the poor.[24] In short, minority interests trump those of the majority. Rationally motivated individuals, not the majority, have constituted the body politic of America. These individuals were also secular minded. Therefore, Christianity—the religion of the majority—cannot play an enduring role in shaping the politics of the republic. (Hartz rarely mentions Christianity in his work, except in the context of the Mayflower Compact, which he dismisses as an unimportant influence.)

The liberal reading of the American founding generally ignores the fact that the vast majority of Americans were neither secular nor particularly liberal, as Barry Alan Shain has documented. Even if leaders of the Revolution like Jefferson embraced deism, they were not exempted from the influence of the Christianity that shaped the souls of the American majority. Indeed, this version of deism was particularly theistic in assuming that a providential God still governed the republic; Jefferson himself famously trembled over the justice of this personal deity.[25] In short, the popular Christianity of the people, which enjoyed full bloom

21. Grant, *Lament for a Nation: The Defeat of Canadian Nationalism,* 64–65.

22. See Willmoore Kendall, *John Locke and the Doctrine of Majority-Rule,* which challenges the traditional view of Locke as a liberal.

23. Pangle, *Spirit of Modern Republicanism,* 27. Shain's analysis of America's communalism in *Myth of American Individualism* critiques the reading of Hartz and Pangle.

24. West, *Vindicating the Founders: Race, Sex, Class, and Justice in the Origins of America.*

25. See Longley, *Chosen People,* 23–24; and Novak, *On Two Wings,* 109–10.

by the time of the Second Great Awakening, left precious little room for the individualism that Hartz and his many followers celebrate as the essence of the founding. Despite the claims of liberals to be walking in the footsteps of Lincoln, they ignore the president's view that Christian charity, rather than reason, must teach morality.

The second influential school of thought on American conservatism can be called *aristocratic conservative.* Like their liberal opponents, supporters of this school are also opposed to majority rule. Unlike their liberal rivals, however, they are skeptical of the wisdom of trusting in the possessive individualism of Americans as the basis for sound politics and are more receptive to the influence of Christianity in the republican tradition. Although the defenders of this school have had far less influence than their liberal opponents, they have been able to tap into the long-established tradition of European conservative thought, particularly its repudiation of the French Revolution, to give weight to their argument. Although aristocratic conservatives would disdain the focus of liberals on self-interested calculation at the expense of tradition, they generally agree with liberals that "We, the People" do not deserve the trust of the leadership class.

The most venerable defender of aristocratic conservatism in America was Russell Kirk, whom many still take "to be the best example" of the American conservative tradition.[26] Kirk taught that the American regime has always accepted the old Burkean assumption that every society needs an aristocracy, which then furnishes an essential understanding of a transcendent order, a class system based on privilege, and a healthy suspicion of change.[27] This elite must teach the people (who are presumably ignorant) the eternal verities of community and honor, even though this same people may have at one time expressed these verities. Belief in both "We, the People" and unbridled Lockean individualism, therefore, is equally anathema to the American conservative mind, as Kirk defines it. "Vestiges of aristocracy" must exist to "temper the impulse of majorities" toward tyranny. At first glance, Kirk sounds no different from Tocqueville in warning about the dangers of unbridled majority rule. Indeed, he invokes the authority of the great French aristocrat in critiquing the worst impulses of the people: to trust

26. Ted V. McAllister, *Revolt against Modernity: Leo Strauss, Eric Voegelin, and the Search for a Postliberal Order,* 10.
27. Kirk, *Conservative Mind,* 8–9.

the judgment of the people in the abstract is a leap of faith "far more credulous than medieval relic-veneration."[28] In practice, only a virtuous aristocracy can restrain the people from embracing a Hitler or a Stalin, a recurrent threat in a democracy.

Kirk did not consider his thoughts on majority rule to be outside of the mainstream of conservative thought. Indeed, he invoked Burke's concept of the ideal majority in a society to be men of property, privilege, and inherited tradition.[29] Yet it is far from obvious that his thought lies in the mainstream of American conservatism.[30] Although the authors of *The Federalist* had no great love for unbridled majority rule, and even celebrated the need for aristocratic leadership, they did not pin their hopes on the virtue of this leadership to maintain a stable polity. Even the most elitist of the founders presupposed that the people must already possess a moral sense, which would take prime place over the authority of an equally fallible leadership class.

Naturally, every school of thought has to explain why historical reality does not cooperate with its theory. Both liberals and aristocratic conservatives (who often blame each other for what is wrong with America) still also point to the same enemy in order to explain why their vision of America has not quite panned out. That enemy is the *people.* More accurately, belief in the sovereignty of the people is, to both liberal and aristocratic minds, a barbaric violation of what is best and most enduring in the American tradition. On the liberal side, Hartz admitted that even the individualistic Lockean creed could become a vicious dogma of conformity in the hands of the American majority.[31]

Other liberal authors have followed suit. The widely respected historian Richard Hofstadter wrote extensively in the 1950s on the need to dismiss as "pseudo-conservatives" those Americans who were hostile to liberal reforms, centralized power in Washington, and a policy of appeasement toward the spread of communism (even though the first two attitudes count as traditions in their own right in American history). Hofstadter believed that these resentful factions did not fit into the American mainstream (conservative or liberal) because their

28. Ibid., 220, 224.

29. Ibid., 59–60.

30. See Paul Edward Gottfried, *Conservatism in America: Making Sense of the American Right,* 2–0.

31. Hartz, *Liberal Tradition,* 284–309. Hartz drew a straight line between Lockeanism and the populist demagoguery of Senator McCarthy.

rebellious attitude opposed the true traditions of the republic: presumably, these traditions were socially "progressive." Indeed, the opponents of these traditions were so far beyond the mainstream that Hofstadter considered these "radical rightists" to be suffering from mental illness.[32]

It may be tempting to dismiss Hofstadter's famous critique of the "radical Right" as an epiphenomenon of cold war politics. After all, he often gave the impression that this right-wing constituency was a minority opinion far beyond respectable mainstream (that is, liberal) thought. Yet Hofstadter was not content to dismiss the radical Right as a mere aberration, for he often ambitiously claimed that the true origin of these extreme tendencies historically lay within the mainstream of American thought. Hofstadter squarely laid the blame for these pathologies at the feet of *Protestant* America, whose inhabitants were definitely not the "virtuous people." All that is ugly with America was attributed to the people to whom Lincoln appealed as the great arbiter of justice and morality. Throughout his major works on American politics, Hofstadter faults the Protestant majority for holding back intellectual and political progress in America. The American disdain for ideas and elevation of irrationality "are inheritances from American Protestantism." At best, this historically frontier culture exemplified manly virtues, at worst a hatred of the mind. While it was a society wedded to practical virtues like "cunning," it was not a society likely "to produce poets or artists or savants," Hofstadter wrote of the people whom Lincoln counted on to practice charity, mercy, and forgiveness.[33] Indeed, he drew a pejorative relation between Lincoln and his fellow Americans, since he convicted the president for living the "Anglo-Saxon" contradiction of revering and destroying institutions and laws at the same time.[34] Although Hofstadter lamented the fact that this pathologically Protestant culture still pervaded much of modern conservatism in America, he fervently hoped that the decline of the Waspish presence would also coincide with the disappearance of this "nativistic" conservatism.[35] Hofstadter's devaluation of American Protestantism fitted well with the thinking of post–World War II elites who were determined to portray the nation as truly cosmopolitan, and not indebted to a particular faith tradition.

32. Hofstadter, *Paranoid Style,* 41–141.
33. Hofstadter, *Anti-Intellectualism in American Life,* 55, 80.
34. Hofstadter, *American Political Tradition,* 133.
35. Hofstadter, *Paranoid Style,* xii, 54.

What Hofstadter found so extremist about this people was simply their opposition to liberalism (just as Hartz excoriated Southerners for resisting this tradition). He faulted them for opposing the liberal reforms of the New Deal and the Fair Deal. He even ridiculed conservatives like Barry Goldwater for holding the absurd view that conservatism is "a system of eternal and unchanging ideas" that requires lasting preservation.[36] (Perhaps unbeknownst to this historian, *The Federalist* makes this assumption several times.) The reader of Hofstadter's works as a whole gets the distinct impression that a true American conservatism in his view must accept liberalism without any Protestant trappings, or else it will face a deserved extinction.

Hofstadter sometimes even expected that these ideological "fundamentalists" were small enough in number to wind up eventually in the dustbin of history. The liberalism of the American founding was simply too powerful for these upstarts to challenge. In direct opposition to Lincoln's trust in the wisdom of the Christian people of America, there is no indication in Hofstadter's work that the American Protestant majority possesses a capacity for virtue. Hofstadter was confident that Waspish conservatism would meet its demise in progressive twentieth-century America, but his admirers who have written on the populist Right since Hofstadter's death in 1970 have been less optimistic.[37] John Lukacs, using language comparable to that of Hofstadter, warned in the post–cold war era that this xenophobic and intolerant (yet strangely popular) movement on the American Right was a false conservatism that, sadly, had nothing to do with the European ancien régime and perhaps even amounted to a Yankee version of national socialism.[38]

On the aristocratic conservative side, warnings about the resurgence of a new populist conservatism have been no less dire. In the same volume on the "radical Right" to which Hofstadter contributed in the 1950s, the self-styled "Tory Democrat" Peter Viereck echoed ominous worries about a new fascism afoot in America. Like Hofstadter, Viereck believed that these rightists were a minority who posed no threat to respectable thought. Although Viereck accused Russell Kirk—another conservative who was suspicious of the popular will—of believing in a

36. Ibid., 94.
37. See David S. Brown, *Richard Hofstadter: An Intellectual Biography,* chap. 2.
38. Lukacs, *Democracy and Populism: Fear and Hatred,* 339–40.

"rootless" conservatism that had no application to America, he seemed to agree with Kirk that true American conservatism (as he defined it) ought to be suspicious of the rabble, and this rabble was Protestant.[39] In concurring with Hofstadter that the *people* are at fault for so easily caving into right-wing radicalism, however, Viereck seemed to worry about the popular roots of what passed for conservatism in America: a "savage direct democracy" that was intolerant of intellectual dissent and aristocratic checks on majority rule.[40]

Like Kirk and Viereck, other self-styled true conservatives have echoed the liberal worry over the dark populist heart of the American people. In the early 1960s, Clinton Rossiter sought to define real conservatism in the manner first prescribed by Kirk and Hofstadter: Rossiter, who followed Hartz in seeing America as a "progressive country with a Liberal tradition," even faulted the mainly Protestant conservatism of Senator Robert Taft for consisting of "assumptions, prejudices, myths, vague longings, and slogans," a conservatism all too reflective of an unimaginative and dangerously radical people. Indeed, Rossiter worried as much as Hofstadter that the most "extreme conservatives" were outdoing the Left in dissenting from the established liberal consensus.[41] In the late 1970s, when the first signs of a well-organized and populist "New Right" were gaining attention, political journalist and self-styled "conservative" Alan Crawford lamented the resentful yet persuasive influence of these new upstarts who were far less concerned with preserving the power of privileged elites and far more interested in overthrowing liberal elites who were faulted for promoting a lax morality, high crime rates, and dependence on federal largesse. In Crawford's polemic, it seemed that both the liberal and the aristocratic conservative readings of America had once again dramatically converged, as they had in Rossiter's analysis. What particularly troubled Crawford (who claimed that Kirk was the classic American conservative) was that the new rightists were as

---

39. Viereck, "The Philosophical 'New Conservatism,'" 188. For a brief yet insightful review of Viereck and other essays in *The Radical Right*, ed. Daniel Bell, see Richard M. Weaver, *In Defense of Tradition: Collected Shorter Writings of Richard M. Weaver, 1929–1963*, 582–83.

40. Viereck, "The Revolt against the Elite," 165.

41. Rossiter, *Conservatism: The Thankless Persuasion*, 182, 262. For his admiration for Hofstadter's analysis of the Right, see 168, 171–72. See also Kendall's critique of Rossiter in *Willmoore Kendall Contra Mundum*, 58–73.

opposed to the old conservative elites as they were to their liberal counterparts. Crawford, who admired Hofstadter's analysis of the populist
Right, despised these pseudoconservatives for rejecting the "elites" who
clearly know better than they how to manage the nation's affairs.[42] In
the same time period, Catholic conservative political theorist Frederick
Wilhelmsen doubted whether the American people, corrupted as they
are by the vices of democracy, are even capable of understanding high
principles like those that constitute natural law ethics. Even a populist
conservative like Kevin P. Phillips (a onetime adviser to President Nixon
on his "southern strategy" to win marginalized white voters in the
South) has warned about the ominous radicalism of "Middle America"
(especially in the South) with parallels to the rise of Nazism during the
Weimar Republic.[43]

In short, both self-professed liberals and aristocratic conservatives
agree that "real conservatism" (whether it is the old liberalism of John
Locke or the old conservatism of the ancien régime) must fear the tyranny of the people, a fear that shows no continuity with the thought of
the founders or Lincoln. Neither liberals nor aristocratic conservatives
demand a high morality from the American people. Liberals are content
to assume that Americans are rational, self-interested individuals who
have no need for religion; aristocratic conservatives insist that virtuous leaders will restrain the masses if they are allowed to reign. When
they regard Americans as a *people* with political authority (rather than
social atoms or cowed subordinates), however, they both tend to fear the
rise of intolerance and ignorance. Each camp fears the vulnerability of
most Americans (especially the old Protestant majority) to demagogic
appeals. Ultimately, both are silent on the capacity of the American people to practice the Christian charity upon which Lincoln attempted to
build a new politics.

42. See Crawford, *Thunder on the Right: The "New Right" and the Politics of
Resentment,* 292–93. For an insightful critique of Crawford's book, see George
W. Carey, "Thunder on the Right, Lightning from the Left."
43. Wilhelmsen, *Christianity and Political Philosophy,* 188; Phillips, *Post-
Conservative America: People, Politics, and Ideology in a Time of Crisis,* 155–64,
193 201. Phillips's most recent work, *American Theocracy,* trumpets the same
fear about the rise of a radical Right (mainly based in the South) in American
politics.

Do the People Need to Be Charitable? The Populist View

Lincoln, who considered himself a conservative preserver of the true founding principles, insisted that charity must be the true morality of Americans. Many on the American Right, who would otherwise heartily endorse Lincoln's trust in the people and his valuation of Christianity, have questioned whether Americans need to be both conservative *and* charitable at the same time. Willmoore Kendall was one of the most famous teachers of this position, an influential theorist who rejected Kirk's aristocratic conservatism as easily as he repudiated Hartz's liberalism. Still, he did not embrace Lincoln's use of Christian morality as a suitable basis for American politics.

I choose to focus on the thought of Kendall for two reasons. First, it represents the most serious objection to the egalitarian legacy of Lincoln, as his longtime opponent, Harry Jaffa, has admitted.[44] Second, his ideas (unlike those of Hofstadter and Kirk) reveal a deeper appreciation for the founding documents (especially *The Federalist*). At present, there are a few signs of a revival of interest in Kendall's thought.[45] The irony is that Kendall, whose thinking has influenced the thought of other critics of Lincoln (Mel Bradford in particular), seemed to share the core assumptions of Lincoln, particularly the defense of majority-rule democracy and an appreciation of the role of Christianity in American thought. Kendall was fond of using a phrase that Lincoln Steffens had made famous: Americans "felt in their hips" a common sense that helped them decide just how important the political issues of the day were.[46] Americans were indeed a *people*, not a collection of atoms accidentally colliding with each other (Hartz), nor were they an unruly mob needful of restraint by wise elites (Kirk). Kendall had no patience with political scientists who despised their own people and advocated the use of statecraft akin to the operation of a "well-run insane asylum" in which the inmates are to be made as comfortable as possible. A conservative in America (or perhaps anywhere) has no right to view "with contempt the generality of the kind of people his society produces." It is simply wrong

---

44. See Catherine Zuckert and Michael P. Zuckert, *The Truth about Leo Strauss: Political Philosophy and American Democracy,* 240–41.

45. See Grant Havers, "Leo Strauss, Willmoore Kendall, and the Meaning of Conservatism."

46. Kendall, *Willmoore Kendall Contra Mundum,* 342.

for conservatives to consider the people as "already corrupt."[47] Lincoln would have happily echoed these sentiments.

Kendall took to heart what *The Federalist* calls the "deliberate sense" of the American people when he constantly railed against both liberal and aristocratic students of the founding for either ignoring or devaluing the idea of popular sovereignty of a prudential citizenry. Liberals, we have seen, prefer to speak of individual rights as the founding premise. Aristocratic conservatives, on the other hand, prefer to speak of wise and benevolent elites who control the vices of the people. These premises are positively alien to American governance, as Kendall articulated it. It is the virtue of the people (rather than individuals or elites) who are best able to prevent tyranny (although, again, there are no guarantees, given human fallibility). All the checks and balances will not prevent this tragedy unless a "certain kind of people" are dedicated to virtue, justice, liberty, and the common good.[48]

Kendall's admonitions about what he sometimes called the "virtuous people" are thoroughly realistic about the limits of majority rule. As a Christian theorist, one might expect him to follow Lincoln on the necessity of having a charitable citizenry. Yet Kendall was oddly silent on the need for the virtuous people to express Christian charity. Nevertheless, Kendall has won a few supporters on the American Right for his hermeneutic of the founding. (Jeffrey Hart calls his teaching on the people's deliberate sense the "core position of American conservatism.")[49]

Still, many more voices across the political spectrum have doubted Kendall's assumptions about the virtues of the people (even though they are grounded in *The Federalist*). Both rightists and leftists have questioned Kendall's faith in the people, an optimism that his former student William F. Buckley calls "baffling."[50] Russell Kirk believed that Kendall was a dangerous Rousseauian.[51] His longtime opponent, Harry Jaffa, accuses Kendall of promoting a consensus theory of politics that is so vague and

47. Kendall and Carey, *Basic Symbols,* 20; Kendall, *Conservative Affirmation,* xxv; Kendall, *Willmoore Kendall Contra Mundum,* 402.

48. Kendall, *Willmoore Kendall Contra Mundum,* 399.

49. Hart, *American Conservative Mind,* 303.

50. Quoted in George H. Nash, "The Place of Willmoore Kendall in American Conservatism," 11.

51. George H. Nash, *The Conservative Intellectual Movement in America since 1945,* 247.

even aprincipled that it might as well be a "distinctive American fascism, or national socialism." Shadia B. Drury associates Kendall's thought with what she considers the "Nazi" philosophy of Carl Schmitt. John Lukacs simply dismisses Kendall's concept of majority-rule democracy as "half-mad."[52] In short, Kendall's faith in the people (which had more in common with Lincoln than perhaps he himself cared to admit) does not appeal to most students of American political science.[53]

Although not all of Kendall's readers have attacked him for imaginary associations with the Far Right, other more admiring critics have found his ideas wanting due to their lack of practicality with respect to the American political system. Samuel Francis contends that Kendall is more of a utopian than a conservative, since he "exaggerated the counterrevolutionary impulses that the mass of the American people harbor." Kendall's former student Gary Wills has faulted his teacher for basing his notion of political discussion on the template of a "faculty meeting" engaged in debate over a protracted period, which poorly serves the interests of impatient minorities in American history. Raymond Tatalovich and Thomas S. Engeman conclude, in their critique of Kendall's "constitutional mythology," that there is nothing fundamentally conservative or prudential in assuming that the people's representatives in Congress will arrive at a just outcome, especially if a legislative majority deprives the president of making important reforms.[54]

It may well be that Kendall's concept of "deliberate sense" is equivalent to a doctrine of majority rule that might oppose the interests of minorities at any given time. Certainly, Kendall admitted that his conservatism was one of process, not abstract principle.[55] In the context of debates over the demands of the civil rights movement in 1964, Kendall described it as the "proper business of the American political system" to place the "good health" of the system over divisive debates on abstract rights.[56] In short,

---

52. Jaffa, *American Conservatism,* 195; Drury, *Leo Strauss and the American Right,* 95–96; Lukacs, *New Republic,* 340.

53. See John A. Murley, "On the 'Calhounism' of Willmoore Kendall," 126–31.

54. Francis, *Beautiful Losers: Essays on the Failure of American Conservatism,* 87; Wills, *Explaining America: "The Federalist,"* 200; Tatalovich and Engeman, *The Presidency and Political Science: Two Hundred Years of Constitutional Debate,* 12–24.

55. Kendall, *Willmoore Kendall Contra Mundum,* 275.

56. Ibid., 362–63.

Kendall opposed as much as Russell Kirk any attempt of the majority (or a determined minority) to impose its will tyrannically, but he was also confident that the necessarily deliberative process of republican governance would minimize this prospect. (For this reason, Kendall praised the judicial review powers of the Supreme Court for curbing the plebiscitary potential in the Constitution.) Like Lincoln, then, Kendall placed his faith in the wisdom of Americans to deliberate on political issues. Still, as some of his critics argue, even a process needs principles that are worth preserving.[57] Did Kendall have an answer to this concern that, he himself admitted, was the "missing section" of *The Federalist*? What exactly should Americans believe in, to make this process work?

Here Kendall had to turn to principles that, he sometimes believed, the American system should cautiously embrace. These amounted to an embrace of a secular state whose citizenry was moderately religious (in the Christian sense). Kendall's attempt to relate biblical principles to the American regime was, in his own view, a reflection of the most important issue in American politics, even though a few of his critics fault him for overemphasizing the Christian origins of the American regime.[58] As he once put it, *the* issue at stake between American conservatives and liberals was over the meaning of reason and revelation.[59] To be sure, Kendall was concerned with the relation, not the *identity*, between religion and the American regime. (The wall between church and state was indeed "porous," but there was still a wall.)

Like Lincoln, Kendall also thought that the American people's religiosity was valuable and even necessary to the workings of this secular political system. They were not allowed to identify religion with politics. Conservatives could not support a quasi-religious state (Kendall faulted Kirk for this error), but conservatives had to support a religion that at least inspired a *prudential* people.[60] Lincoln as well as Kendall also knew that there was no more guarantee that religion would inspire virtue and moderation than there was that the republican system would prevent tyranny.

Unlike Kendall, however, Lincoln demanded that this "deliberate

57. Wills, *Explaining America: "The Federalist,"* 200; Jaffa, *American Conservatism*, 195.

58. See Zuckert, "Natural Rights," 24–27; and Jaffa, *How to Think*, 38.

59. Kendall, *Conservative Affirmation*, 242.

60. Kendall, *Willmoore Kendall Contra Mundum*, 46–47.

sense" be completely based on charity. To be sure, Kendall favored the "Christian picture of man" for presupposing that the people are virtuous. Yet he did not demand quite as high a level of moral excellence as Lincoln had because he legitimately worried about the belief in *chosenness* taking over the deliberate sense of Americans. As he warned in his last work (which he coauthored with George Carey), even secular-minded American leaders might fall for the belief in Americans as a "chosen people." Kendall and Carey warily described this view as the ambition of a "self-chosen people" whose abandonment of belief in God's existence does not deter them from urging Americans to create a "Promised Land" of free and equal human beings, even if it requires "remaking human nature" in the process.[61]

Kendall particularly worried about the "fanatics" in American politics who failed to realize just how religious they were, or how devoted they were to the doctrine of the chosen people. It is undeniable that Kendall had the views of Harry Jaffa in mind, whose work *Crisis of the House Divided* he reviewed in 1959. Kendall rightly worried about the unlimited egalitarian vision that Jaffa implied when he described the divinely sanctioned mission of America in the language of the Mosaic narrative. In Jaffa's terms, the American people were no more worthy of their "mission" than the ancient Israelites, since they had failed to create "a government of equal rights," as the founders had demanded.[62]

Though Kendall (along with many conservatives) wondered how any system could embody "purity of heart," he was confident that this doctrine is a derailment that, influential though it may be, is not fundamental to the American political system or its traditions. Belief in chosenness was an unfortunate accident to which various demagogues throughout history (Kendall blamed Lincoln in particular here) kept contributing. *Pace* Rousseau, Kendall believed that the prudential people did not err: it was a thoughtless leadership that had led an otherwise moderate people into the civil wars and imperialist crusades characteristic of a "chosen people" ideology. Moreover, Kendall squarely blamed Lincoln for contributing to this derailment.[63]

---

61. Ibid., 401; Kendall and Carey, *Basic Symbols,* 152–53.

62. Jaffa, *Crisis of the House Divided,* 230–31. He repeats these claims in *New Birth,* 257–58, 349–50. Kendall's review of *Crisis of the House Divided* is included in his *Conservative Affirmation,* 249–52.

63. Kendall and Carey, *Basic Symbols,* 153–56.

Although it is hard to deny the validity of Kendall's worry that Americans have often disastrously flirted with the myth of chosenness from the time of Winthrop to the present, it is more debatable whether Lincoln himself should share the blame for propagating this myth. As I argued in the last chapter, Lincoln was careful and tentative in not asserting that he possessed actual knowledge of Providence, and placed greater emphasis on the importance of charity (even if he did not always live up to this ethic). Lincoln knew that both sides in the Civil War could invoke the authority of the Exodus narrative (black slaves desired liberation from the "Egyptian" South as much as Confederates desired freedom from the pharaohs of the North). Other presidents, such as Woodrow Wilson, were far more certain that they were acting on the side of God.

Most significant, however, Kendall sets up an extreme dichotomy between a "chosen people" who make impossible demands on the American system of governance *and* a people with a limited commitment to moral principles. This choice is arguably a false one, since it is hard to imagine Americans ever refraining from making morally principled demands on their system of government. Yet Kendall, despite his belief that politics and religion are inexorably linked through a porous wall of separation, also believed that the overriding need for "consensus" in this system trumped any considerations based on moral values. In the context of the civil rights era of the 1960s, Kendall admitted that he had no moral position on the "merits" of the arguments put forth by the marchers and demonstrators within this movement. He felt only that the "proper business of the American political system [was] to adjudicate" these claims to civil rights. The only way to avoid a constitutional crisis, Kendall argued, was to refrain from divisive debates about the rightness and wrongness of abstract principles like equality. Kendall always thought that America, with its great potential for civil war (not least due to the lurking influence of chosenness), would be best served if its leaders did not encourage the untidy integration of ethics with politics using dramatic calls to war upon the sin of prejudice and bigotry "by declaring them criminal."[64]

Although Kendall is justified in warning about the limits of debate

---

64. Kendall, *Willmoore Kendall Contra Mundum*, 362, 382. For a discussion of the high potential for civil war in America, see Ranney and Kendall, *Democracy*, 464–67.

over abstract moral ideals (will these debates ever end?), it is unrealistic to think that Americans should avoid bringing their moral concerns into the process of government altogether. It is hard to imagine that Kendall himself consistently believed this arrangement to be possible, particularly when he celebrated the fact that the "people" (American or not) had every *right* to suppress dissent, a tradition that began with the execution of Socrates, continued on to the time of the libertarian Jefferson's enforcement of the laws against sedition, and forward to the age of Senator McCarthy.[65] Surely, these cases are examples of the "people" relating moral principles and politics in dramatic ways.

The key difference between Lincoln and Kendall (in addition to other populists in American history) is that the president still insisted on a certain willingness on the part of Americans to *relate* morality and politics together. While Kendall celebrated the Christian faith of his people as much as Lincoln did (and even agreed that it was central to maintaining the virtue of the people), he also held that this faith cannot enter the political realm (despite the "porous" nature of the wall between church and state). Surely, one way to address conflicts over morality is to encourage their entrance into the deliberations of the political system. In resisting the fanaticism spurred on by appeals to chosenness, the determination to separate morality and politics altogether is a high price to pay and smacks of the legal positivism that Kendall otherwise despised. It was not sufficient to celebrate the moral sense of Americans, as Kendall did, without demanding that they actually act upon this sense. This Lincoln most certainly demanded. Indeed, if no one makes this demand, then the gap between politics and morality leads to the result that Lincoln most dreaded—the charge of hypocrisy. It is hard to imagine any other culture, apart from one with historically Protestant roots, agonizing over this existential danger.

CONCLUSION

The legacy of Lincoln's trust in the people has not been an overwhelming success as a persistent influence in American political thought. The

---

65. For Kendall's thoughts on Socrates and Jefferson, see *Willmoore Kendall Contra Mundum*, 149–67, 290–302. For his thoughts on McCarthy, see *Conservative Affirmation*, 50–76.

major schools of the American political tradition either do not trust (as in the case of liberals and aristocratic conservatives) or do not demand (as in the case of populist conservatives) the willingness of the people to act in a morally consistent manner, as Lincoln did. Perhaps the demand of the president was unrealistic. Charity, the hardest truth of the Christian worldview, is not easily introduced into the political realm. For this reason defenders of democratic universalism, whose ideas I discuss in the next two chapters, do not usually insist that Americans themselves act charitably, a strange attitude that reflects the willingness of these ideologues to support the spread of democracy while displaying indifference to the more vulgar aspects of popular American culture.

It may be more "realistic" to rely on the enlightened self-interest, deliberate sense, or deference to aristocratic virtue that the people may see fit to practice. Yet none of these attitudes fully resonates with the Christian origins of the American people. None of these ideological factions answers this question: what would happen if America's Christian roots became politically irrelevant? If that were to happen, it is far from obvious that the historic commitment to Christian charity would still survive. It is even less likely that a democracy, detached from the religious moorings that once inspired Americans, could export easily its politics abroad. Lincoln simply assumed that Christianity in America would survive and that no secular substitutes would take the place of this faith. Indeed, an insistence that Americans, both leaders and citizens, act charitably may be the only restraint against ideological rationales for adventurism in foreign policy that strain both the moral fiber and the institutions of the republic.

5

Natural Right, Charity, and Political Realism

> A secularized version of the old religious mille-
> narianism was however not merely intertwined
> with the idea of revolution, it was the very essence
> of that idea.
>
> —Harry V. Jaffa, *How to Think about the American
> Revolution: A Bicentennial Celebration*

> We do not consider ourselves a Christian nation.
>
> —President Barack Obama, April 6, 2009

*M*ost Lincoln scholars agree that there is a deep relation between the principles of charity and equality in the thought of the president. The president's attack on double standards, which were often practiced in the name of a "chosen people," must suggest to anyone that Lincoln was preoccupied with the meaning of Christian ideas for the public square. It also implies that Lincoln must have relied on a vital Christianity in America in order to fulfill the most important credo of the founding, as he understood it. To date, a few scholars agree with Lincoln that this largely Protestant tradition in America is vital to the identity of the republic, and lament its gradual disappearance. Barry Alan Shain has amply documented the early Protestant foundations of the Revolutionary period, a tradition that he believes has yielded to the control of a secular managerial state. Robert Bellah associates the "broken covenant" of America's political creed with the "loss of intellectual creativity" in American Protestantism. Samuel Huntington contends that the political beliefs of the country's citizenry need Christianity more than the latter needs it. Kevin Phillips, who credits Anglo-American Protestantism with the triumph of liberal democracy and the rule of law in the West, laments the passing of this early modern Christian tradition into history, by the end of the twentieth century. James Kurth argues that Protestantism has become "deformed" into an unrecognizably secularized version of itself, whose adherents now replace God's grace with the spread of democracy on a global basis.[1] These authors do not take for granted what Lincoln or Tocqueville did: that the Protestant orthodoxy of the nineteenth century would continue to underpin the American political tradition. Still, at least these authors recognize the palpable influence of faith on the politics of America.

These twentieth-century voices now must compete with a new hermeneutic of the American founding that does not attribute any necessary influence to Christianity. In the post–World War II period, this novel reading of American politics has enjoyed great success in *secularizing* the meaning of the relation between politics and religion in the republic. Defenders of this approach, who would have no sympathy with my overall thesis that Lincoln's usage of charity requires Christianity, declare that America's universalistic principles of liberty and equality are not based on any particular faith. Indeed, defenders of this idea of democratic universalism in the post–World War II era have enjoyed massive success in redefining Lincoln's legacy. In portraying this president as a secular prophet of democratic globalism, as opposed to a Protestant leader who sought to preserve his own nation, this novel approach to Lincoln has convinced even many opponents of the president that he had ambitions to Americanize the world. Therefore, if they can show that Lincoln did not need Christianity, then the historic status of this faith can disappear from the public square without affecting the mores of the republic, in their view.

I shall call this hermeneutic the "natural rightist" reading of twentieth- and twenty-first-century American political thought. In recent history, devotees of the school of natural right have argued for the wholly secular foundation of the republic. The idea of natural right has been one

1. Shain, *Myth of American Individualism*, 55, Bellah, *Broken Covenant*, 90, Huntington, *Who Are We?* 337–40; Phillips, *Cousins' Wars*, 5–8; Kurth, "George W. Bush and the Protestant Deformation."

of the most influential foundations of American political thought over the past fifty years. Indeed, natural rightists unconditionally declare that this idea must be *the* foundation for the true American creed. Moreover, in their view, Abraham Lincoln insisted upon this foundation. The fact that Lincoln saw Christian morality as a precondition for democracy's success receives little attention in the writings of natural rightists. This ideology has grand implications for the world as well, since the very thought of a right being "natural" immediately implies the message of democratic universalism. If rights are indeed natural, then it is illegitimate for anyone to violate these rights or to take credit for their origination. Nature, as the source of right, is the true authority, and mere human authority exists below. Rights do not arise in the political realm: they already exist at the birth of a human being. Natural rights to liberty and equality owe *nothing* to a religious heritage, although it is incumbent upon Americans to support these rights for people everywhere. Moreover, all human beings can comprehend these rights, regardless of historic context. However one understands these rights, they presuppose the free consent of *all* human beings to exercise them as they see fit.

Natural rightists have mightily contributed to the growing debate among academics and the political class in America today about the best way to answer this question: who are we? Are Americans devoted to principles of natural right, a philosophy of liberty and equality that applies universally to all peoples (as the Declaration announces)? Is this creed the answer to the question of America? Or are Americans a particular people wedded more to culture and religion, which cannot be easily universalized across the globe?[2] Does the natural rightist ideal of irreducible human dignity exist on a universal level, ready for acceptance in all cultures?

The ideology of natural right has been so successful in recent years that the very meaning of "conservatism" in America has experienced redefinition. It is now "conservative" (if one is a neoconservative) to invoke the Declaration of Independence—the classic document of American natural right—to justify the quasi-evangelical dissemination of democratic ideals throughout the world, despite the cautionary message of Washington's Farewell Address on the dangers of excessive and irrational interventions abroad. Moreover, the defenders of natural right

2. See Huntington, *Who Are We?*

see no essential role for Christianity to play in this ambitious endeavor. Typically, natural rightists are either silent on or dismissive of the role of religion in spreading democracy. Apparently, all of the world's peoples thirst for democracy, despite religious diversity across cultures.[3] In the words of William J. Bennett (former secretary of education under the first Bush presidency), the "cherished beliefs" of America are also "the world's at large" because they are universal truths that judge the "legitimacy" of governments across the globe. It also became apparent that the Bush II presidency, particularly in its intervention in Iraq, advanced this idea of universal principles (or natural right) more than any other administration in history, as devotees of natural right have observed with satisfaction.[4]

My purpose in this chapter is to scrutinize the natural rightist denial of any necessary relation between the American tradition of natural right and American Christianity. To date, there has been surprisingly little in-depth discussion of this relation. If there is a belief in the historic relation between natural right and Christianity in the republic at all, it is one destined for the dustbin of history, for natural right doctrine is no longer indebted to this discredited religion. This approach is incorrect because it assumes that the success of spreading natural right credos need not rest upon a Christian foundation. These ideologues ignore religious particularity in favor of an abstract and utopian universalism.

The natural rightist teaching about America is the brainchild of the German Jewish political philosopher Leo Strauss, whose numerous studies on the great works of Western political philosophy paid no serious attention to the influence of Christianity on the West. Although I am not the first scholar to argue that Strauss downplayed and even ignored the influence of Christian revelation on modern politics, I believe that there has not been sufficient attention to the relation between this marginalization of America's historic faith and the natural rightist support for ambitious attempts at democracy building as the true mission of the

3. I concede that not all defenders of natural rights in American history support democracy building or downplay Christianity's influence, like twentieth-century natural rightists (as I note in Chapters 2 and 6, Jefferson appreciated Christianity and doubted that democracy is suitable for all peoples). I am focused simply on the contemporary and most influential version of natural rightism in our time.

4. Bennett, "Morality, Character, and American Foreign Policy," 301; James W. Ceaser, *Nature and History in American Political Development: A Debate,* 78.

republic. If it is correct that America owes little to one religious faith, it becomes easier for cosmopolitan elites to portray the nation as truly universalistic, in possession of ideals that all human beings regardless of creed, history, or culture can grasp. For this reason, natural rightists (who are often interchangeable with prominent neoconservatives and liberals of our time) have enjoyed major successes in the post–World War II and post–cold war eras, when America's elites felt the pressure to secularize the nation's history as a truly propositional nation that owes little to the parochial faith of Christianity.

Predictably, natural rightists have looked to Abraham Lincoln for inspiration, although they represent him as a secular politician. Yet the question of historical and religious influence is inescapable, despite the determination of natural rightists to emphasize the ahistorical universality of the creed. Even if it is true that rights exist by *nature,* as opposed to historical tradition, it is also legitimate to ask why it is only in particular contexts (both historical and religious) that these rights enjoy understanding and success. Though Strauss and his numerous students are not the only political scientists who indirectly raise these questions, their considerable influence in America encourages my exclusive focus on their approach to natural right and the defective reasoning behind their attempt to read Christianity out of the American political tradition.

Once again, I am not the first critic of the liberal and neoconservative premise that all peoples have not only a right by nature to democracy but the *desire* for it as well; Lincoln, who knew that the passion for liberty does not translate into passion for everyone else's liberty, was more realistic than Bush. Yet there has been little discussion of the failure of natural rightists, who greatly influenced the Bush administration, to appreciate the historic relation between American democracy and Christianity. If this relation exists, then the universalism of democracy building shatters on the rock of religious particularity. In short, can peoples who lack a Christian understanding of charity welcome the American version of democracy?

Ultimately, the current debate over neoconservative and liberal interventionism is over how universalizable the natural right tradition truly is. This radical universalism, torn from its historic Protestant moorings, is not what Lincoln intended. It is, rather, an attempt to spread these principles of liberty and equality on a global scale without any regard for historic or religious particularity. The creed of natural right calls for a radical transformation of the nation's mission by promoting

American liberal democracy for the entire globe. (This program derives from the same assumption as the global "dignity promotion" that Barack Obama's campaign in 2008 sometimes trumpeted.)[5] Like the prophets and apostles of old, natural rightists believe that the truth is written on the hearts of all human beings. It is thus a gigantic leap of faith, since its devotees assume that all people desire this model of government. Natural rightists often portray Americans as the "chosen people" who will do the job. To my mind, this qualifies natural right as a political creed. (It is interesting that natural rightists are not hesitant to describe their belief as a "creed." Certainly, their critics show no reluctance.) Yet the irony is that this civil faith is portrayed as secular to the core, free of Christian influence.

Defenders of the natural rightist version of universalism, based on the teachings of Strauss, assert that their passion for democracy building is still based on realism as much as idealism. They contend that it is in the interests of the United States to "indoctrinate" the rest of the world in the meaning of democracy (since democracies do not go to war against each other, as President Bush liked to say). As Strauss taught, the morality of the Bible has no place in politics. Its demands are too utopian for the political sphere (an assumption that their hero, Abraham Lincoln, never made!). Yet it is apparently not utopian to demand that nations with diverse values will share the same understanding of democracy as Americans have for more than two centuries. What is particularly contradictory about this allegedly secular doctrine is its reliance on religious credos (like belief in the "chosen people") to justify what is supposed to be an irreligious and realistic policy. Apparently, Americans as the "chosen people" have no need of Christianity as they export a democracy to nations that often lack a biblical understanding of charity. Natural rightists are confident that their ideals alone appeal to all human beings. I intend to explain and target this leap of faith throughout this chapter.

THE INFLUENCE OF LEO STRAUSS IN AMERICA

If any thinker has decisively influenced the debate over the meaning of natural right in the American political tradition, it is Leo Strauss. It is

---

5. See Spencer Ackerman, "The Obama Doctrine."

less often said that Strauss also contributed to the tendency of political theorists in the United States, since World War II, to understate or even ignore the influence of revelation on politics. Strauss, who left Germany in the early 1930s and eventually came to the United States by the end of that decade, is usually credited (or blamed) for inspiring a radically new approach to political philosophy in his newly adopted nation. In teaching that the texts of the great political philosophers (from Plato to the present) taught a *universal* teaching about the art of political rule, Strauss swam against the tide of historicism, progressivism, and relativism that reduce ideas to their contexts and deny any claim to political universalism. Unlike any other comparable émigré intellectual of his time, Strauss spawned a school of thought whose epigones continue to enjoy vast influence on the study of the American regime.

Since the rise of neoconservatism (and especially the start of the Iraq war in 2003), Strauss's ideas have been associated with the project of using religion as a "noble fiction" for political purposes. Presumably, Strauss taught that true leaders (or statesmen) must invoke the authority of God or Providence as the ultimate cynical justification to fool the masses into fighting wars of imperialism. The cynical use of biblical religion is welcome to Strauss, according to these critics.[6] Despite the claims of these readers, I understand Strauss as a thinker categorically opposed to the use of biblical credos in matters of statecraft. Indeed, the only universalism that he supports is one based on a classical pagan tradition, not a biblical one.[7]

Amid the current debate over the meaning of his ideas (when so many readers claim to have figured out his "secret" teachings), it may be futile to emphasize just how original Strauss's contribution to the teaching of political philosophy in America is. While he taught that a return to the teachings of Plato and Aristotle was the ideal means of comprehending the challenges of modernity, he was not the only postwar intellectual to insist on this ambition (his fellow émigrés Hannah Arendt and Eric Voegelin often made similar claims about the superiority of classical

6. See Drury, *Leo Strauss;* Anne Norton, *Leo Strauss and the Politics of American Empire;* and Stephen Holmes, *The Anatomy of Antiliberalism,* 61–87.

7. Grant Havers, "Romanticism and Universalism: The Case of Leo Strauss." For a detailed discussion of Strauss's opposition to the morality of the Bible, see John J. Ranieri, *Disturbing Revelation: Leo Strauss, Eric Voegelin, and the Bible,* 103–30, 158–85.

texts over modern ones). The distinctive challenge of his approach, I believe, lies in his teaching that the Bible is the great *antagonist* to true political philosophy. Scripture lacks the realism necessary for true success in politics. Although this teaching is hardly original (it dates as far back as Machiavelli), it is inventive to claim that this understanding of revelation represents the true American conservative tradition, from the founders to Lincoln. This conservative tradition is presumably based on natural right.

Strauss genuinely lamented the decline of belief in natural right in his newly adopted nation. The universalism of this tradition was naturally appealing to a German Jewish émigré who had escaped the tyranny of Nazism. Yet Strauss taught his many American students in the postwar period that political philosophy, in America or anywhere else, lacks any necessary connection to religion. If anyone rejected Willmoore Kendall's dictum that the wall between church and state ought to be "porous," it was Strauss. To be sure, while Strauss acknowledges that political theorists and leaders invoke religious themes, he cautioned that they did so for purely political purposes, and nothing more. Strauss believed that true political (and philosophical) minds were not sincerely religious. As a result, all of his students who write on Lincoln conclude that the president was not a true Christian. Moreover, the mission of America to protect and spread American democracy does not require a Christian foundation, or even knowledge of Christian charity. Although a few readers of his works have spotted his attempt to read Christianity out of modern political thought, few authors to my knowledge have pursued the implications of this secular hermeneutic for the global application of American natural right credos.[8] The fact that Lincoln appealed to Christianity on a regular basis throughout his political career does not suggest, to the students of Strauss, any need to have a Christian basis for democracy. The morality of natural right is equally intelligible to all people, regardless of creed. Indeed, it is so universal that even pagan political philosophers who supported slavery nevertheless taught the truth of natural right as well, in their view.

It may be odd to many observers to digest the claim that Strauss *opposed* the secularization of biblical themes. His many detractors often

8. See Claes G. Ryn, *America the Virtuous: The Crisis of Democracy and the Quest for Empire.*

contend that Strauss sought to inspire a new political religion of natural right among his students in the United States, which then must be disseminated to all corners of the globe. This popular charge that Strauss is the "godfather" of imperialist designs is related to the view that he saw in biblical religion a useful form of propaganda with which to stabilize a regime. Out of this argument has arisen the charge that Strauss is an "Averroistic" defender of *double truth:* one truth for philosophers, and one fiction for the masses.[9] Presumably, biblical religion is that noble fiction. Yet I shall argue that Strauss is just the opposite of an Averroist, since he saw no common ground between statecraft and revelation. Indeed, in his eyes, the synthesis of the two is a dangerous characteristic of modern thought.

Yet the synthesis of political philosophy and revelation has always characterized American thought. Lincoln taught that charity must be *the* basis of democracy. As I argued in Chapter 3, Lincoln left no doubt that only Christianity can teach charity. Whereas natural right devotees are genuinely opposed to slavery, they also assume that the so-called universal opposition to slavery around the world requires no foundation in Christianity. Even extrabiblical peoples can presumably understand natural rights, since the pagan texts of Plato and Aristotle taught this philosophy as well. Still, in treating the entire world as if it were a large-scale version of the American South, the school of natural right forgets not only the peculiarity of the Civil War but also just how difficult it was for Lincoln to educate his own people on the political implications of an ethics that they already knew. The carnage of the Civil War was hardly a testimony to the success of universalism. The fact that the second inaugural address of the president displayed more modest hopes about the healing of the nation's wounds than the Gettysburg Address's message of a new birth of freedom reveals his awareness of the perils of universalism.[10]

Still, Strauss taught that belief in natural right need not depend on the Bible. Indeed, universalism is based on paganism, an odd choice for

9. See Drury, *Leo Strauss;* and Wilhelmsen, *Christianity and Political Philosophy,* 209–25. Not everyone is convinced that Strauss would be happy with the religious nature of the Republican Party (despite his students' claims to the contrary). See Rogers M. Smith, "What If God Was One of Us? The Challenges of Studying Foundational Political Concepts," 160–61.

10. See Thurow, *Abraham Lincoln,* 87.

a movement dedicated to the spread of human rights, freedom, and equality. Plato and Aristotle—the heroes of the Straussian canon—are decidedly opposed to these concepts. Pagan universalism is unchari-table, hierarchical, and undemocratic, as I discuss below. Although it is rare for Strauss's students to admit these realities about paganism, their understanding of natural right requires them to emphasize the pagan over the biblical: the truth must be known to all by nature. Yet without biblical charity, they end up relying on a universalism that is hostile to both the legacy of Lincoln and the Christian tradition that shaped Lincoln's political philosophy. Indeed, a modern actualization of paganism is more likely to breed exclusivism, as Strauss and his students eventually have to admit.

STRAUSS AND THE BIBLE

It is odd that most readers often portray Strauss as a friend to revela-tion, then, when in fact he harbored deep misgivings over the usage of scripture in modern politics. Although it is true that Strauss showed more respect for revelation than his twentieth-century contemporaries (which is not hard to do in an age of academic positivism), he was ulti-mately respectful at a great distance. The secular bias of Strauss led him to defend political philosophies (usually pagan) that are supposedly free of the authority of religious influences. In the process, he may well have felt uncomfortable in America, where politics and religion are histori-cally inseparable. Indeed, the American political tradition deliberately blurs the distinction between religion and politics in ways that avoid a neatly dualistic approach that Strauss often embraced. At least one criti-cal reader of Strauss has remarked that it was unpersuasive of Strauss to believe that philosophy could be *entirely* free of religion.[11] Though it is partly correct to suggest that philosophy has usually required some degree of religious influence (especially in the medieval and modern periods), this critique misunderstands the teaching of Strauss that true philosophy is *pagan,* the one tradition that (unlike the medieval or the modern) is wholly independent of biblical revelation.

11. Thomas J. Altizer, "The Theological Conflict between Strauss and Voegelin," 269.

Readers familiar with Strauss are well aware of this teaching but generally do not conclude that their master was, therefore, hostile to revelation. After all, Strauss was raised as an orthodox Jew and insisted throughout his life that he respected his ancestral faith. Although he was not a believer (Strauss taught that a philosopher could never be one), he allegedly respected the challenge of faith to reason, and even acknowledged on a regular basis that philosophy cannot refute revelation.[12] Strauss did not want to join the throngs of post-Enlightenment intellectuals who boldly (and imprudently) neglected the chief lesson of the life of Socrates: that religion is required to serve the politics of a regime, and, questions of its irrationality notwithstanding, a prudent political philosopher must support belief if the politics of the regime merit it.

While both detractors and supporters of Strauss tend to interpret his ideas on revelation through the vein described above, I believe that Strauss in fact doubted the political utility of scripture and subtly warned against the influence of revelation in his writings. Strauss was an opponent of political religion, Christian style.[13] Indeed, one of the reasons that motivated him to advocate a return to classical Greek philosophy was his view that only a pagan tradition of natural right (and the modern representations of this tradition) can provide the mainly secular realism to deal with the challenges of politics. Modern political philosophy, despite its denial of dependence on the Bible, is far too subject to this tradition.

It may be tempting to comprehend Strauss, as his students have, as simply a great defender of that cherished American tradition, the separation of church and state.[14] It is true that Strauss desired a separation of political philosophy from revelation, but he also taught that the only political philosophy that accomplished this feat was the tradition that historically predated Christian revelation—the Platonic. If my reading is correct, then Strauss might well be aghast at the efforts of his followers (all devotees of modern natural right) to encourage the spread of

---

12. See Strauss, *Natural Right and History,* 75.
13. See Clark A. Merrill, "Leo Strauss's Indictment of Christian Philosophy"; Havers, "Romanticism and Universalism"; and McAllister, *Revolt against Modernity,* 198–99. Oddly, McAllister, who notes Strauss's reticence to discuss Christianity, still believes (without providing any textual evidence) that Strauss thought that American natural right required the survival of Christian belief (162).
14. See Jaffa, *Original Intent,* 352.

American liberal democracy around the world.[15] Yet Strauss's teachings on the irrelevance of Christianity to politics have indirectly encouraged the position among his mostly American students that the only legitimate mission of America is to spread democracy, without recognition of the historic influence of Christianity. Despite Lincoln, Christianity cannot (and need not) be the precondition for true democracy.

Throughout his studies of modern political philosophy, Strauss emphasizes that the wisest moderns have no great debt to the biblical tradition and have eschewed any attempt to synthesize politics with revelation, except for propagandistic purposes. Natural rightists pride themselves on being realistic about the limits of politics, limits that a religious mind cannot grasp. In his study of Machiavelli, Strauss observes that "the United States of America may be said to be the only country in the world which was founded in explicit opposition to Machiavellian principles."[16] That opposition was based on the tradition of natural right, or the professed commitment, so famously articulated by John Locke, to principles of liberty and equality that all human beings have by nature, as well as their right by nature to oppose tyranny. Because Strauss did not portray Locke as a true Christian, it is fair to say that he doubted that American natural right requires or even enjoys a Christian basis.[17] The success of American democracy lies solely with the *secular* principles of modern natural right.

More than any other political philosopher of the twentieth century, Strauss emphasized the importance of preserving the tradition of natural right against the challenges of historicism, relativism, and nihilism, which deny that any ethic or regime is good *by nature* for humanity. The followers of Strauss have mainly focused on critiquing these ideologies in order to fortify the beleaguered defenses of natural right. Without these defenses, one can justify tyranny as easily as one can justify democracy if one cannot appeal to a standard of what is good by nature. Strauss worried in the postwar years that the truths of the Declaration of Independence, which echoed the noble commitment to natural right and made America "the most powerful and prosperous of the nations of earth," would be vanquished at the hands of its former

15. See Havers, "Strauss, Kendall, and Conservatism."
16. Strauss, *Thoughts on Machiavelli*, 13.
17. Strauss, *Natural Right and History,* 202–51.

enemy Germany, the cradle of historicism and fact-value relativism. "It would not be the first time that a nation, defeated on the battlefield," Strauss states, imposed "the yoke of its own thought" on its conqueror.[18]

One disturbing sign, according to Strauss, is that the academics of this triumphant nation were treating natural right as a matter of individual preference (which was hardly a defense against tyranny) and even as a myth with some beneficial aspects in a utilitarian sense. Strauss believed that the modern triumph of historicism would, at best, favor natural right as a useful fiction but not a necessarily true one, since there is nothing true by nature according to historicists. "Utility and truth are two entirely different things."[19] Still, if Americans no longer believe that their political traditions are true—only useful—then they may not muster the commitment to be good citizens.

Perhaps Strauss's students have interpreted this teaching as a call to arms, since they give the impression that the only way to preserve the ideals of the republic from ideological enemies (within and without) is to universalize them. For this reason, I spy an *evangelical* imperative within their hermeneutic of modern natural right, or a secularized faith that demands a relentless attempt to make the world American in the noblest sense, presumably without the help of Christianity. (Oddly enough, this imperative clashes with the emphasis on realism that is supposed to characterize natural rightism.) As a Platonist, Strauss would not object to the political use of religion, but it depended on the *type* of religion. There is no evidence whatsoever that Strauss thought revealed religion was politically useful. Indeed, he acknowledged as much when he dismissed this use of scripture as "either stupid or blasphemous."[20]

At first glance, this claim is a strange one for a Platonist to make. Why shouldn't biblical credos be used for political purposes? Why, in the same essay, does Strauss warn against identifying America as a nation founded upon "divine premises"? Is there anything in scripture that is too hot for a politician to handle? Is it true, as one critic has argued, that Strauss "seemed set upon minimizing the period from the Christian era [of political thought] to Machiavelli"?[21]

---

18. Ibid., 1–2.
19. Ibid., 6.
20. Strauss, "Progress or Return?" 298–99.
21. Ibid., 257; Francis G. Wilson, "The Political Science of Willmoore Kendall," 39.

What troubled Strauss about the Bible as a whole (and not just Christianity) is that it may discourage citizens from becoming fervent supporters of their polity. Because the regime is, ostensibly, the highest authority, the idea of a God above this city would be distinctly subversive. The political religion of a pagan polis spies no tension between the gods and the regime itself. A biblically based political religion would be oxymoronic, since the immanence of the political must clash with the transcendence of the religious. Indeed, the most subversive element of this transcendent God is that he loves his creation. This personal God, who exists above the political, is universalistic in expressing his love for all of humanity, even the lowest and most oppressed.[22] If a political regime, then, does not reflect this universal love, God must judge it accordingly. Natural rightists therefore spy an irresolvable tension between God and the city.

In asserting that true political philosophy (based on natural right) is not indebted to scripture, Strauss may have sincerely thought that he was saving revelation from the very modernist temptation to misuse biblical credos for political purposes. The tough morality demanded by scripture—especially its call for "purity of the heart"—simply is not compatible with the tragic and heartless world of pagan politics.[23] Yet the full application of his hermeneutical separation between political philosophy and the Bible has not been a plausible one in a nation in which the most widely read book has always been the Bible. Nevertheless, Strauss thought that the politicization of revelation sternly demands a level of virtue that no regime can embody, since the Christian "City of God" requires a "certainty and definiteness" that classical philosophy never promised. No pagan lawgiver, for example, prophesied the onset of redemption for humanity.[24] Strauss typically taught that the classics never promised *certainty* in politics. The best regime exists only as an ideal, not a reality. No one should confuse an actual regime with the best regime. As Strauss pithily remarks, students of philosophy "must drink wine, not in deed, but in speech."[25] It is not that political philosophers

22. Nygren, *Agape and Eros*, 731.
23. Strauss, "Progress or Return?" 279.
24. Strauss, *Natural Right and History*, 144.
25. Strauss, *What Is Political Philosophy?* 31. As Schall has astutely remarked, Strauss's rejection of Catholic natural law theory lies in his view that this tradi-

lack a sense of the transcendent, but that this notion is different from that of revealed religion. As seekers of the eternal, political philosophers must never declare that this search is over and that an existing regime is the *final, best regime.* The Bible clearly promises a cessation of evil that no political regime can afford to put into practice. Whereas the classics taught the primacy of thought, the "Bible asserts the primacy of deed." Strauss was adamant that this noble sentiment would have disastrous consequences in the political realm. For this reason, the ancients never made this promise; even the Platonic best regime "will not include the cessation of war" that Isaiah (2:2–4) prophesies.[26] A biblical regime, then, is fraught with tension, because it fails (unlike pagan thought) to understand the basic right to self-preservation, which cancels out any pretension to either universal peace or cosmopolitan acceptance of all other nations. The classical authors were too realistic to believe in political utopianism.

What is astounding about the Straussian hermeneutic is that its most influential supporters in America have followed the master's teachings on classical realism (and the lack of any equivalent in revelation) *while* they have embraced liberal democracy as the best regime whose triumph ends "History," or meaningful debates about politics. Students of Strauss have been notoriously selective readers of his teachings, especially since they end up embracing a mission of democratization that ignores the master's views on both the realism of classical political philosophy and the unrealism of biblical revelation. Although natural rightists have followed Strauss in ignoring the contribution of Christianity to the West, their attempt to build a program of democratic universalism on a bizarre synthesis of pagan natural right and the biblical credo of the "chosen people" has resulted in a perversely ahistorical utopianism in foreign policy. Yet their assumption that pagan natural right is the true source of a moral democracy (as Lincoln understood it) is an untenably romanticist view of pagan history and thought.

---

tion offers too much "precision" in the area of ethics (*Christianity and Politics,* 220–21). I take this to mean that the Christian, not Aristotelian, dimension of Thomism is too demanding on politics, in Strauss's view.

26. Strauss, "Progress or Return?" 294; Strauss, "Jerusalem and Athens: Some Preliminary Reflections," 172.

Is Pagan "Natural Right" Charitable?

Strauss believed that the classics had founded political philosophy in a time of grave political crisis.[27] The founder of political philosophy, Socrates, had fatally challenged the gods of the state. Thus, the relation between politics and religion was every bit as intertwined in classical Athens as it was for moderns. Yet this relation was still different, for the old pagan gods never promised the radical change that the God of the biblical tradition did. No personal god who loved all of humanity existed for the pagans. No promise of everlasting peace was possible in cyclical time, the tragic movement from fortune to misfortune without respite. The believers in scripture were certain, despite grueling crises of faith, that all would be well under the sovereignty of God.

Strauss could even spy prudence in the biblical vision, which taught a stern morality and thus self-restraint.[28] Yet *prudentia* existed in the biblical sense only if there was no attempt to synthesize biblical ethics with the order of politics. Strauss freely granted the "heartless" nature of the classics, at least compared to the prophets and apostles. Indeed, the Greek philosopher—if his model is truly a god in the Greek sense— must be "self-sufficient," or must extinguish the need for love, especially from the teeming multitude.[29] (For this reason, there is always a tension between political philosophy and democracy.) Aristotle's God is pure thought, with neither love nor hatred for man, who is not the highest creation in the cosmos anyway.[30] Unlike the God of revelation, the unmoved mover is beyond good and evil.

What is revealing about Strauss's thought is the occasional indication that pagan natural right is not particularly democratic or universalistic in any liberal sense. His students always insist that the truth of natural right is independent of revelation, and indeed more universalistic, since revelation is the source of faiths that exclude other peoples. Yet Strauss, in the spirit of Machiavelli, willingly admitted that even a nation devoted to universalism often "deviated" from this high ideal, as in the case of the Louisiana Purchase and the treatment of Native Americans.[31] It might be

27. Strauss, *What Is Political Philosophy?* 92.
28. Strauss, *On Tyranny, Including the Strauss-Kojève Correspondence,* 191. See also his "Progress or Return?" 273.
29. Strauss, *On Plato's "Symposium,"* 58.
30. Strauss, "Jerusalem and Athens"; Strauss, *Thoughts on Machiavelli,* 208.
31. Strauss, *Thoughts on Machiavelli,* 14.

tempting to respond that the exclusion of Native Americans from republican liberty was an unfortunate deviation that does not cast any serious doubt on the overall universalism of natural right. Yet Strauss does not necessarily believe that these deviations are aberrant. No regime, not even one dedicated to the liberty and equality of all human beings, can afford to be completely open and inclusive of all human beings, especially those who may lack a knowledge of natural right in the first place. Since natural right "presupposes the cultivation of reason," it may not be known universally, particularly among the "savages" to whom teachers of natural right have always made reference, in Strauss's view.[32]

Strauss of course knew that the West has often prided itself on being "the only culture which is open to all cultures and which does not reject the other cultures as forms of barbarism."[33] Yet he did not necessarily believe that this ideal is possible to actualize; indeed, he sympathized with Oswald Spengler's famous prophecy that the West would go down, despite this openness. In any case, a commitment to universal freedom does not necessarily contradict exclusivist policies at times. The American regime, then, requires careful leaders ("statesmen") who know when to apply natural right principles, and to the most appropriate people. Even a supposedly egalitarian regime like the American republic has every right *by nature* to be a closed polity, at least one closed to "savages."

Yet the many students of Strauss, most of whom hail from the United States, usually portray the master's teaching as the most persuasive defense of the superiority of liberal democracy. They are convinced that Strauss's occasional support for universalism amounts to support for democracy as the best regime. In an essay on classical political philosophy, Strauss emphasizes that Aristotle's judgment of "barbarians" does not deter him or any other like-minded Greek thinker from admiring other civilizations or assuming that these are just as capable as the Greeks of the "perfect city."[34] The students of Strauss find this teaching of the master to be the central one, although they conclude that somehow he portrays democracy as the best regime (as a devotee of Plato, Strauss could never consistently claim this!). Presumably, it would not

32. Strauss, *Natural Right and History,* 9.
33. Strauss, *The City and Man,* 2.
34. Strauss, *What Is Political Philosophy?* 87–88. Yet Strauss also warns that "one nation may have a greater natural fitness for political excellence than others" (87).

bother them that their own teacher also pointed to the belief that natural right through the ages is perfectly compatible with a belief that there will always be "savages" who can rarely be transformed into good citizens. If it is true that all human beings desire freedom by nature, then it must be possible to persuade all human beings of justice (a precondition for the establishment of a stable regime). Do the pagan texts teach this lesson?

Perhaps the dialogue between Socrates and Thrasymachus in the *Republic* (338b–354c) would be the foundation of this leap of faith that all peoples—even the most "savage"—can become citizens. Socrates eventually "persuades" his spirited interlocutor—who dogmatically holds to "might is right" or "justice is the advantage of the stronger"— that the just life (which is not reducible to the will of the stronger) is superior to the unjust life. As Strauss puts it in an essay on Plato, "It could seem that the foundation of the good city requires that Thrasymachus be converted into one of its good citizens."[35] Even the savage personality of a Thrasymachus is open to the force of rational persuasion.

The boldest natural rightist of all, Harry Jaffa (who, we shall see, argues that America's mission is to liberate the world from Thrasymachean tyrants), sees no difference between the attempt of Socrates to persuade Thrasymachus and that of Lincoln to persuade Senator Douglas on the evils of slavery.[36] I believe, however, that there is a world of difference between the two cases, which parallels the difference between pagan and biblical views of authority. What becomes clear in this text is that classical political philosophy cannot possibly provide a rationale for universalizing a regime like liberal democracy. The "realism" of Athens cancels out the utopianism of modern natural rightists. Moreover, the Platonic teachings contrast sharply with the hopeful message of Lincoln on political change.

It may well be true that both Thrasymachus and Senator Douglas attest to the truth of "might is right." Yet the Socratic attempt to persuade his opponent is decisively different in content from that of Lincoln. As I argued in Chapter 3, Lincoln always appealed to the principle of charity to persuade Southerners that slavery was immoral. Lincoln obviously assumed that professed Christians like Douglas and others already knew what charity is (it is written on their hearts). What exactly is written on the heart of Thrasymachus? Does he already know what justice is? This is not necessarily the case, since Strauss himself admitted that Socrates

---

35. Strauss, "Plato," 192.
36. Jaffa, *Crisis of the House Divided*, vi; Jaffa, *Original Intent*, 314.

had not even defined what justice is by the end of their dialogue.[37] For this reason, Socrates did not truly convince Thrasymachus of anything. Indeed, Strauss emphasized that Thrasymachus was convinced of nothing, except perhaps of the fact that Socrates was superior as a speaker. Excellence in speech, however, is not excellence in reason. Socrates may well indeed have been the "stronger" of the two, but he may not necessarily have been the wiser. In submitting to Socrates, Thrasymachus was showing his weakness, not his acceptance of his interlocutor's position.[38] Still, the fact that Glaucon feels compelled in book 2 of the *Republic* to offer a more sophisticated version of the position of Thrasymachus indicates the failure of Socrates to persuade.

It is often said that *Republic* is a long refutation of the base principle that "might is right." Yet justice ultimately ends up serving the advantage of the stronger—the wise few guardians who reign over the truly perfect city. They successfully persuade the other classes (auxiliaries, craftsmen) that their rule is best. This triumph of speech does not refute the Thrasymachean principle. It reminds the reader only that Socrates is a more clever speaker than Thrasymachus: this superiority of rhetoric is a more sophisticated version of "might is right."

Why did Socrates not appeal to the inner moral conscience *(daimon)* of Thrasymachus, which would tell him what justice is? The Straussian position is that such an appeal would be futile, because it rests on the level of belief in religion in a community.[39] If too few Greeks believed in the gods, then this appeal would have no force.

Yet it is one thing to appeal to the corrupt gods of Olympus but quite another to appeal to a God who demands justice. The failure of Socrates to appeal to Thrasymachus's notion of justice (inscribed on his heart by a loving divine authority) lies in the fact that no concept of incarnate love exists in the first place. The gods are certainly not the source of justice. As Plato's *Euthyphro* demonstrates, the gods are every bit as unjust as mortals. Absent in the soul of every single speaker in the *Republic* or any other Platonic dialogue is the awareness of a personal God who demands that human beings act charitably toward the other. (Indeed, charity is missing in the great discussion of the various expressions of

37. Strauss, *The City and Man*, 83.
38. Jaffa, *Crisis of the House Divided*, vi. See also Stanley Rosen, *Plato's "Republic": A Study*, 51.
39. Rosen, *Plato's "Republic": A Study*, 42.

love in the *Symposium*.)[40] Neither Socrates nor Thrasymachus need fear the wrath of the gods if he sins against his fellow men, for the gods do not punish sinfulness. If sin is indeed the deliberate act of violating the law of a *just God*, then the Greek pagans do not, technically, "sin."

The fact that Plato ultimately defends a regime of rigid natural hierarchy in no way challenges the original principle of Thrasymachus. Nor does it testify to the presence of charity in the just regime. The wise few never put themselves in the position of the lower souls who also occupy the city. Why would Socrates empathize with a disordered soul like that of Thrasymachus? (The pagan fear of contamination due to contact with inferior souls is real.)[41] If they teach virtue to these others, virtue comes down to knowing one's place *(telos)* within the hierarchy. Although I do not doubt that Plato or Aristotle thought that regimes outside of Greece could accomplish this feat of hierarchy, this universalism is far different from the biblical universalism that Lincoln demanded of his people.

It is significant that the *Republic* holds out no hope for the survival of the just regime: it is fated to perish like any other according to the cycles of time, as Socrates suggests at the end of book 8. Indeed, a just regime will in time become a tyranny (after devolving into timocracy, oligarchy, and democracy). The *Republic* thus fails to refute Thrasymachus, for eventually the just (who once ruled the just city) are no longer the strong but are now the weak (who are ruled by the unjust tyranny).[42]

As early as his Lyceum speech, Lincoln was only too aware that a democracy can fail to appease the Thrasymachean personality, "the family of the lion or the tribe of the eagle."[43] For this reason, a "political religion" must restrain the personality who "thirsts and burns for distinction." It would be tempting to believe (as Jaffa does) that Lincoln is simply filling the role of the wise few in the *Republic,* who use the authority of religion to restrain spirited individuals who threaten a regime with conquest and revolution. If that is the case, then Lincoln is merely advocating "might is right" once again. Yet Lincoln hopes for an outcome that would never occur to Socrates: that this cycle of violence must end one day, lest the republic perish.

---

40. For a detailed discussion of the absence of charity as a concept within the Platonic understanding of love, see Nygren, *Agape and Eros.*
41. Strauss, *On Tyranny,* 201.
42. See Brayton Polka, *The Dialectic of Biblical Critique.*
43. Lincoln, *Collected Works,* 1:114.

How can Lincoln hope for this seemingly unrealistic goal? First, he believes in one God who shall deliver humanity from this bondage of the soul; second, his people already know (in their hearts) of this God's great commandment, to love in charity. Lincoln can judge his fellow Americans for precisely the same reason that Socrates can neither judge nor refute Thrasymachus: a Christian people will agonize over injustice because they fear the judgment of the Lord who revealed and commanded the practice of love. The pressure of agape, enforced by a tough-minded God, is ever present upon this people. Unlike Jefferson, Thrasymachus never trembles over the justice of a loving God.

Given the absence of belief in a personal loving god, it is no surprise that the pagan world, as Jaffa himself must admit, lacks any knowledge of charity.[44] A regime based on natural right in the pagan sense will indeed face "savages" in its midst. At first glance, that observation sounds realistic. Is it not utopian to anticipate the end of savagery? In demanding that charity be the precondition of true democracy, Lincoln makes an appeal that no pagan author ever did. If Fustel de Coulanges is correct in his analysis of classical Greece and Rome, the pagan city lacks a concept of extending justice to enemies and even strangers.[45] The limits of moral obligations to others could not possibly encourage the sense of charity that Lincoln assumed.

Socrates makes this discovery in the *Crito,* when he emphasizes that his own city of Athens can appeal to no authority above the unjust gods (whose authority the *Euthyphro* pilloried). If there is any universalism in the pagan cosmos, it is the recognition that the regime has every right to exclude the *other.* (For this reason Socrates dismisses the idea that he can escape to other cities.) Paganism leaves no room for a concept of the stranger as one's brother.[46]

Clearly, such a vision of the relation between God and humanity would have no chance of success in a Christian nation. Strauss, who thought highly of Coulanges's study, faulted it nevertheless for failing to distinguish between a "prephilosophic" and "philosophic" understanding

---

44. Jaffa, *Thomism and Aristotelianism: A Study of the Commentary by Thomas Aquinas on the "Nicomachean Ethics,"* 28–30. I discuss Jaffa's ideas in detail below.

45. Coulanges, *The Ancient City: A Study of the Religions, Laws, and Institutions of Greece and Rome,* 155.

46. Ibid., 95.

of the city, or, the difference between religious particularity and philosophic universalism.[47] Yet rationalists like Socrates do not transcend the city (as Coulanges describes it), for there is no god in paganism who will liberate him from this regime. Socrates refuses to escape from prison (as Plato recounts in the *Crito*) for precisely this reason. The gods of Athens are the only gods that Socrates knows.

The paradox of Lincoln's political use of charity is that the God of this regime is *above* it. Charity elevates authority above the political. This God judges both ruler and ruled, not for necessarily violating the laws of the city, but for violating his law of charity. By contrast, the natural rightist followers of Strauss deny that their ideology requires a Christian basis, as they spread democratic principles throughout the world. Yet Lincoln discovered just how resistant even Christians in his own nation could be toward the call of charity (as he understood it). This resistance has magnified as Americans have encountered peoples who historically lack an egalitarian Christian background. Natural rightists so far have felt no need to reconcile the tragic limitations of pagan political philosophy with the utopianism of their democracy building on a global scale.

CHRISTIANITY NO, CHOSENNESS YES

Ultimately, the only way to make sense of the natural rightist adulteration of paganism at the expense of any appeal to Christianity is to examine this school's *selective* use of scripture. Although it is certainly true that natural rightists have attempted to marginalize Christianity, they have found it convenient to make use of another biblical credo, the idea of the "chosen people." In this sense, their ideas bear more resemblance to those of Thomas Paine, who far preferred to employ the myth of the chosen people against the English "pharaoh," instead of the Christian ethic of charity, which he tended to despise. Without this myth, natural rightists would be forced to rely on pagan political philosophy to justify an ambitious project of democracy building. Yet the Greek texts do not support this mission. Therefore, the secularization of chosenness is absolutely essential as a rationale for disseminating the ideals of natural right. At the same time, natural rightists do not feel compelled to insist

47. Strauss, *The City and Man*, 240–41.

on charity as a worthy restraint upon the zealotry of the democratizing ways of the chosen people.

In fairness, natural rightist followers of Leo Strauss are not the only famous thinkers to underrate the influence of Christianity in America. In her famous study of the American founding, Hannah Arendt claims that the Revolution had nothing to do with Christianity, since this religion is apolitical (even though she also believes that Christian love is the most important understanding of love in the Western tradition!). Indeed, believers care nothing for politics, "since the contents of Christian teachings" do not constitute the origin of modern revolution. Moreover, Christians are indifferent to the "spectacles" of secular history. Near the end of this study she concludes that "freedom from politics" is the greatest legacy of the Christian heritage. The most famous exponent of the liberal interpretation of America, Louis Hartz, similarly argues that America's historic linkage to the Mayflower Compact does not change the fact that the "master assumption of American political thought"—Lockean individualism—is absolutely secular. Former ambassador to the United Nations Jeane J. Kirkpatrick has insisted that political doctrines rather than the core values of Christianity influence modern regimes.[48]

Nevertheless, natural rightists do not believe that *all* biblical credos have lost their force, although they sometimes give that impression. To be sure, the most secular minded of the natural rightists (who deny any historical connection between revelation and the American founding) are most prominent. James W. Ceaser contends that "Sacred History" dominated the American consciousness before 1776, but did not survive in any politically important sense after the Revolution. Apparently, any references to religion *after* the Revolution are either unimportant or insincere. In his study of the founding, Thomas L. Pangle dismissively refers to public proclamations of God's sovereignty as mere "carryovers from the Christian heritage." Moreover, the founders are not the "continuers of Christian morals and politics." In his best-selling defense of America's political traditions, Allan Bloom celebrates the decline of Christianity as central to the success of the American Revolution: "The domesticated churches in America preserved the superstition of

48. Arendt, *On Revolution*, 16–17, 272; Hartz, *Liberal Tradition*, 61; Kirkpatrick, *Dictatorships and Double Standards: Rationalism and Reason in Politics*, 14.

Christianity, the overcoming of which was perhaps the key to liberating man." Furthermore, religion disappears or becomes dim when "bathed in the light of natural rights." In their respective works on bioethical debates, Francis Fukuyama and Leon Kass acknowledge the importance of America's biblical heritage and that believers as well as natural right-ists share the same goals in preserving human dignity and the sanctity of life. Yet they ultimately conclude that natural right philosophy can stand on its own merits, without recourse to revealed religion. Walter Berns, who doubts that either the founders or Tocqueville put any particular value in Christianity, asks in the context of the entire Revolutionary era, "What did it mean to say that Christianity was part of the common law? Very little, as it turns out."[49] Even public intellectuals sympathetic to the importance of the biblical origins of America—like David Gelernter— do not believe that the Bible has any *lasting* importance, since belief in the "American Religion" does not require belief in the Almighty in any orthodox sense.[50] Indeed, one student of Strauss praises President Bush for abandoning the historical link between Christianity and democracy, as most Americans (at least since the age of Tocqueville) have understood it.[51] In fine, Christianity has little if any importance to the American founding, before or after the Revolution.

In their view, Abraham Lincoln completed the work of the founders by fashioning a theology of politics whose content and success do not require a persistently strong foundation of Protestant Christianity. As Lucas E. Morel contends, Lincoln's attack on the evil of slavery was not in need of the "authority of the Bible or any other religious text."[52] As we have seen, even many admirers of Lincoln doubt that he was a

---

49. Ceaser, *Nature and History,* 16; Pangle, *Spirit of Modern Republicanism,* 21, 81; Bloom, *The Closing of the American Mind: How Higher Education Has Failed Democracy and Impoverished the Souls of Today's Students,* 161, 27; Fukuyama, *Our Post-Human Future: Consequences of the Biotechnology Revolution,* 89, 111; Kass, *Beyond Therapy: Biotechnology and the Pursuit of Happiness,* 308–9; Berns, *Making Patriots,* 33. Berns adds that the founders appealed to Christianity only in order to placate the great mass of Americans, even though the former knew that Christianity had no connection to natural rights (42–43). Apparently, even Tocqueville valued only religion, but not Christianity in particular (43)!

50. Gelernter, *Americanism,* 4. I discuss Gelernter's ideas in more detail in Chapter 6).

51. See Clifford Orwin, "The Unraveling of Christianity in America," 34–36.

52. Morel, *Lincoln's Sacred Effort,* 69.

sincere Christian, or that he saw any true importance in the *apoliteia* of scripture.

It is hard to believe that these writers have understood American history, given the role that Christianity has played in the republic's most important periods of struggle and change. It is also difficult to grasp the degree to which they deny the political implications of revelation on Americans. (Have they ever reflected upon William Jenning Bryan's "Cross of Gold" speech?) My explanation for this fact is that these scholars have focused on the founding texts of America while ignoring what the great mass of Americans has believed from 1620 to the present. In a Marxian sense, they have studied the texts of the "ruling class" without bothering to examine what ordinary Americans actually thought about religion, before or after 1776. It is also inconceivable to them that Lincoln could ever have been influenced by the mass of Christian believers whom he governed; presumably, a truly "god-like" statesman would not allow this to happen. Why is it so easy for these natural rightists to dismiss the overwhelming influence of Christianity on Americans throughout their history?

Natural rightists may dismiss these claims with the response that they adhere to the authority of "Nature," not "History." In following the teachings of Strauss, they are inclined to focus on Nature (which promotes what is universally good) over History (which simply stresses what is ephemerally good). Generally, the real threat for them is summed up in one word: *historicism.* This ideology, which reduces all ideas and principles to epiphemonena of particular historic periods, denies any claim to universalism and focuses entirely on particularity. Natural right theorists insist that any claim of indebtedness to tradition is historicist. The high price of insisting that sacred political truth is based on nature is the denial that America had any historical traditions that contributed to its revolutionary founding. Historicists are also enemies of the "natural rights" of liberal and bourgeois societies.[53]

Historicists, from this perspective, are not simply teaching the importance of learning history (even natural rightists often write works of history), but setting up History as the ultimate authority. History in this categorical sense must then devalue any claim to the truth by

---

53. Michael Palmer, "Historicism, Relativism, and Nihilism versus American Natural Right in *Casablanca*," 36.

nature. Historicists must deny that there is a permanent human nature. According to natural right theorists, every single assault on natural right tradition in American history has a historicist basis (from Calhounism in the antebellum period to Progressivism in the twentieth century). By confusing the appeal to historical antecedents or traditions with historicist denials of truth and morality, natural rightists are reluctant to engage any questioning of the beginnings of their doctrine.[54] These same theorists argue for the *originality* of the American Revolution, whose heroes were the first founders in history to invoke Nature, not History. The founders brought "nature down from the realm of philosophy" to create a new regime free of historical influences like revelation.[55]

The natural rightist critique of historicism deserves considerable scrutiny, since its devotees are quite content to make use of chosenness, a biblical idea that surely rests on the authority of History rather than Nature. As major thinkers from Hegel to Eric Voegelin have argued, the idea of chosenness celebrates the dramatic movement toward liberation of the oppressed in *history,* and thus foreshadows modern progressivism. A great deal of natural rightist thought depends more on a biblical worldview than its avatars are willing to admit. *Pace* Voegelin again, modern appeals to "paganism" still betray indebtedness to biblical credos.[56]

When natural rightists are enthralled with the idea of new beginnings or new births of freedom, of which Lincoln famously spoke at Gettysburg, they reveal just how dependent they are on the story of the chosen people. They correctly observe that 1776 was a new beginning in history. Yet the very idea of a novel beginning in history is biblical, not pagan. The idea of hoping that other nations embrace novel principles is based on linear time. Only biblical credos can hope for liberation from the cycles of fortune, or "might is right." This reliance on biblical symbolism—usually unacknowledged by natural rightists—often contributes to a brash optimism about the capacity of cultures or nations to understand and even appreciate the Declaration. Certainly, the founders did not believe (not even Jefferson) that all peoples desire natural rights. Yet if the Declaration is based on a *nature* common to all of humanity, then why is there so much resistance to truths supposedly self-evident

---

54. It is not obvious that Strauss himself made this mistake. See Havers, "Strauss, Kendall, and Conservatism."

55. Ceaser, *Nature and History,* 22.

56. Voegelin, *New Science of Politics,* 107.

to all human beings? Natural rightists also ignore Lincoln's warnings of the perils of chosenness, with the self-serving assumption that God is on the side of the chosen (as the president knew all too well, both sides in the Civil War claimed this blessing).

Despite the anxiety of natural rightists over the survival of this creed, it is unlikely to find a major politician in America today who would doubt the universality of this faith. The widely invoked rhetoric of America's universalistic and egalitarian "creed" that sounded through the air on the evening of Barack Obama's victory in the 2008 election confirms the survival of this consensus. This broad agreement lies in the assumption that "Nature" commands this task to take on this "special role" as a chosen people. Although natural rightists do not always openly acknowledge their indebtedness to the Exodus narrative, the messianic implications of their vision (which have no counterpart in paganism) are plain to see. Harry Jaffa has insisted that people everywhere must receive "indoctrination" in the philosophy of natural rights, since America's security depends on it. Allan Bloom portrays World War II as an "educational project" to force reluctant nations to embrace these credos. James Pontuso proclaims that the only opposition left to natural rights, after liberal democracy defeated fascism, communism, and monarchy, lies in "fanatical theocracies" who vainly desire to turn back the "tide of history" in favor of liberal democracy. Carnes Lord is confident that liberal democracy can and must be "exported" to nations with only "minor adjustments" needed in cases where people have no experience of this regime. Francis Fukuyama most famously believes that the "nature of man as man" requires the triumph of liberal democracy. David Gelernter is certain that not only do American credos belong to all of humanity, but it is up to the republic to "bring them" to the entire world.[57]

These adherents of natural rights are absolutely confident that liberal democracy is the *last and best regime,* and that the mission of America is to establish this fact for all peoples. Perhaps with the prophecy of Isaiah in mind, they expect this regime to bring peace to the world. It is ironic that natural rightists hark back to the Greeks for support of

---

57. Jaffa, *Crisis of the House Divided,* 326; Bloom, *Closing of the American Mind,* 153; Pontuso, "*Casablanca* and the Paradoxical Truth of Stereotyping: Rick and the American Character," 99; Lord, *The Modern Prince: What Leaders Need to Know Now,* 48; Fukuyama, *End of History,* 50; Gelernter, *Americanism,* 4.

their universalism, since no Greek political philosopher ever considered democracy to be the best regime (it was second only to tyranny as the lowest of all regimes). Gone is any Platonic caution about the movement of cyclical time (all regimes must come to an end), the relation between democracy and tyranny (the first is always leaning toward the second), and the need to recognize that the best regime exists only in speech (Plato's ideal regime is a far cry from democracy!). Most significant, American Christianity plays no essential role in encouraging these beliefs.

Whatever the validity of their reading of the tradition of political philosophy, the practicality of their project is also open to question. As we have seen, Strauss taught that natural rightists are tough-minded realists about politics. Yet one is tempted to conclude that if these rights and duties are *natural* (and all of humanity can grasp their meaning), then it is up to peoples other than Americans to fight for them on their own: if "nature's God" will bring democracy into existence, then the United States has no special duty to do so. These authors, however, are not inclined to wait around for nature. It is up to the republic to spread these doctrines, based on what Jaffa calls the "messianic theme" in American political traditions. Despite Jaffa's obvious appeal to chosenness here, he is more comfortable in appealing to Nature's God than the apolitical God of creation.[58] Although most natural rights theorists (including Jaffa at times) have made a great effort to distance themselves from the biblical tradition of America, ironically they end up creating a *secularized* political theology that still presupposes a biblical foundation.

As I have argued, Lincoln's political ideas implicitly stress the need to be aware of both particularity and universality. Lincoln never addressed a non-Christian audience in his life, a fact that should give pause to any natural right utopian. Lincoln also gave much reason to doubt whether a nation torn apart over the truth of scripture could ever transplant its ideals elsewhere.

Natural rightists obviously admit that their hero made use of Christian ideas, although they tend to portray this use as purely Machiavellian (see Chapter 3). They are willing to acknowledge typical statements of the president in defense of Christianity, as in the case of his first inaugural address. The fact that Lincoln makes use of Christian themes has not discouraged natural rightists, however, to advocate a bold mission for America to universalize its ideals on a global basis without relying

58. Jaffa, *How to Think*, 56–62.

on Christian faith. In short, Lincoln's occasional tentative allusions to chosenness interest them far more than his much deeper reliance on Christian morality.

Therefore, it would be false to claim that natural rightists abandon the Bible altogether, for their favored biblical idea of natural rightists is chosenness. In *A New Birth of Freedom*, Jaffa even declares that God himself sanctions the Declaration, and that regimes that do not fully respect this principle are not "in harmony with the divine government of the universe." As a religious nation, America is bound to live up to the *identical* promises of scripture and the Declaration on the equality of all by committing to the task of fulfilling this ideal on a global level.[59] Although he admits that Lincoln never truly believed in the equality of the races, Jaffa is determined to show that the full implications of Lincoln's views on equality must lead to the conclusion that it is an ideal whose absolute fulfillment must be at least attempted: "'Perfect' equality was the goal to be approximated, even if never reached."[60]

In the mind of Jaffa, there cannot be any compromise of this ideal. Anyone who questions this principle, or doubts that global implementation of this principle is the mission of America, is guilty of "an unjust motive." Jaffa has made it clear that those skeptical of the global implementation of equality are "confederates," or worse.[61] Jaffa appeals to the authority of revelation to justify his hermeneutic of the American regime's mission. In *Crisis of the House Divided*, Jaffa poses a stark choice between majority rule and this political religion, and he makes it abundantly clear to the reader what the proper choice must be. Jaffa contends that Americans will suffer divine punishment if they ever stray from the principle of equality. Lincoln was only the first Moses to lead Americans and the entire world to the promised land of democracy. Once again, the American people are "not worthy of their mission" if they decide to postpone the fulfillment of equal rights for all Americans; like the Israelites, they will be punished if they fail.[62] The political religion of equality, which commands reverence, is the best restraint upon the will

---

59. Jaffa, *New Birth*, 123. Jaffa maintains that both Christianity and the Declaration of Independence embody the same "promises to all men" (164). In short, both documents promise liberation from slavery.

60. Ibid., 340.

61. See Jaffa, *How to Think*, 18–25, 197.

62. Jaffa, *Crisis of the House Divided*, 230–31; Jaffa, *New Birth*, 257–58, 349–50.

of an irrational majority who may not be fully committed to this credo. Religion is still useful, even if it is not true, when it encourages grand appeals to act as the chosen people. Jaffa gives the impression that it is possible and even essential to know the mind of God. He is *certain* that Providence dictates the mission of America to universalize its credos. As a few historians have documented, various pastors and preachers also made claims to know the will of the Almighty during the Civil War, much to Lincoln's chagrin.[63] The fact that Lincoln famously referred to an "almost chosen people" does not deter natural rightists like Jaffa (and many others) from fully affirming the unambiguous nature of the chosenness of Americans.

The subtlety of the president's thought, however, is lost on natural rightists. The difficulty of building a republican democracy even on Christian soil was all too apparent to Lincoln. Whereas the president publicly affirmed the moral sense of Americans—the "better angels of our nature" in his first inaugural address—he also knew that opposition to slavery was not a guaranteed sentiment among his people, much less among the peoples of the world, as I discussed earlier. Even though Lincoln believed that everyone is capable of understanding the basic biblical ethic of charity, just how universal was the practice of this great principle?

Charity requires the honesty and the willingness to put oneself in the position of the other. Lincoln consistently pointed out that no slave owner (and even few Northerners) had ever done this. In his eyes, people who prayed to the same God still refused to understand the suffering that they inflicted on the least of their brethren. Supporters of slavery demanded that charity be practiced toward them, but they did not demand this of their own actions. The scandal so appalling to Lincoln was that this denial of charity was expressed in the name of the Bible, which, on a literal level, sanctioned slavery (although not the enslavement of one race by the other necessarily). There was no excuse for an ostensibly Christian people to love God *while* they despised their fellow man.

Natural rightists are confident that all of humanity can and should embrace the universal principles of liberty and equality. Their confidence rests on their knowledge of providential sanction for America's

---

63. See Mark A. Noll, *America's God: From Jonathan Edwards to Abraham Lincoln*, 434–38; and Guelzo, *Abraham Lincoln: Redeemer President*, 322.

mission in the world. Yet they neglect the lesson of Lincoln that we cannot know Providence, nor can we teach humility and charity unless people first believe in a Christian God (and there are no guarantees that this belief will translate into justice automatically). Although natural rightists occasionally admit that Christianity alone fosters an appreciation of the democratic value of individual freedom (since all individuals have a personal relationship with God), they typically (and inconsistently) assert that this faith is apolitical.[64] Still, if Christianity is first needed among a people for natural right ideology to have a hope of success, should America necessarily embark on crusades to spread the gospel?

Lincoln referred to himself as a "humble instrument of the Almighty" in the same speech in which he also referred to Americans as the "almost chosen people."[65] The grave cost of the Civil War to both sides suggested to Lincoln—as it did not to many Northerners flush with the taste of victory—that Providence had not necessarily been on the side of the North, at least unconditionally. The second inaugural address made this patently clear. Lincoln hoped that his own people would have enough understanding of humility and charity to see themselves as "almost chosen" but never chosen. Naturally, this understanding presupposes a biblical grasp of what chosenness actually is.

Yet these biblical ideas must be built into a civilization that enjoys an entrenched Christian influence. The fact is that these ideas are not universal across civilizations. Even Saint Thomas Aquinas, who struggled more than any other philosopher of the West to discover universal principles of "natural law" that all peoples shared, had to admit that ideas like charity and humility were not so universally shared. The pagan thought of Aristotle simply does not accommodate such virtues. As Harry Jaffa contends in his study of Thomism, the meekness and humility of Christ had no counterpart among the pagans who celebrated "noble pride." The political consequences of the disjunction between pagan and Christian are enormous for the natural rightist camp, since any claim to universal justice breaks apart on this disjunction. Because pagans do not, in the spirit of humility or charity, see all of humanity as their brethren, their regimes must be inaccessible to all except their own noble citizens. Even Jaffa admits (in terms reminiscent of Coulanges)

64. Jaffa, *The American Founding as the Best Regime: The Bonding of Civil and Religious Liberty*, 24; Jaffa, *New Birth*, 144.
65. Lincoln, *Collected Works*, 4:236.

that the "closed society" of classical paganism is hard to reconcile with an ethic that proclaims the brotherhood of all humanity. Presumably, the realm of a pagan Caesar has nothing to do with the realm of Christ.[66]

If Lincoln's political thought has any meaning at all, it is the imperative to break down the wall between Caesar and Christ (recall Willmoore Kendall on the "porous" wall of separation between church and state). Yet the pagan mind must believe that all belongs to the political (Caesar), nothing belongs to a religion of brotherhood (Christ). This double-mindedness has no room for the true ethic of charity. Once again, Jaffa must admit that the pagan philosopher has no horizon beyond the political regime, whereas the believer places the universal ethic of Christ above any regime.[67] It was Lincoln's hope that political virtues would no longer be distinguishable from religious ones. Both realms must be subject to the law of charity; otherwise, the Revolution would make no sense as an act of liberation of all of humanity. It is not obvious to natural rightists, however, that a knowledge of Christian charity is required as the "chosen" people strike out to conquer the world.

Generally, natural rightists must depend far more on the idea of the chosen people, destined to spread democracy, than the decidedly undemocratic and exclusivist pagan tradition to which they pay lip service. Natural rightists are not as secularist as they appear to be. Yet the fact that they refuse to give equal weight to the apparently apolitical faith of Christianity bodes ill for America. Chosen peoples typically have a poor record for liberating others, especially if they simply assume that other nations and cultures share the same ideals. This presumption contradicts the humility necessary to a truly charitable foreign policy. Belief in chosenness is also a poor substitute for realism in global affairs, despite the apparent tough-mindedness of Strauss's followers.

CONCLUSION

Strauss was fond of quoting Nietzsche's view that a biblical morality

---

66. Jaffa, *Thomism and Aristotelianism*, 28–29. For an elaboration of the Caesar-Christ distinction in politics, see Larry Arnhart, "Statesmanship as Magnanimity: Classical, Christian, and Modern"; and Carson Holloway, "Christianity, Magnanimity, and Statesmanship."
67. Ibid., 30.

presupposes belief in a biblical God.[68] If that claim is true, then natural rightists would do well to pay more attention to the indispensability of Christian belief as they disseminate the universal credos of freedom and equality. Without the restraining force of the deity, biblical morality has no meaning. Indeed, a supposedly biblical program of democracy building will more likely unleash the worst passions of a self-proclaimed chosen people.

After Lincoln delivered his second inaugural address, he worried that his listeners would not respond well to his position that the Almighty had designs of his own. As he confessed to his friend Thurlow Weed, "Men are not flattered by being shown that there has been a difference between the Almighty and them."[69] If any statement sums up the president's attempt to distinguish between charity and chosenness, this is it. It is always easier to believe that one is divinely favored than it is to love one's enemies (which Lincoln called upon all Americans to practice, now that the war was nearing its end). It requires charity (along with humility) to admit that one is ignorant of Providence, and that all we can know of God is his command to practice the law of love. It is also more difficult to convince the "chosen" that their claims to divine favor may be false—how can reason refute revelation?—even if the acts of the "chosen" are brazenly immoral. Whereas an act of hypocrisy is intelligible to all, one's status as a chosen people is obvious only to a special elect. Charity is all that God can reveal as the truth; chosenness is a leap of faith.

The limitations of Lincoln's political theology seem lost on natural rightists, who betray no shadow of a doubt that God favors the chosen people. One critic of Strauss has noted that his students desire the benefits of Christianity without the religion.[70] Still, if the practice of charity is more important than the belief in one's chosenness, the self-proclaimed people of God would do well to disseminate Christian ethics *before* they embark on grand attempts to reconstruct the world. As the next chapter illustrates, natural rightists are not the only faction to privilege chosenness over the virtue of charity.

---

68. Strauss, "Progress or Return?" 265.

69. Lincoln, *Collected Works*, 8:356. Some admirers of the president are certain that America faces punishment if it fails to fulfill the promise of equality. See Bellah, *Broken Covenant*, 143.

70. See Wilhelmsen, *Christianity and Political Philosophy*, 213.

6

Charity and Chosenness

> After three millenniums of defections and
> returns, of reforms, renaissances, and revisions, of
> Christian gains and modern losses of substance,
> we are still living in the historical present of the
> Covenant.
>
> —Eric Voegelin, *Israel and Revelation*

*T*here have been two distinct yet related principles in the history
of the American usage of scripture for political ends: a belief in
the "chosen" destiny of the republic and a belief in the morality of charity. The first credo has received infinitely greater attention
and acclaim than the second. Yet very few commentators have seen the
need to study the tension between the two beliefs, especially in the vast
literature on Lincoln. This situation may well be due to the fact that the
president himself did not *always* see a tension between the two principles. On a theological level, after all, why should a chosen people act
in any other spirit than one informed by charity? In this chapter, I argue
that the tension between the two credos is not only important for properly understanding the complexity of Lincoln's thought but crucial for
identifying the distortions that admirers have made of his legacy from
Woodrow Wilson to today's neoconservatives. In the twentieth century,
not only have natural rightists fervently believed that every human
being desires democracy and invoked Lincoln as their inspiration for

this faith. Liberals have also displayed this grand hope about human nature, as I shall argue throughout this chapter. Even stripped of the grand rhetoric of natural rights, however, this usage of Lincoln's legacy does not bear scrutiny.

Lincoln, we have seen, was usually hesitant in making grand claims about the chosenness of the American people. His famous phrase "the almost chosen people" suggests a subtlety of mind that sharply contrasts with the triumphalist tones of Julia Ward Howe's "Battle Hymn of the Republic." His last inaugural address emphasized the need to mend the wounds, avoid the vindictive actions of a self-righteous victor over a vanquished foe, and repudiate claims that God preferred one side over the other. As a politician who grew up during the Second Great Awakening, Lincoln grasped the dangers of invoking chosenness too easily, especially if the rhetoric inspired a false sense of certainty about the designs of Providence among the chosen. Unlike the radical abolitionists (including Frederick Douglass) of his time, Lincoln did not join in praising the bloody actions of John Brown. Instead, he displayed nothing but contempt: "An enthusiast broods over the oppression of a people till he fancies himself commissioned by Heaven to liberate them." As he forcefully reminded the abolitionist Horace Greeley early on in the war, he would not end the injustice of slavery unless the preservation of the Union was at stake (certainly, he was echoing the founders on this truth). If the Union could survive without the liberation of one slave, the president would not end slavery.[1] Lincoln clearly did not presume to possess the knowledge of the Almighty who called upon him to use his office to liberate the slaves.

It would, of course, be false to deny that Lincoln *sometimes* appealed to the authority of Providence with a certainty that he otherwise condemned in his abolitionist foes.[2] When the president allegedly declared, after he issued the Emancipation Proclamation, that "it is a momentous thing to be the instrument, under Providence, of the liberation of a race," the president sounded certain about the side of the war that God

---

1. Lincoln, *Collected Works*, 3:541, 5:388.

2. Holland claims that Lincoln was never guilty of asserting "certitudes" about the meaning of Providence (*Bonds of Affection*, 254–55). That reading is partly true, but it ignores the fact that Lincoln occasionally made claims about America as a chosen people. In contrast to Holland, Noll claims that Lincoln never abandoned a belief in chosenness (*America's God*, 431–35).

intended to bless and support.[3] Still, despite the occasional allusions that Lincoln made to his role as an instrument of the Almighty, he usually resisted the temptation to claim the unmitigated assistance of God. His unpublished "Meditation on the Divine Will" (which he composed in late 1862, at a time when the Union was losing the war) was as tentative about the meaning of Providence as his second inaugural address: "In the present civil war it is quite possible that God's purpose is something different from the purpose of either party—and yet the human instrumentalities, working just as they do, are of the best adaptation to effect His purpose."[4]

The fact that Lincoln cautioned against the brash use of chosenness and claims to know the mind of God has not deterred his many readers—both friend and foe—from possessing *certainty* about the president's legacy, particularly his intent to advance the cause of equality in America. In fairness, these readers can be partly forgiven, since the president sometimes at the rhetorical level gave the impression that there were no limits that must stand in the way of fulfilling the goal of equality: "They [the authors of the Declaration] meant to set up a standard maxim for free society which should be familiar to all: constantly looked to, constantly labored for, and even though never perfectly attained, constantly approximated and thereby constantly spreading and deepening its influence and augmenting the happiness and value of life to all people, of all colors, everywhere." Although this passage does not suggest a particularly religious theme, Lincoln was sometimes bold enough to declare that God would stand for nothing less than the granting of full equality to all of his creation. In a debate with Senator Douglas, he declared that God "set that up as a standard, and he who did most towards reaching that standard, achieved the highest degree of moral perfection. So I say in relation to the principle that all men are created equal, let it be as nearly reached as we can."[5]

Supporters of the president have interpreted claims such as these as nothing less than a call for the chosen to undertake permanent revolution, under the benevolent sanction of a higher power. When the

---

3. Quoted in Elton Trueblood, *Abraham Lincoln: Theologian of American Anguish,* 26. This statement does not appear in *Collected Works* but was attributed to the president by Col. James McKaye.

4. Lincoln, *Collected Works,* 5:404.

5. Ibid., 3:301, 2:501.

planners of the Lincoln bicentennial of 2009 refer to the necessity of completing the "unfinished work" of fostering equality, they are simply the latest figures in a long tradition of pushing for greater social egalitarianism. Woodrow Wilson, a few years before he became president, called on his fellow Americans to be the true "fellow countrymen of Lincoln" by living every day "as if that were the day upon which America was to be reborn and remade." Harry Jaffa is only one of many admirers who calls for the full universalization of equality in the footsteps of Lincoln, both at home and abroad. Leftist theologian Robert Bellah agrees with Jaffa that the founding documents embody the moral faith of a "covenant people" to order its political regime "by the highest standards of which it is capable." David Gelernter, who considers Lincoln's thoughts and actions the single greatest attempt to defend "American Zionism," is certain that the "almost chosen people" must never cease trying to follow the will of God in liberating all of humanity. Elton Trueblood, who praises the president for avoiding easy claims to know Providence, nevertheless also credits him for taking on the role of the "instrument" of God's will in freeing the slaves. Joseph Fornieri is confident that Lincoln's legacy calls for the full and equitable distribution of all of the "privileges and immunities of society" and an endless war "against new forms of idolatry." Matthew Holland, in his admirable study of Lincoln's use of biblical ethics, asserts that the president demanded the eradication of all "artificial handicaps" (like slavery and much else besides) to fulfill the identical demands of charity and liberty.[6] Barack Obama, in his campaign for the Democratic presidential nomination, defended the attempt to narrow the gap between ideals of equality and political reality as a permanent and necessary struggle in American history, with the ultimate goal of securing the goal of a "more perfect" (and thus more egalitarian) union.[7] In the eyes of these figures, not all of whom are leftists, the chosen people's achievement of justice must face neither limit nor compromise.

The critics of Lincoln are only too happy to agree with his supporters

6. Wilson, "Abraham Lincoln: A Man of the People," 105; Bellah, *Broken Covenant,* 62; Gelernter, *Americanism,* 111, 176; Trueblood, *Abraham Lincoln,* 31–32; Fornieri, *Abraham Lincoln's Political Faith,* 149, 173; Holland, *Bonds of Affection,* 191.

7. Senator Obama gave this speech on March 18, 2008, near Independence Hall.

on the *unlimited* nature of the president's designs. Willmoore Kendall faults Jaffa's version of Lincoln for launching the nation into a "future made up of an endless series of Abraham Lincolns" who promote endless civil wars in order to achieve equality. M. E. Bradford contends that Lincoln's "second founding" threatens "the prospect of an endless series of turmoils and revolutions," all of which require newer and more radical redefinitions of equality. George Carey is convinced that Lincoln, who freed the slaves based on ideology rather than "circumstances," requires of his successors the eradication of "lesser inequalities" that oppressed the freed slaves as well as "those unforeseen inequalities" that have arisen long after the Civil War.[8]

All of these interpreters of Lincoln are certain about one thing: that the president's legacy is perfectly clear, especially the imperative to render all human beings equal. Yet it is far from clear what Lincoln meant exactly by equality, beyond his eventual goal of freeing the slaves. Even a sympathetic biographer of the president has arrived at the conclusion that Lincoln never defined what equality was, nor did he reveal his clear intentions on the future of the former slaves in America.[9] The best evidence for the ambiguity surrounding the meaning of equality in the thought of the president is clearly the issue of *colonization,* or the long-standing intention of Lincoln to tie eventual emancipation of the slaves to the goal of their deportation to Africa or Central America, where they would establish their own nations. For defenders of Lincoln, this issue is the thorniest of all, since the removal of the freed slaves is hard to reconcile with the ethic of charity, the principle of equality, or the actions of a liberating chosen people. Frederick Douglass, who demanded equal rights for black Americans usually without much regard for political exigencies, considered Lincoln's thoughts on colonization to be evidence of his "canting hypocrisy."[10]

8. Kendall, *Conservative Affirmation,* 252; Bradford, *A Better Guide than Reason: Studies in the American Revolution,* 42; Carey, introduction to *Basic Symbols,* by Kendall and Carey, xxi.

9. Guelzo, *Abraham Lincoln: Redeemer President,* 373, 454.

10. For a discussion of Douglass's disappointment with Lincoln, see James Oakes, *The Radical and the Republican: Frederick Douglass, Abraham Lincoln, and the Triumph of Antislavery Politics,* 194–95. See also George M. Frederickson, *Big Enough to Be Inconsistent: Abraham Lincoln Confronts Slavery and Race,* 103–14.

A few attempts have been made to justify this intended action on Lincoln's part. Harry Jaffa has argued that newly freed slaves had the right to emigrate but not the right to stay.[11] Yet this defense sounds like a very selective and hypocritical appeal to rights: why should the right to emigrate be more important than the right to stay? The fact that Lincoln encouraged black Americans to fight for the Union suggests to at least some of his defenders that he could not sincerely have gone through with dispensing the bitter reward of colonization to freed slaves after they performed military service.[12] Predictably, even this defense has not satisfied Lincoln's most visceral critics, who argue that there cannot possibly be any ethical rationale for the original intent of Lincoln to deport the slaves, even if he later changed his mind in light of circumstances.[13]

The issue of colonization is of great importance for all Americans to consider, especially if they admire Lincoln and support his dual rhetorical commitment to both "the almost chosen people" and "charity for all." The policy of deportation, once again, appears to contradict central premises of the American creed, as Lincoln defined it. What the colonization issue reveals, as I argue in this chapter, are two pivotal lessons about Lincoln's legacy: that chosenness, as Lincoln understood it, does not necessarily call for the aggressive liberation of other peoples, and that "charity for all" is not always the same as full equality. The invocation of chosenness as a rationale for democratic universalism is a post-Lincoln phenomenon, a figment in the minds of his twentieth- and twenty-first-century admirers. The automatic identification of charity with equality also has more to do with the modern reading of Lincoln than with the ideas of the man himself. Moreover, Lincoln's views on colonization hardly qualify as a rationale for the democratic universalism that both friend and foe attribute to the president's thought.

As a lifelong admirer of his political mentor, Henry Clay (who founded the Colonization League), Lincoln gave every impression in his prepresidential career that colonization was charitable to *both* races. Colonization was indeed an act of liberation for both black and white, the consummation of a liberation that would commence only with emancipation. As he remarked in his eulogy for Clay in 1852, "If as the

11. Jaffa, *Crisis of the House Divided,* 380.
12. Stephen B. Oates, "A Momentous Decree: Commentary on 'Lincoln and Black Freedom,'" 201.
13. DiLorenzo, *Real Lincoln,* 19–20.

friends of colonization hope, the present and coming generations of our countrymen shall by any means, succeed in freeing our land from the dangerous presence of slavery; and, at the same time, in restoring a captive people to their long-lost father-land, with bright prospects for the future; and this too, so gradually, that neither races nor individuals shall have suffered by the change, it will indeed be a glorious consummation." Lincoln always attached the condition that colonization must benefit both blacks and whites (no one "shall have suffered by the change"). In a debate with Douglas six years later, he reiterated his view that the act of colonization would be in the interests of both races. This time, however, Lincoln added a dose of scripture to buttress his claim: "The children of Israel, to such numbers as to include four hundred thousand fighting men, went out of Egyptian bondage in a body."[14] This brief allusion to the Exodus narrative suggests that the president saw black Americans as an "almost chosen" people whose destiny lay beyond the shores of the republic. Indeed, this understanding of chosenness—despite the claims of his democratic universalistic defenders like Jaffa and Gelernter—suggests that he would never sanction the idea of a chosen people destined to liberate the world of tyranny. If there is any meaning to this invocation of Exodus, it is that "chosen peoples" need to liberate themselves!

It would be easy to claim, as so many critics of the president have, that Lincoln was a hypocrite here, that he was unwilling to accept black Americans as full equals in the republic after the war ended, and that the only thing that changed his mind were the difficult logistics of deporting millions of former slaves. These charges ignore one pivotal concern of the president: the prevention of violence in the republic, a concern of his as early as the Lyceum speech of 1838, always took precedence over the fulfillment of equality. This goal, the preservation of the Union, is impossible to separate from the policy of colonization. At least in the mind of Lincoln, there would be no point in achieving full equality if it led to further racial violence. Indeed, this is where charity and equality parted company in the mind of the president: it is uncharitable to all Americans if equality becomes more important than the peace and preservation of the republic.

The above claim may be hard for many friends and foes of the president to swallow, since Lincoln often associated the survival of the Union with the fulfillment of equality. Yet Lincoln did not *always* make this

14. Lincoln, *Collected Works*, 2:132, 409.

association. In contrast to the radical abolitionists, Lincoln was not prepared to identify charity and equality at all times, for charity (as he understood it) also called for the survival of the nation. There were other goods besides equality. Lincoln doubted that the Civil War—even with a Union victory—would put an end to racial violence. Moreover, the full emancipation of black Americans would only pour gasoline on the fire. It is this message that Lincoln was trying to convey to black American leaders who met with the president in August 1862. Lincoln appealed to the moral sense and self-interest of these leaders as he explained the advantages of colonization. Despite the apparent disadvantages of such a scheme, "you ought to do something to help those who are not so fortunate as yourselves. There is an unwillingness on the part of our people, harsh as it may be, for you free colored people to remain with us. . . . If we deal with those who are not free at the beginning, and whose intellects are clouded by Slavery, we have very poor materials to start with."[15] In coaxing the black American emissaries to lead the way, on a voluntary basis, to encourage their less fortunate brethren to build a new nation of their own (a goal of some black leaders in Lincoln's age and black nationalists in the twentieth century as well),[16] Lincoln revealed his pessimism about the future of race relations after the Civil War was concluded. There is no evidence that he abandoned this pessimism, even if he eventually abandoned the scheme of colonization and supported limited suffrage for those whom he considered particularly intelligent black Americans in the state of Louisiana.[17] His worry about future violence is obvious to anyone who reads the second inaugural address with care. As he had suggested in his debate with Douglas, America would still be Egypt to black Americans even after their liberation.

In the words of one critic, there was something "fantastically improbable" about colonization, since it was "more of a rhetorical gesture than a practical agenda."[18] Nevertheless, Lincoln was uncannily prophetic and realistic about the violence that later characterized the Reconstruction period in the South. The carpet-bagger governments certainly manipulated those whose intellects were "clouded by Slavery." It was not charitable, although perhaps egalitarian, to allow newly freed slaves to

---

15. Ibid., 5:372.
16. Merrill D. Peterson, *Lincoln in American Memory,* 350.
17. Lincoln, *Collected Works,* 7:243.
18. Oakes, *Radical and Republican,* 45, 193.

work with opportunistic and vengeful politicians bent on oppressing Southern whites. The goal of equality became a rationale for revenge, not the incarnation of charity for all. It is well known that the vindictive nature of the Radical Republicans and the rigidity of President Andrew Johnson (who also had no great love for the South) combined to demolish the charitable spirit that, had Lincoln lived, may well have spared both former slaves and former Confederates great misery.[19]

Few historians of the Reconstruction period, even those who exude little sympathy for the plight of the postbellum South, can honestly claim that the Radical Republicans acted with goodwill toward Southern whites, particularly when they employed the assassination of Lincoln as a pretext for punishing Dixie. The Radical Republican control of Congress by 1867, which enfranchised former slaves even as it disenfranchised Southern whites, effectively destroyed any pretense of mercy for the South while it encouraged violent response; resistance of the Ku Klux Klan did not arise until after the Radicals imposed racial egalitarianism in voting and land distribution.[20] As one famous admirer of Lincoln remarked on this period, Reconstruction left "a legacy of bitterness and hatred greater by far than that produced by four years of war," particularly when the governments of occupation insisted that whites would not be allowed to vote unless they accepted full civil rights for former slaves.[21] Another famous admirer, who later modeled his foreign policy on Lincoln's principles (as he understood them), wrote that the process of Reconstruction "was in almost every instance much worse than what had to be endured under military rule."[22] It was simply not charitable to actualize "a more perfect" equality if this program reduced the original master class of Southern whites to the position of an oppressed group;

19. See Holland, *Bonds of Affection*, 237–38. Thomas Nelson Page, the novelist and pro-Confederate Virginian, admitted that the death of Lincoln left the South without any other "potent friend" ("The Southern People during Reconstruction," 307).

20. Harvey Wish, introduction to *Reconstruction in the South, 1865–1877: Firsthand Accounts of the American South after the Civil War, by Southerners and Northerners*, xxiii–xxxvii; Thomas H. O'Connor, *The Disunited States: The Era of Civil War and Reconstruction*, 246–52.

21. Winston S. Churchill, *A History of the English-Speaking Peoples: The Great Democracies*, 241. See also Page, "Southern People," 313.

22. Woodrow Wilson, "The Reconstruction of the Southern States," 21.

in the long run, the sting of resentment against egalitarian reform also contributed to greater oppression of the former slaves.

It is obviously impossible to know exactly how Reconstruction would have fared had Lincoln lived; not everyone is convinced that the president's survival would have sufficiently mitigated the vindictiveness of the Radical Republicans.[23] Nevertheless, it is not a matter of speculation to recognize that Lincoln's policy on Reconstruction was associated with his approval of colonization. The difficult lesson that few readers of Lincoln grasp is that, whatever the merits and defects of colonization, this policy reflected the president's view that no objective—not even equality—justifies the destruction of a nation. The Radical Republican policies during Reconstruction threatened to replace one master class with another. If equality devolves into "might is right," or simply the war of one race for entitlements against another, then equality is a mere political weapon that has no relation to charity.[24] Although Lincoln can sometimes be understood as a leader who closely identified equality with the very survival of the nation, he cannot be faulted for *always* making this claim. No self-described chosen people have the right to destroy the nation in the name of the good.

Sadly, in the twentieth century, presidents like Woodrow Wilson did not learn this lesson well, and took Lincoln too literally on the absolute identity of metaphysical abstractions with the mission of the republic. Wilson and his supporters were far more confident about the primacy of a chosen people spreading universal credos than Lincoln ever was.

Woodrow Wilson and the Legacy of Lincoln

Friend and foe of President Woodrow Wilson tend to agree that his presidency marks a turning point in the history of the United States. He was the first president to steward the republic's entry into a controversial and unpopular world war. He was also the first president to *universalize* the mission of the United States on theological grounds. After Wilson, it became much more tempting for various politicians on the Left and the Right in America to identify the mission of America with

23. DiLorenzo, *Real Lincoln,* 204–11.
24. Francis, *Beautiful Losers,* 208–21.

that of a "chosen people" (not just an "almost chosen people") whom God commands to spread democracy all over the globe. The fact that Wilson failed to accomplish this lofty goal (and according to his harshest critics made the world safe for the enemies of democracy) has not deterred many American politicians from continuing the divinely sanctioned mission of democratizing the world in the image of America.[25]

It has been enormously tempting for supporter and defender alike to associate Wilson with the legacy of Lincoln. Wilson was a lifelong admirer of Lincoln, who praised the president for making it possible to believe in democracy while he embodied the tough realism necessary for guiding the nation through a near-fatal conflict.[26] Critics of Lincoln and Wilson have faulted both leaders for establishing an "Imperial Presidency" that put America on the road to crusades for democracy on a global scale.[27] The usual parallels drawn between the two men lie in the fact that both presidents aggressively defended the principles, not just the interests, of the republic. The supporters of both presidents at the time of Wilson's decision to enter World War I hailed Wilson for continuing the legacy of Lincoln in universalizing the "new birth of freedom" worldwide. Americanism became a "true world religion" for the first time, thanks to Wilson.[28] Germany became simply a European version of the old American South that had stood in the way of progress and moral universalism. In the eyes of Wilson's mainly liberal Protestant supporters, this righteous war against "pagan" tyranny reached from Gettysburg to the western front.[29]

The fact that both presidents made ambitious use of biblical symbolism has only encouraged natural comparisons of the two leaders. Wilson often sounded like his illustrious predecessor when he claimed that he was acting in the service of God (though without the qualifications that Lincoln often imposed on this political theology). Just as Lincoln referred to himself as a "humble instrument in the hands of the

25. See Jim Powell, *Wilson's War: How Woodrow Wilson's Great Blunder Led to Hitler, Lenin, Stalin, and World War II*.

26. Jaffa, *Crisis of the House Divided*, 190; Ronald J. Pestritto, *Woodrow Wilson and the Roots of Modern Liberalism*, 57–58, 209–10.

27. DiLorenzo, *Real Lincoln*, 270; Gamble, "Problem of Lincoln," 74–80.

28. Gelernter, *Americanism*, 148.

29. Gamble, *War for Righteousness*, 174; see also 146, 172–75. See too Peterson, *Lincoln in American Memory*, 198.

Almighty," so Wilson represented himself (while he was defending the need for the League of Nations) as the "personal instrument of God."[30] Although Wilson failed to persuade a skeptical American public that the Almighty wanted the League of Nations to be supported by the Senate, many other Americans were enthusiastic supporters of the president's attempt to identify the mission of Christianity with that of democracy. The claims of Wilson and many of his cabinet (especially Elihu Root) that America had a divine mission to democratize the world resonated with the progressivist Protestant clergy of the nation.[31]

There have also been attempts to fault Wilson for not pursuing Lincoln's alleged moral universalism, which rested on a faith in Americans as the chosen people, with sufficient verve and vigor. (Conversely, there were a few from the South who praised Wilson for defending the principle of self-determination that Lincoln had violated during the Civil War.)[32] Wilson's hatred of Germany also sharply contrasts with Lincoln's call to forgive the South and even acknowledge Northern complicity for slavery.[33] Wilson's failures, then, are usually contrasted with Lincoln's successes.

Critics tend to fault Wilson for choosing faith in his own righteousness over realism in arrogantly dismissing anyone who questioned the League of Nations or his faith in democracy building (at least among European peoples). Apparently, Wilson's lack of realism (and complicity in the Treaty of Versailles) makes the president at best naive and at worst a hypocrite. Even today's neoconservatives, who are often associated with the legacy of Wilson, fault the president for not properly tempering his idealism with a hearty dose of realism.[34] On the goal of democratizing the world, however, there is little debate. Few of these critics question Wilson's overall goal of liberating the world: there is usually just a questioning of the means and strategy.

---

30. Lincoln, *Collected Works*, 4:236; Marvin Olasky, "Woodrow Wilson's Folly: The Private and Public Life of a President," 7.

31. Gamble, *War for Righteousness*, 160–61, 177, 229.

32. Peterson, *Lincoln in American Memory*, 253.

33. W. Miller, "Lincoln's Second Inaugural," 335.

34. George F. Will, "The Slow Undoing: The Assault on, and Underestimation of, Nationality," 139; James W. Ceaser, "The Great Divide: American Interventionism and Its Opponents," 38; Fukuyama, *America at the Crossroads*, 9–10. For the neoconservative indebtedness to Wilson, see Paul Edward Gottfried, "The Invincible Wilsonian Matrix: Universal Human Rights Once Again."

What is also missing, surprisingly, in this typical critique of Wilson is his failure to distinguish belief in a "chosen people" with charity for all human beings. In the minds of his supporters and even critics who praise his goals while faulting his choice of means, Wilson was still justified in believing in Americans as the "chosen people." He was justified in reducing charity to the social gospel doctrine of spreading democracy all over the world.[35] Hardly any of his supporters and sympathetic critics question the dubious theology upon which Wilson (along with so many other presidents in the twentieth century) built his foreign policy.

The fact is that Wilson and his many supporters (some of whom can be critical to some degree) had no doubt that all Christians should support democracy building. Therefore, if one spreads democracy, one must also be spreading the basic principle of Christianity. Yet one can turn this theology on its head. If charity is the true test of a democracy, as Lincoln taught, then is it not even more difficult for a chosen people to build a democracy in a nation that lacks a historic Christian foundation? If people must be committed to charity at least in principle (as American Southerners were) *before* true democracy blooms, then political universalism stands or falls on belief in religious universalism.

Wilson always taught that the principles of America were the principles of mankind. The messianic tone of this universalism is obvious to anyone who carefully reads the president's second inaugural address. After declaring that the values of America are not "the principles of a province or of a single continent" but those of a "liberated mankind," Wilson predicts that the conflict raging overseas will test not just the nation's mettle but its commitment to fulfilling the imperatives of the Almighty. In "God's providence," Wilson predicted that his fellow Americans would be "purged of faction and division" and "purified" of partisanship. A "new unity" would be forged as a result.[36] In short, Americans must act as one people sanctioned by God, and true unity must lie in universalizing the values of the republic. Although Wilson had not yet declared war on Germany at this point in his presidency, he was laying the theological groundwork for intervention.

The tragedy of Wilson is that the messianic version of moral universalism, which wedded Christianity with democracy, had been tested

35. Gamble, *War for Righteousness,* 73, 204.
36. Wilson, "Second Inaugural Address," 332.

and found wanting in his political experience even before World War I. In defending his controversial decision to colonize the Philippines, President McKinley had claimed that the Almighty had responded to his anxious prayers about what the best course of action would be with the command to educate, uplift, and "Christianize" the natives.[37] In 1899, in a speech on patriotism that he gave soon after the start of the Filipino intervention, Wilson doubted that democracy in the Philippines could be "spread by manuscripts."[38] Three years later, in a speech on the ideals of the republic, Wilson elaborated on his earlier doubts. The president was not only aware that Americans had "yet to learn the things we would teach" about self-government but also admirably skeptical about whether self-government could ever be "given" to a people, particularly if that people had not earned this process of statecraft from "the hard school of life" by their own designs.[39]

Wilson was admirably self-critical here in recognizing that Americans themselves may not be infallible teachers of democracy and may therefore lack the moral authority to impose it upon an alien culture. (One is tempted to draw a parallel between Wilson's doubts about the readiness of all peoples to embrace democracy and Lincoln's doubts that all Americans were ready for full equality for blacks after emancipation, which explains his support for colonization.) Amazing as it may sound to contemporary readers, in light of his reputation for democratic universalism, the president-elect in 1912 faced criticism for expressing the "hope that the frontiers of the United States might soon be contracted."[40]

During his presidency, Wilson was forced to discover the stubborn reality that not all peoples think or act as moral universalists, at least not in the American Protestant sense. The relativity of culture and ethics inevitably clashes with the universalism of the chosen people on a global scale. Wilson found this out the hard way time and time again in his presidency. It was sobering for the president to discover that peoples as diverse as the French and the Filipinos were not devoted to

---

37. See Drinnon, *Facing West*, 279. Senator Albert Beveridge echoed these sentiments about the Filipinos' need for Anglo-American Christianity. See Bellah, *Broken Covenant*, 37–38.

38. Erez Manela, *The Wilsonian Moment: Self-Determination and the International Origins of Anticolonial Nationalism*, 28.

39. Wilson, "The Ideals of America," 222–23.

40. Drinnon, *Facing West*, 301.

moral universalism, as Wilson understood this ideology. Europeans and non-Europeans alike were in no hurry to embrace principles of liberty, forgiveness (especially after the Versailles Treaty), or respect for the rule of law. Indeed, even historically Christian peoples did not share the Wilsonian conflation of Christianity with the spread of republican democracy. The universalism of America's ideals oddly depended on the faith of liberal Protestant Christians in democracy; this faith was absent elsewhere in the world.

Yet Wilson has been blamed for occasionally doubting (unlike Lincoln, presumably) the capacity of all human beings regardless of creed or culture to build successful democracies (Wilson was often ethnocentric on the extent to which dark-skinned peoples could evolve into good liberal democrats). To natural rightist critics, Wilson is at fault for embracing a "progressivist" or "historicist" ideology, one focused on historical conditions that often affect the capacity of some peoples to embrace democracy more effectively than others. It was simply "ethnocentric" on the part of this president to qualify his democratic universalism (both as a young academic in the early twentieth century and as a president committed to fair negotiations after World War I) in insisting that not all peoples by "nature" desire or practice democracy. As a historian, Wilson taught that the most successful democracies require the English tradition of respect for self-government: in the eyes of his critics, this view amounts to racism.[41] Given the aftermath of World War I, in which ethnic tribalism across Europe made a mockery of the compatibility of democracy with moral universalism, one can lament the fact that Wilson was not persistent enough in qualifying his democratic universalism!

Significantly, Wilson is not the first president to qualify, at times, the alleged American faith in the capacity of all human beings to work successfully for democracy. Despite the attempts of the "natural right" school to portray Wilson as the first president to abandon or restrict democratic universalism, Thomas Jefferson—who is widely credited and faulted for pressing the influence of natural right principles in the founding years—was at least as inconsistent as Wilson in adhering to the belief that all human beings are ready for democracy. Jefferson doubted that the capacity for self-government was innate, or that "habit and long training" could be avoided altogether in the process of democratization.

41. Manela, *Wilsonian Moment.* See also Pestritto, *Woodrow Wilson*, 253–66. Pestritto is a natural right theorist.

This devotee of natural right also doubted, toward the end of his life, that the French and the Russians—two historically Christian peoples— could grasp the meaning of natural rights.[42] Even so, Wilson's own qualifications were fleeting. In defending the peace treaty of 1919, Wilson sounded as if he had forgotten his older cautionary remarks about democratic colonization. Instead, he affirmed that God had led America into the destiny of being a great power: "America shall in truth show the way. The light streams upon the path ahead, and nowhere else."[43]

Despite this high-blown rhetoric, the most sophisticated liberal defenders of Wilson today have faulted the president for not practicing a version of charity toward those whom he attempted to serve (for example, historically oppressed peoples) or those who disagreed with him on pivotal issues like the League of Nations (his conservative opponents in America). In their post–cold war study of the president's legacy, Robert S. McNamara and James G. Blight contend that Wilson can be legitimately faulted for self-righteous disdain for his enemies, lack of understanding of the complexity of ethnic nationalistic politics, and compromising with nations (Britain and France) who sought to preserve their colonial empires at the expense of his own ideal of national self-determination. Most relevant to my purposes is their charge that Wilson showed a lack of *empathy* toward his adversaries. Wilson preached rather than listened, failed to learn the history and culture of peoples who would be affected by his decisions, showed ignorance of historical grievances, and did not treat all human beings as equals worthy of dignity and respect.[44] In short, Wilson did not put himself in the "skin" of other human beings (both friend and foe), as the ethic of charity requires.

Yet it is significant that McNamara and Blight never question Wilson's overall goal of democratic universalism; only the president's means and attitudes toward achieving this end are critiqued. Does true empathy,

---

42. For a discussion of Jefferson's highly qualified universalism, see C. Miller, *Jefferson and Nature*, 257–58.

43. Quoted in Gelernter, *Americanism*, 175.

44. McNamara and Blight, *Wilson's Ghost: Reducing the Risk of Conflict, Killing, and Catastrophe in the Twenty-first Century*, 65–66. Other liberal Wilsonians have recently followed suit in defending the need for the formation of multilateral military forces that impose liberal democratic ways on governments that are not popular, accountable, or respectful of rights. See G. John Ilkenberry and Anne-Marie Slaughter, *Forging a World of Liberty under Law: U.S. National Security in the Twenty-first Century*.

then, require the assumption that every human being is a potential democrat waiting to be liberated? Without a hint of irony, McNamara and Blight support a policy of "liberal imperialism" (as a continuation of Wilson's uncompleted legacy) in which the values of what I have called democratic universalism are imposed on a people. The "liberal values of tolerance, pluralism, and democracy" must be imposed on failed states. Liberals must act as "benevolent dictators" until these values bloom.[45]

The reader has a right to expect McNamara and Blight to show how liberal imperialism relates to their ethic of empathy. Yet the authors never explain how this mode of imperialism is an act of empathy. It does not occur to them, despite their own legitimate criticism of Wilson's lack of understanding of ethnic nationalist politics, that many cultures that lack a tradition of "liberal values" may actively (and indefinitely) resist them. Indeed, Wilson at least showed more wisdom (with respect to the Philippines anyway) than his defenders on the folly of forcing a people to be free. That imperialism undertaken in the name of democratic ideals can still be unrealistic and oppressive is lost on McNamara and Blight. It is also likely that a powerful liberal democracy may not consistently exercise wisdom in defining what is and is not a "murderous failed state," and which states require intervention. (Would these authors agree that the United States must put an end to all tyrannies, as President George W. Bush declared in his second inaugural address?) McNamara and Blight also fail to recognize that true empathy might require the recognition that not all human beings are historically suited for a liberal democracy (as Wilson sometimes understood). The act of putting oneself in the "skin" of a people may lead to the unpleasant discovery that there is no democrat waiting to break out of captivity. It may well be uncharitable to condemn peoples who refuse to cooperate with liberal imperialism, especially since the imposed regime is not of their own making. In short, democratic universalism and charity (empathy) may often part company as ideals. (To date, attempts at "liberal imperialism" in the Balkans and the Middle East have been resounding failures.) Although democratic universalists today (whether liberal or neoconservative) often resent the charge of being "naive Wilsonians"

---

45. McNamara and Blight, *Wilson's Ghost*, 153. It is noteworthy that the late secretary of defense Robert McNamara has opposed the Iraq war, despite his policy of "liberal imperialism."

who ignore the particularities of history and culture, not one prominent avatar of this ideology has abandoned the optimistic view that democracy is the best regime for all human beings in the long run.[46]

Despite the record of history, democratic universalists today are disappointed with Wilson for failing to put into practice grand rhetoric about the chosen nation. It is thus tempting for them to look back to Lincoln as a consistent avatar of democratic universalism, as neoconservatives (and even paleoconservatives) typically do. Yet Lincoln never claimed that America had a mission to democratize the world (a decidedly unrealistic objective during a time of civil war). The fact that Lincoln related democracy and Christianity more closely than any of his predecessors should not suggest that he intended to put America on the path to democratic universalism. Indeed, when the president insisted that a true democracy already requires the presence of charity, this arguably made it more difficult to justify the cause of democracy crusades. The fact that the "almost chosen people" enjoyed a common faith did not prevent its members from killing each other for four bloody years. If the presence of Christianity cannot guarantee the success of a democracy, what can?

THE PERILS OF SELECTIVE CHOSENNESS

The failure of Wilson has not encouraged democratic universalists to abandon the idea of America as a chosen people. After all, they take comfort in recalling that Lincoln too had failed to achieve peace in his time (through no fault of his own).[47] Indeed, the lesson of the Civil War, that common agreement on issues of faith does not lead to the seamless establishment of democracy, has been lost on democratic universalists. Moreover, few American politicians and media commentators to date have questioned the validity of belief in America as a chosen people.

This last claim is not a denial of the fact that there are critiques of the politicization of chosenness. Indeed, there are. Yet these critiques are usually ideologically selective. Right-wing chauvinistic versions of the chosen people, particularly those expressed by European fas-

---

46. See Irwin Stelzer, "Neoconservatives and Their Critics," 10–11; and Paul Wolfowitz, "Statesmanship in the New Century," 320–21.

47. Gelernter, *Americanism*, 148.

cist movements, garner most of this critical attention. In the Anglo-American context, the Puritans' invocation of chosenness as a rationale for exterminating Irish Catholics and Native Americans is a particularly well-studied period of history.[48] Yet leftist critics of rightist versions of chosenness are not dissuaded enough to abandon the idea of chosenness altogether for their own political purposes.

Leftist theologian Robert Bellah (an admirer of Lincoln's "covenant" for social change) associates the sinister side of chosenness with expansionist wars and oppression of minorities at the hands of the Right (especially the Puritans), not the Left. In his study of the politics of Exodus, Michael Walzer blames right-wing Zionists and devotees of Christian eschatology for subverting the liberating meaning of chosenness; the true meaning of chosenness has been best understood by liberation theologians on the Left. In his detailed study of the Anglo-American use of the myth of the chosen people, Clifford Longley considers "political correctness" on the Left to be a valid form of chosenness in our own time; he does not hesitate to embrace the overall liberating implications of this secularization of chosenness. In particular, Longley praises Martin Luther King as a "theologian of chosenness" who rightly saw a "grand design" for America, in which the "mantle of the elect" could be shared by all human beings. Longley's predictable conclusion, that the chosen people shall one day include all oppressed peoples and groups (women, homosexuals, the disabled, the elderly, and others) who are happy to lay the blame for their oppression on the original chosen people of early modernity (white Anglo-Saxon Protestants), confirms the worst fears of the conservative opposition to Lincoln: that there is no foreseeable end to claims of chosenness (which, in practice, translate into ever increasing demands for entitlements).[49]

I have argued throughout this work that Lincoln ambitiously elevated charity above all other values. Yet the meaning of his legacy is contradictory. Although he sometimes associated charity with equality for blacks and whites, he did not consistently do so (especially in the context of colonization). While he sometimes invoked the power of the chosen people guided by Providence, he also knew that his fiercest enemies did

---

48. Drinnon, *Facing West*, 3–61; Longley, *Chosen People*, 101–28; Phillips, *Cousins' Wars*.

49. Bellah, *Broken Covenant*, 36–60, 179; Walzer, *Exodus and Revolution*, 144, 149; Longley, *Chosen People*, 278–79, 255.

the same. There is no hard evidence to support the claim of friend and foe that Lincoln advanced the cause of democratic universalism, the secularization of the myth of chosenness.

A correct understanding of Lincoln's rhetoric and actions should suggest the need for caution about the extent to which a nation can universalize its ideals, especially since a democratic Christian nation almost failed to maintain them during the Civil War. Yet, as David Donald once quipped, Lincoln is "everybody's grandfather."[50] Leftists and rightists alike have read into Lincoln's ideas rationales for their own parochial agendas. Both camps have forgotten the historical and religious specificity of Lincoln's age.

It may be tempting to respond here that I have concluded that there is nothing *timeless* to learn from the legacy of Lincoln, that his thought and deed are mere epiphenomena. That would be an unfair conclusion, for I believe that the ethic of charity is indeed universal and that Lincoln was correct in teaching its primary importance. The fact that Lincoln himself was compelled to act uncharitably at times in no way teaches the irrelevance of charity. Indeed, critics of Lincoln are quite happy to invoke charity against the president when it suits them. What we can also learn from the president is the need to distinguish charity from the idea of a chosen people. It is not simply that the historical record includes few examples of liberating cases of the use of chosenness (usually, chosen peoples take vengeance on their victims, after all). It is also sobering to recognize that the ambiguity of chosenness is so gaping that one can justify the most horrible crimes in its name. No political system, not even a democratic one, can long survive the strains imposed by belief in chosenness. Indeed, the irony is that the very first chosen people in history failed to establish stable political kingdoms, as the Old Testament reveals.

AMERICAN POLITICS AND THE FUTURE OF THE CHOSEN PEOPLE

I have argued throughout this work that Abraham Lincoln was the first president to politicize, at least in his most important speeches during his political career, the ethic of charity. To be charitable to all Americans meant the liberation of all. No one is free unless are all free to enjoy

50. Donald, "Getting Right with Lincoln," 3–18.

the blessing of equality (whose meaning remains ambiguous). It was the duty of the American political system to bring this blessing to all Americans. No other president had insisted on the falsity of separating moral consistency from political praxis as brilliantly and eloquently as Lincoln.

Lincoln also invoked the biblical concept of the "almost chosen people" in order to underscore his call for liberating the slaves. Despite his many attempts to play down the message of self-righteousness and triumphalism so often recurrent in the application of chosenness, the Civil War helped to solidify the idea of Americans as a "chosen people" (not simply an "almost chosen people") whose ideals must liberate the entire world, under the watchful and approving guidance of the Almighty. Although Lincoln was too intelligent not to see the spurious and often lethal foundations of chosenness, the crucible of the republic's bloodiest conflict persuaded many Americans that their mission was the very mission of mankind.[51] (Still, the first great venture to remake the world after the Civil War—the war with Spain—did not occur for another three decades.)

There may be readers at this point who still do not doubt the natural complementarity of chosenness and charity. They may be skeptical about the need to separate the two beliefs. Cannot a chosen people be charitable? If a chosen people refuses to be charitable, does not the Bible teach that God will punish this backsliding? I am inclined to believe, nonetheless, that a long-held belief in one's chosenness as a people tends to undermine the basic practice of charity.

The historical record suggests, overwhelmingly, that self-described chosen peoples eventually become imperialistic, tyrannical, and xenophobic. It is well documented that the very first chosen people to settle in North America invoked the powerful symbolism of Exodus in order to drive Native Americans off their lands. Over time, the imperative of being charitable toward others simply becomes obscured or ignored altogether. Although the idea of chosenness is obviously appealing to peoples who have been historically oppressed and who need the assurance that God loves them best while the world's powers despise them,

---

51. It is worth observing that many other Americans had no thought of a "grand strategy" to remake the world even after the Civil War, as even some democratic universalists occasionally admit. See Robert Kagan, *Dangerous Nation: America's Place in the World, from Its Earliest Days to the Dawn of the Twentieth Century*, 286.

it is undeniable that chosen peoples who eventually acquire great influence tend to take vengeance on their vanquished enemies. Although natural rightists like Harry Jaffa are inclined to believe that chosen peoples deserve punishment only when they fail to spread the value of liberty, one can just as easily claim that a chosen people fail if they force others to be free.[52] Lincoln feared that this vindictive expression of chosenness would characterize the aftermath of the Civil War; tragically, his fear was realized during the Reconstruction period.

It may be tempting to believe, as many secularist intellectuals do in our age, that we can effectively resist any usage of biblical religion in politics. As I have argued, this temptation has never been a realistic option in the American experience, especially since the age of Lincoln. The current debate over America's status as a "propositional" or "creedal" nation reflects the inescapability of biblical influences. Traditional (or "paleo-") conservatives typically argue that America has a distinctive identity that defies universalization. The ideals of the republic are distinctively rooted in a particular faith (Christianity), culture (Anglo-Saxon), and language (English). America's indebtedness to Western (particularly British) civilization makes it difficult and even undesirable to spread its credos of democracy and liberty to cultures that lack these foundations. Neoconservatives and liberals tend to agree that the American creed requires that the world be transformed in the image of the republic, that the very survival of the nation requires this ambitious dissemination of its values. To make both America and the world safe and free, the republic's leaders must unleash the desire of all human beings for America's values and institutions.[53]

It is not hard to spy the indebtedness of both camps to the idea of chosenness. The traditional conservatives desire to protect the nation's distinctive culture from the influence of the outside world, lest America's identity as a people wither and die. Liberals and neoconservatives believe that America's uniqueness requires the spread of its values on a global scale. Both camps are convinced, however, that America is *special*. Indeed, since the values of America are superior to those of every other nation, its leaders must take special care to protect its identity, either through isolationism or global democracy building. Certainly, both camps agree

---

52. Jaffa, *Crisis of the House Divided*, 230–31; Jaffa, *New Birth*, 257–58, 349–50.
53. See Huntington, *Who Are We?* 46–49; and Ceaser, "Great Divide," 25–43.

that America can be a light to the rest of the world, whether this requires the isolationist preference for being a noninterventionist role model or the neoconservative preference for being an activist imperial power.

It may also be tempting to suggest that this debate over particularity and universality in America is peculiar to this republic, and thus reflects the apparently stronger influence of religion in the United States.[54] Yet the idea of chosenness took root in the Western world long before the inception of the republic and persists as an influence far beyond the country's shores. Certainly, European nationalistic movements have invoked chosenness in order to justify taking back their nations from outside influences. (One irony about the politics of Far Right anti-Semites is that they often use the Exodus narrative for their own purposes.)[55] As we have seen, leftist movements have regularly invoked the Exodus narrative as a rationale to justify the liberation of all oppressed minorities who have run afoul of a once dominant Christian hegemony. As Eric Voegelin persuasively documents in his study of Exodus, modern politics has not transcended the Covenant. Despite the efforts of Jews and Christians through the ages to downplay the political implications of Exodus, the relation between politics and biblical faith is inescapable even in a secularized age. Although the prophets and the early church alike had to warn their brethren not to equate political triumph with true service to God, the fact is that they both felt the pressure to *separate* religion from politics precisely because it was so tempting for their followers to *identify* the two.[56]

This often idolatrous temptation to identify God with Man's politics (or the New Jerusalem) has haunted both the American and the Western experience of religion in modernity. It would be false, therefore, to argue that only religious folk are prone to this idolatry of chosenness. As we have seen, Willmoore Kendall and George Carey rightly worried whether chosenness "without God" is more dangerous than more traditional belief. If Americans no longer believe (as Lincoln did) in a God who restrains the worst human temptations toward idolization of a political program, then the secularization of belief may not be the pathway to peace and enlightenment after all. As Voegelin warned in

54. Michael O'Meara, *New Culture, New Right: Anti-Liberalism in Postmodern Europe,* 154–55.

55. See Werner Sombart, *The Jews and Modern Capitalism,* 224; and Burleigh, *Sacred Causes,* 95, 121.

56. Voegelin, *Israel and Revelation,* chapter 6.

his studies of "political religions," secularization not only fails to banish religious influences but may even radicalize them.

A pertinent example for our time is the idolization of democracy. In his tome *Americanism: The Fourth Great Western Religion*, David Gelernter identifies "American Zionism" (or Americanism) with the mission to spread democracy all over the world. In contrast to the natural right school, Gelernter rushes to embrace theological rhetoric without appeal to the authority of "nature." Still, it is abundantly clear that Gelernter sees no need for traditional religious belief as a rationale for this endeavour. Though he admits that the biblical narrative of chosenness historically inspires and buttresses the democratizing mission of Americans as a chosen people, today's Americans do not have to believe in God or any religion in particular, save the political religion of Americanism. To be sure, they can use the Bible as they see fit. What matters, however, are the conclusions that Americans *draw* from the Bible, not the truth of this hermeneutic. Additionally, belief in God, even a God of revelation, is unimportant as long as one believes in the "beautiful blossoms" of Americanism. Belief in democratic "Man" everywhere is essential.[57] The message is that the most successful "Americanists" will be individuals who do not hold traditional beliefs but are adept at using biblical language and credos to justify a political program that has utterly no place in scriptural teachings. (It does not bother Gelernter that Romans 13 calls on believers to obey all regimes, democratic or not.) Most disturbing, the idolization of "Man" is a precondition for Americanism: if the democratic version of "Man" does not command belief, then America will lose its way.

Gelernter, who praises Lincoln as "America's last and greatest founding father," supports ideas that were unthinkable to his hero. Lincoln not only believed in the primacy of the biblical God over the interests of humanity but also insisted on the importance of charity over chosenness (even if his actions were not always charitable). Without the restraining influence of belief in a God of love, Gelernter's version of a political religion will respect no limits and even confirm the Old Testament prophecy on the dangers of sinful pride (this author mentions charity only once in a book otherwise overwhelmingly devoted to chosenness). To be sure, belief in God did not deter progressivist Christians from supporting World War I as a divinely sanctioned conflict against tyranny.

57. Gelernter, *Americanism*, 20, 97, 109.

Nevertheless, it is hard to imagine that belief in "man" would foster more humility and charity than belief in God.

Secularized chosenness, then, can be just as fanatical as religious expressions of the Exodus narrative. Indeed, as Hegel observes in his discussion of the Mosaic history, chosenness can become most destructive when the people no longer believe in God. Once the Israelites successfully built political kingdoms (for a time), they no longer needed to believe in a liberating God. Only when their kingdoms failed did they return to the consolation of the Almighty.[58] This lesson is lost on democratic universalists (or what Gelernter calls "American Zionists"), who believe that one nation is so free and virtuous that no obstacle (not even God) can stand in the way of its ultimate triumph. The simple message of the history of the Israelites (as Spinoza and Hegel both well understood) is that chosen peoples are chosen only for a time, before they slide back into self-righteousness and imperialism. If Hegel's reading is correct, chosen peoples who become oppressors are no longer the truly chosen.

Chosen peoples are not usually known to be open to criticism. Indeed, there is no reason to be self-critical if one assumes, as most neoconservatives do, that it is simply "natural" for all human beings to desire freedom as Americans define it (see Chapter 5). As Michael Ledeen, Francis Fukuyama, and other leading neoconservatives have often intoned, the majority of Muslims today desire such freedom and would seek to become "Americanized" if they did not face oppression in their native lands. These same commentators are genuinely puzzled at the resistance to American democracy building in Iraq and elsewhere, as well as the persistence of oppressive practices in Muslim nations that have some semblance of democracy. As avatars of a political religion, they cannot grasp how the chosen people can make enemies of those whom they seek to liberate.

Yet the presumption that all human beings desire freedom is not a charitable one, if by "charitable" one means taking the time to understand the history, religion, and culture of a people who may have correspondingly different concepts of the meaning of freedom. Even a self-described "liberal imperialist" like Robert McNamara calls on his citizens to empathize with the enemy, to understand the other's position. (Lincoln, we have seen, called on Northerners to understand

58. G. W. F. Hegel, *Early Theological Writings*, 158–59. See also Longley, *Chosen People*, 245–46; and Bellah, *Broken Covenant*, 43.

Southerners for the same reason.) The most disastrous ventures in American history—the Vietnam and Iraq wars—are largely failures to learn this lesson. Even tough-minded realists who have little patience with moral sentimentalism have pointed out the dangers of this failure. Maj. Gen. Edward Geary Lansdale, the CIA agent who is credited with helping to save the Philippines from communist insurgency in the 1950s, later taught his comrades during the Vietnam War that a faith in American democracy is no excuse for failing to understand the distinctive particularities of a people. Lansdale bemoaned (as did McNamara in retrospect) the fact that most Americans in Vietnam, even at the highest levels, lacked a basic knowledge of the Vietnamese people. His own love of American republicanism, which tempted him to associate democracy building with biblical credos, nevertheless did not blind him to the fact that the primary tradition of ethics in Vietnam (Confucianism) should be the basis for a successful regime.[59]

Only a few politicians of stature have dared to observe that America's leaders have failed to understand the Muslim world, especially since the beginning of the Iraq war. To date, it is very risky to fault neoconservative democracy builders for failing to understand the historical grievances of Muslim peoples against the West, lest one is accused of appeasing theocrats and terrorists. Even though neoconservatives acknowledge that support for dictatorships in the Middle East has damaged the image of America and made it vulnerable to the charge of hypocrisy, they stand accused of failing to make the effort to understand Muslims from their own perspective. In calling for empathy (as opposed to approval), a defender of charity does not condone the often violent and irrational attitudes of many Muslims. The American killing of Muslims (not just terrorists) in the name of democracy does not exactly reflect an understanding of the Muslim fear of a return of Christian crusaders to occupy the holy lands of Islam, nor does it reflect an attempt to understand what many Muslims want from a democracy.[60] The American attempt to remake the Middle East is apparently an act of liberation, not a replay

---

59. Lansdale, *In the Midst of Wars: An American's Mission in Southeast Asia,* 363. Lansdale's fellow CIA agent Willmoore Kendall lamented in the 1950s the agency's lack of understanding of the dictum "know one's enemy," or the need to get into the mind of one's adversary ("The Function of Intelligence").

60. See Akbar S. Ahmed, *Islam under Siege: Living Dangerously in a Post-Honor World,* 23–45.

of old historical conflicts, in the eyes of its supporters. Most Muslims have not seen this policy as an act of charitable liberation so much as a new form of Western Christian tyranny. Most important, it has been too easily assumed that Muslims possess the same understanding of (and desire for) democracy as Western liberals; it is often forgotten that the liberal version of democracy is not the only possible expression. Majority-rule democracy, with its intolerance of individual rights, is another alternative model.[61] In short, the divide between the North and South of Lincoln's time is a crevice compared to the chasm between Western and Muslim views of politics and history. A simple act of empathy might have prevented the formation of naive and ignorant assumptions about the universal desire for freedom, American style.

It may be tempting to argue that a call to be charitable and avoid hypocrisy would lead to an orgy of self-critique that already paralyzes the Christian mind in the West. The fact that Christians today often fall over themselves attempting to atone for past injustices inflicted upon Muslims (the late Pope John Paul II apologized for the Crusades) and other minorities has provoked the charge that charity has become the equivalent of excessive guilt-tripping, particularly when no apologies are forthcoming on the other side.[62] Although this attitude reflects the most leftist versions of Christianity in the West, it dubiously reflects the spirit of Lincoln's thoughts on charity. It is not even obvious that charity must encourage a posture of pacifist acceptance of an aggressor's actions. As Willmoore Kendall argues in an essay on the Christian opposition to pacifism, one may have to use violence against an enemy to show that one cares about his moral and spiritual health.[63] Charity does not encourage indifference to injustices committed by others: in the baldest terms, it is a two-way street. If Muslims are incensed at the interference of the West in their historic lands for the sake of oil (and "democracy"), they too must show a charitable understanding of Western fears that radical Muslims desire a holy war against liberal democracy. Chosenness as expressed by jihadists must also face condemnation on all sides. To

---

61. See Fareed Zakaria, *The Future of Freedom: Illiberal Democracy at Home and Abroad.*

62. See Paul Edward Gottfried, *Multiculturalism and the Politics of Guilt: Toward a Secular Theocracy,* 39–70.

63. Kendall, *Conservative Affirmation,* 134–35.

judge the other *and* oneself is an act of charity; chosen people rarely have the stomach for this moral consistency.

In fine, friends and foes of Lincoln do an injustice to the president if they fail to grasp that his true theological legacy makes a forcible distinction between chosenness and charity. The president, like all Americans, saw his people as special. Their history rests on a specific faith that is the source of the tension between these two great biblical credos. Moreover, the president never suggested that America's special status must be endlessly reproduced across the world. (It would be very dangerous and confusing to export this tension between chosenness and charity.) Moreover, the fact that no human being (Lincoln included) is consistently charitable should remind Americans that it is all too easy to justify immorality in the name of God (or Man). Political religions, or secularized expressions of chosenness, never consider the other side of the debate. This failure inflicts irreparable harm on both the citizens who are unfortunate enough to live under the hegemony of ideologues and the world at large.

It has always been tempting for some Christians to embrace an apolitical stance, after exhausting periods of secularist idolization and distortion of biblical credos; certainly, scripture can often justify a stance of obeying political realms while refraining from creating new regimes (Rom. 13:1–5). Yet the stance of what Hegel calls the "beautiful soul" who falsely exists beyond the political is likely not an option for most believing Americans, particularly after Lincoln. Engagement in the world, however, need not embrace the opposite extreme of belief in a chosen people reshaping the world through democratic universalism. A commitment to charity need not lapse into what Voegelin called the "gnostic" tendency of some Christians (particularly on the Left) to embrace revolutionary programs of eliminating every trace of injustice on the face of the earth. Perhaps the most charitable action to which Americans can commit themselves today is to support other peoples to liberate themselves on their own *if* the latter possess a desire for liberation. If they do not, the problems of other nations should not be America's eternal challenge, despite the claims of George Bush and Barack Obama. Lest anyone consider this attitude an act of cold isolationism, it does not seem particularly kind to raise expectations that few nations, no matter how chosen their citizens believe themselves to be, can fulfill.

7

Conclusion:
The Future Past of a Charitable Politics

American nationalism is that of an exceptional nation founded on a universal principle, on what Lincoln called "an abstract truth, applicable to all men and all times."

—William Kristol and David Brooks, "What Ails the Right?"

*A*t least since Lincoln, there has been some attempt in the American political tradition to understand the relation between charity and democracy. If I have been correct in my analysis, Lincoln believed that charity was a necessary precondition of this regime. Unfortunately, the most zealously secular avatars of the American creed have ignored this ethic in favor of the belief in Americans as a chosen people. Lincoln's demand that Americans act as a charitable people has become gradually detached from its religious moorings and replaced with recurrent demands for the chosen to go out into the world and force people to be free. Moreover, friends and foes of Lincoln's legacy now widely understand his legacy to be one that is at once secularist and globalist. Morality itself has become virtually synonymous with the spread of liberal democracy. Indeed, these developments are related and emerged at the same time in American history, in the post–World War II era. Although defenders of democracy-building consider their ideology to be both ethical and realistic, the tragedy is that it is often neither.

GLOBALIZATION AND AMERICAN PROTESTANTISM

It is undeniable that America's rise as a superpower after 1945 in part explains the attempts of scholars and commentators to read the Protestant tradition of the nation out of its history; indeed, some of these efforts have enjoyed the cooperation of the historically Protestant elites who feel no compunction to water down their theology to fit secular political goals.[1] Using arguments that foreshadowed those made by neoconservatives in the Bush II years, liberals and leftists (as well as a few rightists) in the early cold war argued that America's image as an egalitarian and cosmopolitan nation would suffer if it were too closely tied to its historic faith tradition. Historians with the prestige of Richard Hofstadter led this fight to marginalize and vilify the oldest faith tradition of the republic in order to portray America as a nation that does not require any particular commitment to one religious creed. In the perilous times of the cold war, Hofstadter and others believed that America required a secular creed, in order to win the support of diverse peoples who may be tempted to embrace the siren song of Soviet communism. When Hofstadter asserted, "It has been our fate as a nation not to have ideologies but to be one," he was speaking for many cold war intellectuals on the need for the republic to universalize its ideals with an ideology that appeals to all of humanity, not just the Protestant people whom Lincoln generally addressed.[2] If America were indeed a propositional nation, it would have to abandon historic and religious barriers (for example, Protestantism) that would impede its struggle to win peoples away from the blandishments of the communist bloc. The historic precedent that only Western Protestant Christianity contributed to the rise of respect for the dignity and freedom of the individual, as Ernst Troeltsch argued, did not deter polemicists like Hofstadter from imagining the survival of American values without need of their historic roots.[3]

---

1. Kurth, "Bush and the Protestant Deformation."

2. Quoted in Huntington, *Who Are We?* 46. Huntington includes Hofstadter among many cold war intellectuals who played up the cosmopolitan origins of the republic in the post–World War II era.

3. Ernst Troeltsch, *Protestantism and Progress: The Significance of Protestantism for the Rise of the Modern World*, 30–32. See also Page Smith, *Rediscovering Christianity: A History of Modern Democracy and the Christian Ethic.*

The irony of the attempts of many cold war intellectuals to portray America as a chosen nation whose destiny was to universalize democratic ideals is that this ideology itself is a secularized version of the old biblical belief in chosenness. However, it has been advantageous for America's intelligentsia to downplay any debt to particular religious histories as much as possible, in order to avoid thorny questions about the true universalism of the ideals. For this reason, I believe, natural rightist ideology could have become the powerful influence it is only in a period of American globalism, when the nation was under pressure to win the hearts and minds of all peoples, regardless of creed, color, or belief.

LINCOLN'S CHANGING LEGACY

It is also instructive to evaluate the debate over the legacy of Lincoln in the context of America's path to superpower status in the mid-twentieth century. Just as there have been ambitious attempts to read the nation's Christian heritage out of its history, so were there concerted efforts on the part of intellectuals during the cold war to portray the president as a globalist leader who was firmly committed to the universalization of American democracy. It seems that a Lincoln who comes across as too Protestant is not an attractive candidate who would inspire millions of people to understand the republic's values as their own. The preferred image of Lincoln is that of a leader who was a democratic universalist (although, admittedly, a leader who also made use of Christian ideas for political purposes).

Looking back at the history of this debate over the legacy of Lincoln, which commenced almost immediately after his assassination, one can make a case that America's ascendancy to globalism has encouraged a *monolithic* debate over the president's lasting influence. Leftists and rightists alike in the cold war period converged most dramatically in their shared assumption that the president set the nation on the path of making the world American. The Left and Right in America in the nineteenth century sharply disagreed over Lincoln's views on socialism and capitalism—the biggest issue of their time.[4] No comparable divergence of opinion can be found in the literature on the "globalist" Lincoln today.

4. Peterson, *Lincoln in American Memory,* 155–63.

American presidents who first contemplated the emergence of the nation as a superpower found it useful to portray themselves as leaders walking in the footsteps of Lincoln (we already saw this dynamic of emulation in the Wilson presidency). The famous Lincoln biographer Carl Sandburg persuaded President Franklin Delano Roosevelt during World War II to draw parallels between the war against tyranny in Europe and Lincoln's "irrepressible conflict." Even in the early years of the cold war, however, it was not obvious to every American of influence that Lincoln's presidency had globalist implications. When Adlai Stevenson (as governor of Illinois) celebrated the eighty-eighth anniversary of the Gettysburg Address by asserting that Lincoln's stewardship during the Civil War served the hopes of all mankind, the feisty editor of the *Chicago Tribune,* Col. Robert McCormick, dismissed this claim as "preposterous."[5]

Nevertheless, by the 1960s, a discernible hardening of the terms of debate was apparent. Particularly within the conservative movement, a consensus was building around the assumption that Lincoln's presidency represented the first dramatic moment in the nation's history in which a globalist creed of democracy building had taken root. Undoubtedly, the publication of Harry Jaffa's *Crisis of the House Divided* in 1959 can take much credit (or blame) for this sea change in the debate over Lincoln. Jaffa persuaded liberals and conservatives alike that Lincoln's aims were universalistic and unlimited, in bringing America's ideals to the entire world for the sake of its own survival as a free nation, in a study that a few Lincoln experts still consider "the greatest Lincoln book of the century."[6] Indeed, Jaffa convinced conservatives like Frank Meyer and Willmoore Kendall (both regular contributors to *National Review* in the 1950s and 1960s) that Lincoln's use of executive powers had forged what later became termed the "Imperial Presidency," or the mission of presidents to invoke extraordinary (and even unconstitutional) powers to save a nation from crises. To be sure, many conservatives did not think that this legacy of Lincoln was a good one: Meyer and Kendall blamed the president for setting the stage for the erosion of American democracy.[7] Nevertheless, Jaffa's portrait of Lincoln as the aggressive

5. Ibid., 321, 325.
6. Guelzo, *Abraham Lincoln: Redeemer President,* 469.
7. For Meyer's critique of Lincoln (and Jaffa), see Nash, *Conservative Intellectual Movement,* 345–47; and Peterson, *Lincoln in American Memory,*

universalist won over friend and foe alike across the ideological spectrum well past the end of the cold war period. Robert Bellah on the Left sympathizes with Jaffa's portrait of Lincoln as an ardent racial egalitarian (which fits well with Bellah's call for America to bring its "covenant" of freedom and equality to the world). Thomas J. DiLorenzo on the libertarian Right has similarly accepted the position of Jaffa that Lincoln harbored radical global ambitions for the nation, an interpretation that paleoconservative commentators Mel Bradford and Sam Francis also endorsed (although all three writers lament the long-term implications of this mission).[8]

In short, it is very rare to find a major writer on Lincoln's legacy today who does not draw a straight line between his presidency and the policy of democracy building in our time. Hardly any conservative or liberal today dissociates Lincoln from the legacy of the strong presidency with imperial ambitions. (Conservatives like Irving Babbitt and Richard Weaver who made this dissociation are hardly read anymore in the literature on Lincoln).[9] The fact that there is plenty of reason to portray Lincoln as a "realist" on foreign policy, who weighed the pros and cons of giving support to democratic movements around the world, has not deterred globalist readers of the president from making exotic claims about his legacy. Neoconservative writer Robert Kagan has praised Lincoln for claiming that it would be "meritorious" for America to intervene against Russia in 1852 to prevent the czarist crushing of the Hungarian revolution; Kagan sees this onetime statement of Lincoln as evidence of a consistent love of "universal human equality" on the president's part.[10] Yet Kagan omits the more inconvenient fact that Lincoln, as president, made no move to support Poland's rebellion against Russian tyranny in 1863. Although he had once championed Polish independence, he did not stop his secretary of state, William Seward, from reassuring the Russians that America's friendship with the nation

---

334. On Kendall's acceptance of Jaffa's version of Lincoln, see his *Conservative Affirmation*, 17; and Murley, "On the 'Calhounism' of Kendall," 126–29.

8. See DiLorenzo, *Lincoln Unmasked: What You're Not Supposed to Know about Dishonest Abe,* 143–48; Bradford, "Dividing the House: The Gnosticism of Lincoln's Political Rhetoric," 21; and Francis, *Revolution from the Middle,* 111, 139.

9. See Babbitt, *Democracy and Leadership,* 275–76; and Weaver, *The Ethics of Rhetoric,* 114.

10. Kagan, *Dangerous Nation,* 263.

(and appreciation of Russia for not interfering in America's affairs) would keep America from interfering in this conflict.[11] Nevertheless, the reinvention of Lincoln as the premier globalist president fits well with cosmopolitan elites in America who need to justify the dissemination of democracy on a world scale, just as the trumpeting of America as a "propositional" nation, which owes little of enduring value to its Protestant roots, is a convenient form of propaganda. (The paleoconservative acceptance of Lincoln as a protoneoconservative in the postwar era has only helped the cause of democratic universalism as well.)

CHARITY AND GLOBAL DEMOCRACY BUILDING

In addition to the triumph of this revisionist hermeneutic on Protestantism and Lincoln, the very meaning of charity has become altered. As I have argued, not even Lincoln simplistically identified charity with the globalist spread of equality (as his views on the proposed colonization of freed slaves illustrates). Certainly, the most universalistically minded of America's leaders, like Jefferson, did not make this connection. Yet in debates over foreign policy in the cold war period, there were subtle attempts to associate the spread of Christian charity with support for democracy itself. Although there had also been similar efforts on the part of Protestant clergymen during World War I, they tended to lack intellectual rigor and faced popular disillusionment with interventionist policies after the war ended.

The conflict between two schools of foreign policy in the post–World War II period provides a context for conventional thought on the changeable meaning of democracy, charity, and Lincoln's legacy in an age of American global hegemony. The emergence of the "realist" school in foreign policy has usually been portrayed as one largely premised on national self-interest, without regard for moral concerns or commitments. In perfect juxtaposition, a "moral" or "idealist" school emerged during the cold war that called on America to support the cause of democratization and therefore live up to the nation's most cherished ideals. Obviously, this dualism is a simplistic one, since few idealists have been totally oblivious to the limits imposed by reality. Yet it has

11. Gottfried, "Invincible Wilsonian Matrix," 250.

been highly advantageous for American leaders who are committed to democracy as the best regime to portray the realists as uncharitable proponents of a cold-blooded foreign policy that does an injustice to the ideals of the republic, especially the legacy of Lincoln.

The influential liberal Christian theologian Reinhold Niebuhr portrayed realism in just this light, particularly in his critique of the ideas of that classic defender of realism in foreign policy, George Kennan. Niebuhr, who prided himself on being a realistic opponent of abstract utopians in politics—those whom he branded the "children of light"—faulted Kennan for simply advocating a realpolitik policy of "national interest." The foundation of this policy was pure "egotism." Niebuhr chastised Kennan for advising Americans to be "less certain that we know what is good for others." As a result of this "egotistical" thinking, Kennan was merely advocating the employment of "technocratic skills" rather than "genuine charity" to guide foreign policy.[12]

As an admirer of Lincoln, Niebuhr believed that the president rightly understood charity as the recognition that all human beings are too flawed to justify a "simple moral resolution" to complex problems of injustice.[13] Niebuhr therefore prided himself on following "Lincoln's model" of avoiding both the Scylla of heartless realism and the Charybdis of naive moral sentimentalism. Yet Niebuhr was not necessarily as resistant to utopianism as it may appear, for he never doubted that American democratic ideals are the best ideals for all of humanity, even though he had doubts about their particular implementation during the cold war. As his neoconservative admirer Michael Novak has contended, Niebuhr was certain that a truly healthy society, not just for Americans but for all human beings, requires the "trinity of goods": freedom, community, and justice. Liberty and equality for all constitute the principle of justice. In short, it is America's mission to actualize this trinity for the world: Novak's critique of socialist liberation theology of the 1970s takes its inspiration from Niebuhr's support for liberal democratic capitalism as the only viable regime for all human beings. Moreover, Niebuhr was convinced that a true American Christian must support this type of regime.[14] Indeed, his most famous statement on democracy implied as much: "Man's capacity for justice makes democracy possible, but man's

12. Niebuhr, *The Irony of American History,* 147–50.
13. Ibid., 171–73.
14. See Novak, *The Spirit of Democratic Capitalism,* 318–24.

inclination towards injustice makes democracy necessary." It is "necessary," then, for believers to support one regime over all others, since only this regime can restrain human sinfulness.

Like Novak, Niebuhr's many admirers (on the Left and Right) have praised his political theology for striking the right balance between realism and idealism. Still, how realistic and ethical is it to support just one type of regime for all of humanity? Kennan, whose ideas Niebuhr and others falsely stereotyped as amorally realistic, challenged the idea of democratic universalism on both realistic *and* charitable grounds. In warning that Americans must never assume that they know what is good for others, Kennan was appealing to charity, not, as Niebuhr thought, to mere power politics. In one of his earliest postwar studies of American-Soviet relations, Kennan warned his countrymen to refrain from judging foreigners "by the extent to which they contrive to be like ourselves."[15] This temptation came out of the dubious assumption that all human beings are potential democrats at heart. Well into the 1970s, when Kennan was reflecting on a possible thawing in the cold war, he still warned that Americans should not assume that democracy "is the natural state of most of mankind." Moreover, it is far from obvious that democracy is the "best course" for peoples who have no experience of politics apart from authoritarian rule. Finally, America should not "guarantee" the liberties of the world on a global scale.[16]

Kennan's influence has largely dissipated since the end of the cold war, particularly in a context when it is no longer fashionable to question democratic universalism, even though Kennan defended a position that old-style conservatives welcomed during the cold war.[17] What likely accounts for this diminished appreciation for Kennan, whom neoconservative and liberal critics still stereotype as a realist without concern for ethics, is the failure to understand that Kennan was invoking true charity as the basis for a realistic foreign policy.[18] His critic Niebuhr could

15. Kennan, *American Diplomacy, 1900–1950,* 135. See also his *Realities of American Foreign Policy,* 99.

16. Kennan, *The Cloud of Danger: Current Realities of American Foreign Policy,* 41–43.

17. See Scott McConnell, "The Good Strategist."

18. See Natan Sharansky, *The Case for Democracy,* 69–72. There are exceptions. In *Wilson's Ghost,* McNamara and Blight portray Kennan as an "anti-Wilsonian" who still believes that America should lead by "moral example" while refraining from telling others how to run their affairs (164).

never explain how it is charitable to assume, without evidence, that all human beings desire a liberal democratic capitalist regime. Moreover, Niebuhr's use of Lincoln is suspect, since this president never systematically equated charity with democracy on a global scale, and was quite content to show "realism" toward Russian-Polish relations of his time. The fact that Kennan simply advised that Americans make the effort to study other peoples on their own terms, not just American terms, sounds more akin to humility and honesty than just cold-blooded realism. Such an investigation might be uncomfortable to democratic universalists who believe in a common human nature crying for liberty and equality: certainly, Kennan's view that Americans and Chinese have different ideas of sin and mercy would be politically incorrect today.[19] In setting up a simplistic opposition between tyranny and democracy, any regime that is not a democracy must be inferior. (Certainly, neoconservative admirers of Leo Strauss tend to consider tyrants as "mad," as Plato taught, and therefore not worthy of relation with America.) A more informed foreign policy of true charity could only help America's relations with the world.

In contrast, if America's leaders simplistically equate ethics with a quasi-religious mission to spread democracy, they may continue to harm the very image and stability of the nation. The brutal fact is that even a superpower cannot end tyrannies on a global scale, as President Bush declared in 2005. If the end of tyranny became the stated policy of the United States, then the nation must be committed (for the sake of moral consistency) to pressure its allies, many of whom just happen to be dictatorships, to become more democratic over time. The potential for charges of hypocrisy is enormous. When liberal democrats in the years immediately following World War II pressed for the democratization of Franco's Spain, they faced the legitimate accusation that this new policy turn was a radical departure from the ease with which America had been aligned with a far worse tyranny, that of Stalin's Russia during World War II.[20] If the spread of democracy is truly the mission of America, then any support for tyranny, no matter how prudent, must be a sin. This political theology can only strain a political system like America's.

19. McConnell, "The Good Strategist," 9–10.
20. See Kendall, *Conservative Affirmation*, 230–31; and Kendall, *Willmoore Kendall Contra Mundum*, 255–70.

In the simplest terms, many peoples may not have a hankering for freedom, as Western democracies have defined it. Liberals who look forward to the "realism" of the Obama presidency, after having faulted the Bush administration for irresponsibly managing wars of democratic liberation, should pose some tough questions: Do *all* peoples charitably desire freedom for themselves as well as others? Do they understand freedom in the same way? It will be difficult, even after a period of failed interventions, for many Americans to abandon the mythology of a cross-cultural love of freedom that enjoys acceptance among Republicans and Democrats alike. If America's leaders are still tempted, even after the folly of the Iraq war, to read into Lincoln's legacy universalistic pretensions for democracy building that are neither realistic nor charitable, they will continue to distort both the republic's past and its future.

Bibliography

⟿

Ackerman, Spencer. "The Obama Doctrine." *American Prospect,* March 24, 2008.

Adams, John. *The Political Writings of John Adams: Representative Selections.* Ed. George A. Peek Jr. Indianapolis: Bobbs-Merrill, 1954.

Ahmed, Akbar S. *Islam under Siege: Living Dangerously in a Post- Honor World.* Cambridge: Polity, 2003.

Altizer, Thomas J. "The Theological Conflict between Strauss and Voegelin." In *Faith and Political Philosophy: The Correspondence between Leo Strauss and Eric Voegelin, 1934-1964,* ed. Peter Emberley and Barry Cooper. University Park: Pennsylvania State University Press, 1993.

Anastaplo, George. *Abraham Lincoln: A Constitutional Biography.* Lanham, Md.: Rowman and Littlefield, 1999.

Anderson, Dwight G. *Abraham Lincoln: The Quest for Immortality.* New York: Alfred A. Knopf, 1982.

Arendt, Hannah. *On Revolution.* London: Penguin, 1990.

Arnhart, Larry. "Statesmanship as Magnanimity: Classical, Christian, and Modern." *Polity* 16 (Winter 1983): 262–83.

Aron, Raymond. "The Secular Religions." In *The Dawn of Universal History.* Chicago: University of Chicago Press, 2002.

Babbitt, Irving. *Democracy and Leadership.* Indianapolis: Liberty Fund, 1979.

Barton, William E. *The Soul of Abraham Lincoln.* 1920. Reprint, Urbana: University of Illinois Press, 2005.

Bary, Wm. Theodore de. *The Trouble with Confucianism.* Cambridge: Harvard University Press, 1985.

Bellah, Robert N. *The Broken Covenant: American Civil Religion in Time of Trial.* 2d ed. Chicago: University of Chicago Press, 1992.

Bennett, William J. "Morality, Character, and American Foreign Policy." In *Present Dangers: Crisis and Opportunity in American Foreign and Defense Policy,* ed. Robert Kagan and William Kristol. San Francisco: Encounter Books, 2000.

Berns, Walter. *Making Patriots.* Chicago: University of Chicago Press, 2001.

Bloom, Allan. *The Closing of the American Mind: How Higher Education Has Failed Democracy and Impoverished the Souls of Today's Students.* New York: Simon and Schuster, 1987.

Bloom, Harold. *The American Religion: The Emergence of the Post-Christian Nation.* New York: Touchstone Books, 1992.

Bradford, M. E. *A Better Guide than Reason: Studies in the American Revolution.* LaSalle, Ill.: Sherwood Sugden, 1979.

——. "Dividing the House: The Gnosticism of Lincoln's Political Rhetoric." *Modern Age* (Winter 1979): 11–24.

——. "The Lincoln Legacy: A Long View." In *Lincoln's American Dream: Clashing Political Perspectives,* ed. Kenneth L. Deutsch and Joseph R. Fornieri. Washington, D.C.: Potomac Books, 2005.

Brown, David S. *Richard Hofstadter: An Intellectual Biography.* Chicago: University of Chicago Press, 2006.

Bryan, William Jennings. "The Prince of Peace." In *William Jennings Bryan: Selections,* ed. Ray Ginger. Indianapolis: Bobbs-Merrill, 1998.

Burleigh, Michael. *Earthly Powers: The Clash of Religion and Politics in Europe, from the French Revolution to the Great War.* New York: Harper Perennial, 2005.

——. *Sacred Causes: The Clash of Religion and Politics, from the Great War to the War on Terror.* New York: HarperCollins, 2007.

Carey, George W. "Thunder on the Right, Lightning from the Left." *Modern Age* (Spring 1981): 132–42.

Ceaser, James W. "The Great Divide: American Interventionism and Its Opponents." In *Present Dangers: Crisis and Opportunity in American Foreign and Defense Policy,* ed. Robert Kagan and William Kristol. San Francisco: Encounter Books, 2000.

——. *Nature and History in American Political Development: A Debate.* Cambridge: Harvard University Press, 2006.

Churchill, Winston S. *A History of the English-Speaking Peoples: The Great Democracies.* New York: Bantam, 1958.

Cooper, Barry. *New Political Religions; or, An Analysis of Modern Terrorism.* Columbia: University of Missouri Press, 2004.

Coulanges, Fustel de. *The Ancient City: A Study of the Religions, Laws, and Institutions of Greece and Rome.* Garden City, N.Y.: Doubleday Anchor, 1956.

Cox, Harvey. *The Secular City: Secularization and Urbanization in Theological Perspective.* New York: Macmillan, 1965.

Crawford, Alan. *Thunder on the Right: The "New Right" and the Politics of Resentment.* New York: Pantheon, 1980.

Crozier, Michael, Samuel P. Huntington, and Joji Watanuki. *The Crisis of Democracy: Report on the Governability of Democracies to the Trilateral Commission.* New York: New York University Press, 1975.

DiLorenzo, Thomas J. *Lincoln Unmasked: What You're Not Supposed to Know about Dishonest Abe.* New York: Crown Forum, 2006.

——. *The Real Lincoln: A New Look at Abraham Lincoln, His Agenda, and an Unnecessary War.* New York: Three Rivers Press, 2003.

Donald, David. "Getting Right with Lincoln." In *Lincoln Reconsidered: Essays of the Civil War,* ed. David Donald. New York: Vintage, 1961.

Drinnon, Richard. *Facing West: The Metaphysics of Indian-Hating and Empire Building.* Norman: University of Oklahoma Press, 1997.

Drury, Shadia B. *Leo Strauss and the American Right.* New York: St. Martin's Press, 1997.

Fackenheim, Emil L. *To Mend the World: Foundations of Future Jewish Thought.* New York: Schocken Books, 1982.

The Federalist. New York: Modern Library, 1937.

Feldmann, Linda. "Candidate Clinton Goes Public with Her Private Faith." *Christian Science Monitor,* December 20, 2007.

Fornieri, Joseph R. *Abraham Lincoln's Political Faith.* DeKalb: Northern Illinois University Press, 2003.

Fortin, Ernest L. "Rational Theologians and Irrational Philosophers: A Straussian Perspective." In *Classical Christianity and the Political Order: Reflections on the Theologico-Political Problem,* ed. J. Brian Benestad. Lanham, Md.: Rowman and Littlefield, 1996.

Fox-Genovese, Elizabeth, and Eugene D. Genovese. *The Mind of the Master Class: History and Faith in the Southern Slaveholders' Worldview.* Cambridge: Cambridge University Press, 2005.

Francis, Samuel. *Beautiful Losers: Essays on the Failure of American Conservatism.* Columbia: University of Missouri Press, 1993.

——. *Revolution from the Middle.* Raleigh: Middle American Press, 1997.

Frederickson, George M. *Big Enough to Be Inconsistent: Abraham Lincoln Confronts Slavery and Race.* Cambridge: Harvard University Press, 2008.

Freud, Sigmund. *Civilization and Its Discontents.* Trans. James Strachey. New York: W. W. Norton, 1961.

Frohnen, Bruce P. "Lincoln and the Problem of Political Religion." In *Lincoln's American Dream: Clashing Political Perspectives,* ed. Kenneth L. Deutsch and Joseph R. Fornieri. Washington, D.C.: Potomac Books, 2005.

Fukuyama, Francis. *America at the Crossroads: Democracy, Power, and the Neoconservative Legacy.* New Haven: Yale University Press, 2006.

——. *The End of History and the Last Man.* New York: Simon and Schuster, 1992.

——. *Our Post-Human Future: Consequences of the Biotechnology Revolution.* New York: Farrar, Straus, and Giroux, 2002.

——. *Trust: The Social Virtues and the Creation of Prosperity.* New York: Free Press, 1995.

Gamble, Richard M. "The Problem of Lincoln in Babbitt's Thought." *Humanitas* 15, no. 1 (2002): 69–80.

——. *The War for Righteousness: Progressive Christianity, the Great War, and the Rise of the Messianic Nation.* Wilmington, Del.: ISI Books, 2003.

Gelernter, David. *Americanism: The Fourth Great Western Religion.* New York: Doubleday, 2007.

Gottfried, Paul Edward. *Conservatism in America: Making Sense of the American Right.* London: Palgrave, 2007.

——. "The Invincible Wilsonian Matrix: Universal Human Rights Once Again." *Orbis* (Spring 2007): 239–50.

——. *Multiculturalism and the Politics of Guilt: Toward a Secular Theocracy.* Columbia: University of Missouri Press, 2002.

——. *The Strange Death of Marxism: The European Left in the New Millennium.* Columbia: University of Missouri Press, 2005.

Grant, George. *Lament for a Nation: The Defeat of Canadian Nationalism.* 1965. Reprint, Ottawa: Carleton University Press, 1991.

Guelzo, Allen C. *Abraham Lincoln: Redeemer President.* Grand Rapids: Eerdmans, 1999.

Hart, Jeffrey. *The Making of the American Conservative Mind: "National Review" and Its Times.* Wilmington, Del.: ISI Books, 2005.

Hartz, Louis. *The Liberal Tradition in America: An Interpretation of American Political Thought since the Revolution*. New York: Harcourt Brace, 1955.

Havers, Grant. "Leo Strauss, Willmoore Kendall, and the Meaning of Conservatism." *Humanitas* 18, nos. 1–2 (2005): 15–25.

———. "The Meaning of 'Neo-Paganism': Rethinking the Relation between Nature and Freedom." In *Humanity at the Turning Point: Rethinking Nature, Culture, and Freedom,* ed. Sonja Servomaa, 159–69. Helsinki: Renvall Institute of Publications, 2006.

———. "Romanticism and Universalism: The Case of Leo Strauss." *Dialogue and Universalism* 12, nos. 6–7 (2002): 155–67.

———. "Was Spinoza a Liberal?" *Political Science Reviewer* 36 (2007): 143–74.

Hegel, G. W. F. *Early Theological Writings.* Trans. T. M. Knox. Philadelphia: University of Pennsylvania Press, 1948.

Hertz, Emanuel. *The Hidden Lincoln: From the Letters and Papers of William H. Herndon.* New York: Viking Press, 1938.

Himmelfarb, Gertrude. *The Roads to Modernity: The British, French, and American Enlightenments.* New York: Vintage, 2004.

Hofstadter, Richard. *The American Political Tradition and the Men Who Made It.* New York: Vintage, 1989.

———. *Anti-Intellectualism in American Life.* New York: Vintage, 1963.

———. *The Paranoid Style in American Politics, and Other Essays.* New York: Vintage, 1967.

Holland, Matthew. *Bonds of Affection: Civic Charity and the Making of America—Winthrop, Jefferson, and Lincoln.* Washington, D.C.: Georgetown University Press, 2007.

Holloway, Carson. "Christianity, Magnanimity, and Statesmanship." *Review of Politics* 61 (1999): 581–604.

Holmes, Stephen. *The Anatomy of Antiliberalism.* Cambridge: Harvard University Press, 1994.

Huntington, Samuel. *Who Are We? The Challenges to America's National Identity.* New York: Simon and Schuster, 2004.

Ilkenberry, G. John, and Anne-Marie Slaughter. *Forging a World of Liberty under Law: U.S. National Security in the Twenty-first Century.* Princeton: Woodrow Wilson School of Public and International Affairs, 2006.

Jaffa, Harry V. *American Conservatism and the American Founding.* Claremont, Calif.: Claremont Institute, 1984.

———. *The American Founding as the Best Regime: The Bonding of Civil and Religious Liberty.* Claremont, Calif.: Claremont Institute, 1990.

———. *Crisis of the House Divided: An Interpretation of the Issues in the Lincoln-Douglas Debates.* Chicago: University of Chicago Press, 1982.

———. *How to Think about the American Revolution: A Bicentennial Celebration.* Durham: Carolina Academic Press, 1978.

———. *A New Birth of Freedom: Abraham Lincoln and the Coming of the Civil War.* Lanham, Md.: Rowman and Littlefield, 2000.

———. *Original Intent and the Framers of the Constitution.* Washington, D.C.: Regnery Gateway, 1994.

———. *Thomism and Aristotelianism: A Study of the Commentary by Thomas Aquinas on the "Nicomachean Ethics."* Chicago: University of Chicago Press, 1952.

Jefferson, Thomas. "First Inaugural Address." In *The Inaugural Addresses of the Presidents,* ed. John Gabriel Hunt. New York: Gramercy Books, 1997.

———. *The Life and Selected Writings of Thomas Jefferson.* Ed. Adrienne Koch and William Peden. New York: Modern Library, 1998.

Kagan, Robert. *Dangerous Nation: America's Place in the World, from Its Earliest Days to the Dawn of the Twentieth Century.* New York: Alfred A. Knopf, 2006.

Kass, Leon. *Beyond Therapy: Biotechnology and the Pursuit of Happiness.* New York: ReganBooks, 2003.

Kendall, Willmoore. *The Conservative Affirmation in America.* Chicago: Gateway Editions, 1985.

———. "The Function of Intelligence." *World Politics* 1, no. 4 (July 1949).

———. *John Locke and the Doctrine of Majority-Rule.* Urbana: University of Illinois Press, 1965.

———. *Willmoore Kendall Contra Mundum.* Ed. Nellie D. Kendall. New York: University Press of America, 1994.

Kendall, Willmoore, and George W. Carey. *The Basic Symbols of the American Political Tradition.* Washington, D.C.: Catholic University of America Press, 1995.

Kendall, Willmoore, and Frederick D. Wilhelmsen, "Cicero and the Politics of Public Orthodoxy." In *Christianity and Political Philosophy,* ed. Frederick D. Wilhelmsen. Athens: University of Georgia Press, 1978.

Kennan, George F. *American Diplomacy, 1900–1950.* Chicago: University of Chicago Press, 1951.

——. *The Cloud of Danger: Current Realities of American Foreign Policy.* Boston: Little, Brown, 1977.

——. *Realities of American Foreign Policy.* Princeton: Princeton University Press, 1954.

Kesler, Charles R. "Democracy and the Bush Doctrine." In *The Right War? The Conservative Debate on Iraq,* ed. Gary Rosen. Cambridge: Cambridge University Press, 2005.

Kirk, Russell. *The American Cause.* Wilmington, Del.: ISI Books, 2002.

——. *The Conservative Mind: From Burke to Eliot.* 7th ed. 1953. Reprint, Washington, D.C.: Regnery Gateway, 2001.

Kirkpatrick, Jeane. *Dictatorships and Double Standards: Rationalism and Reason in Politics.* New York: AEI Press, 1982.

Kristol, Irving. "The American Revolution as a Successful Revolution." In *The American Revolution: Three Views.* New York: American Brands, 1975.

Kristol, William, and David Brooks. "What Ails the Right?" *Wall Street Journal,* May 22, 2001.

Kurth, James. "George W. Bush and the Protestant Deformation." *American Interest* 1, no. 2 (Winter 2005): 4–16.

Lansdale, Edward Geary. *In the Midst of Wars: An American's Mission in Southeast Asia.* New York: Fordham University Press, 1991.

Levine, Andrew. *The American Ideology: A Critique.* New York: Routledge, 2004.

Lincoln, Abraham. *The Collected Works of Abraham Lincoln.* Ed. Roy P. Basler. 8 vols. New Brunswick: Rutgers University Press, 1953.

Longley, Clifford. *Chosen People: The Big Idea That Shapes England and America.* London: Hodder and Stoughton, 2002.

Lord, Carnes. *The Modern Prince: What Leaders Need to Know Now.* New Haven: Yale University Press, 2004.

Lukacs, John. *Democracy and Populism: Fear and Hatred.* New Haven: Yale University Press, 2005.

——. *A New Republic: A History of the United States in the Twentieth Century.* New Haven: Yale University Press, 2004.

Mahdi, Muhsin. *Alfarabi and the Foundation of Islamic Political Philosophy.* Chicago: University of Chicago Press, 2001.

Manela, Erez. *The Wilsonian Moment: Self-Determination and the International Origins of Anticolonial Nationalism.* Oxford: Oxford University Press, 2007.

McAllister, Ted V. *Revolt against Modernity: Leo Strauss, Eric Voegelin, and the Search for a Postliberal Order.* Lawrence: University Press of Kansas, 1995.

McConnell, Scott. "The Good Strategist." *American Conservative,* June 6, 2005, 7–10.

McNamara, Robert S., and James G. Blight. *Wilson's Ghost: Reducing the Risk of Conflict, Killing, and Catastrophe in the Twenty-first Century.* New York: PublicAffairs, 2001.

Merrill, Clark A. "Leo Strauss's Indictment of Christian Politics." *Review of Politics* 62, no. 1 (2000): 77–106.

Miller, Charles A. *Jefferson and Nature: An Interpretation.* Baltimore: Johns Hopkins University Press, 1988.

Miller, William Lee. "Lincoln's Second Inaugural: The Zenith of Statecraft." In *Lincoln's American Dream: Clashing Political Perspectives,* ed. Kenneth L. Deutsch and Joseph R. Fornieri, 333–50. Washington, D.C.: Potomac Books, 2005.

Morel, Lucas E. *Lincoln's Sacred Effort: Defining Religion's Role in American Self-Government.* Lanham, Md.: Lexington Books, 2000.

Murley, John A. "On the 'Calhounism' of Willmoore Kendall." In *Willmoore Kendall: Maverick of American Conservatives,* ed. John A. Murley and John E. Alvis. Lanham, Md.: Lexington Books, 2002.

Murray, John Courtney. *We Hold These Truths: Catholic Reflections on the American Proposition.* Lanham, Md.: Rowman and Littlefield, 1960.

Nash, George H. *The Conservative Intellectual Movement in America since 1945.* New York: Basic Books, 1976.

——. "The Place of Willmoore Kendall in American Conservatism." In *Willmoore Kendall: Maverick of American Conservatives,* ed. John A. Murley and John E. Alvis. Lanham, Md.: Lexington Books, 2002.

Niebuhr, Reinhold. *An Interpretation of Christian Ethics.* New York: Living Age, 1959.

——. *The Irony of American History.* New York: Charles Scribner's Sons, 1962.

Noll, Mark A. *America's God: From Jonathan Edwards to Abraham Lincoln.* Oxford: Oxford University Press, 2002.

——. *The Civil War as a Theological Crisis.* Chapel Hill: University of North Carolina Press, 2006.

——. "The Contingencies of American Republicanism: An Alternative Account of Protestantism and the American Founding." In *Protestantism and the American Founding,* ed. Thomas S. Engeman and Michael P. Zuckert. Notre Dame: University of Notre Dame Press, 2004.

Norton, Anne. *Leo Strauss and the Politics of American Empire.* New Haven: Yale University Press, 2004.

Novak, Michael. *On Two Wings: Humble Faith and Common Sense at the American Founding.* San Francisco: Encounter Books, 2002.

———. *The Spirit of Democratic Capitalism.* New York: Madison Books, 1991.

Nygren, Anders. *Agape and Eros.* Trans. Philip S. Watson. New York: Harper and Row, 1969.

Oakes, James. *The Radical and the Republican: Frederick Douglass, Abraham Lincoln, and the Triumph of Antislavery Politics.* New York: W. W. Norton, 2007.

Oates, Stephen B. "A Momentous Decree: Commentary on 'Lincoln and Black Freedom.'" In *The Historian's Lincoln: Pseudohistory, Psychohistory, and History,* ed. Gabor S. Boritt. Urbana: University of Illinois Press, 1996.

Obama, Barack. "Renewing American Leadership." *Foreign Affairs* (July–August 2007).

O'Connor, Thomas H. *The Disunited States: The Era of Civil War and Reconstruction.* 2d ed. New York: Harper and Row, 1978.

Olasky, Marvin. "Woodrow Wilson's Folly: The Private and Public Life of a President." In *Philosophy, Culture, and Society.* Washington, D.C.: Capital Research Center, 1998.

O'Meara, Michael. *New Culture, New Right: Anti-Liberalism in Postmodern Europe.* Bloomington, Ind.: IstBooks, 2004.

Orwin, Clifford. "The Unraveling of Christianity in America." *Public Interest* 155 (Spring 2004).

Page, Thomas Nelson. "The Southern People during Reconstruction." In *Reconstruction in the South, 1865–1877: Firsthand Accounts of the American South after the Civil War, by Southerners and Northerners.* New York: Noonday Press, 1965.

Paine, Thomas. *The Age of Reason: Being an Investigation of True and Fabulous Theology.* Ed. Moncure Daniel Conway. Mineola, N.Y.: Dover, 2004.

———. *Common Sense.* Mineola, N.Y.: Dover, 1997.

Palmer, Michael. "Historicism, Relativism, and Nihilism versus American Natural Right in *Casablanca.*" In *Political Philosophy Comes to Rick's: "Casablanca" and American Civic Culture,* ed.

James Pontuso. Lanham, Md.: Lexington Books, 2005.

Pangle, Thomas L. *The Spirit of Modern Republicanism: The Moral Vision of the American Founders and the Philosophy of Locke.* Chicago: University of Chicago Press, 1988.

Pestritto, Ronald J. *Woodrow Wilson and the Roots of Modern Liberalism.* Lanham, Md.: Rowman and Littlefield, 2005.

Peterson, Merrill D. *Lincoln in American Memory.* New York: Oxford University Press, 1994.

Phillips, Kevin P. *American Theocracy: The Perils and Politics of Radical Religion, Oil, and Borrowed Money in the Twenty-first Century.* New York: Simon and Schuster, 2006.

——. *The Cousins' Wars: Religion, Politics, and the Triumph of Anglo-America.* New York: Basic Books, 1999.

——. *Post-Conservative America: People, Politics, and Ideology in a Time of Crisis.* New York: Random House, 1982.

Pierard, Richard V., and Robert D. Linder. *Civil Religion and the Presidency.* Grand Rapids: Zondervan, 1988.

Podles, Leon J. *The Church Impotent: The Feminization of Christianity.* Dallas: Spence, 1999.

Polka, Brayton. *Between Philosophy and Religion: Spinoza, the Bible, and Modernity.* Vol. 1, *Hermeneutics and Ontology.* Lanham, Md.: Lexington Books, 2007.

——. *Between Philosophy and Religion: Spinoza, the Bible, and Modernity.* Vol. 2, *Politics and Ethics.* Lanham, Md.: Lexington Books, 2007.

——. *The Dialectic of Biblical Critique.* New York: St. Martin's Press, 1986.

Pontuso, James. "*Casablanca* and the Paradoxical Truth of Stereotyping: Rick and the American Character." In *Political Philosophy Comes to Rick's: "Casablanca" and American Civic Culture.* Lanham, Md.: Lexington Books, 2005.

Powell, Jim. *Wilson's War: How Woodrow Wilson's Great Blunder Led to Hitler, Lenin, Stalin, and World War II.* New York: Crown Forum, 2005.

Ranieri, John J. *Disturbing Revelation: Leo Strauss, Eric Voegelin, and the Bible.* Columbia: University of Missouri Press, 2009.

Ranney, Austin, and Willmoore Kendall. *Democracy and the American Party System.* New York: Harcourt, Brace, 1956.

Rosen, Stanley. *Plato's "Republic": A Study.* New Haven: Yale University Press, 2005.

Rossiter, Clinton. *Conservatism: The Thankless Persuasion.* 2d ed. New York: Vintage, 1962.

———. *Seedtime of the Republic: The Origin of the American Tradition of Political Liberty.* New York: Harcourt, Brace, and World, 1953.

Ryn, Claes G. *America the Virtuous: The Crisis of Democracy and the Quest for Empire.* New Brunswick, N.J.: Transaction, 2003.

Schall, James V. *Christianity and Politics.* Boston: Daughters of St. Paul, 1981.

Scotchie, Joseph. *Revolt from the Heartland: The Struggle for an Authentic Conservatism.* New Brunswick, N.J.: Transaction, 2004.

Shain, Barry Alan. *The Myth of American Individualism: The Protestant Origins of American Political Thought.* Princeton: Princeton University Press, 1994.

Sharansky, Natan. *The Case for Democracy.* New York: PublicAffairs, 2006.

Sharlet, Jeff. "Through a Glass Darkly: How the Christian Right Is Reimagining U.S. History." *Harper's,* December 2006.

Smith, Page. *Rediscovering Christianity: A History of Modern Democracy and the Christian Ethic.* New York: St. Martin's Press, 1994.

Smith, Rogers M. "What If God Was One of Us? The Challenges of Studying Foundational Political Concepts." In *Nature and History in American Political Development: A Debate,* ed. James W. Ceaser. Cambridge: Harvard University Press, 2006.

Sombart, Werner. *The Jews and Modern Capitalism.* Trans. M. Epstein. Kitchener, Ontario: Batoche Books, 2001.

Spinoza, Benedict. *Spinoza's Theologico-Political Treatise.* Trans. Martin D. Yaffe. Newburyport, Mass.: Focus Philosophical Library, 2004.

———. *"A Theologico-Political Treatise" and "A Political Treatise."* Trans. R. H. Elwes. New York: Dover, 1951.

Steigmann-Gall, Richard. *The Holy Reich: Nazi Conceptions of Christianity, 1919–1945.* Cambridge: Cambridge University Press, 2003.

Stelzer, Irwin. "Neoconservatives and Their Critics." In *The Neocon Reader,* ed. Irwin Stelzer. New York: Grove Press, 2004.

Strauss, Leo. *The City and Man.* Chicago: University of Chicago Press, 1964.

———. "Jerusalem and Athens: Some Preliminary Reflections." In *Studies in Political Philosophy,* ed. Thomas L. Pangle. Chicago: University of Chicago Press, 1983.

——. *Natural Right and History.* Chicago: University of Chicago Press, 1953.

——. *On Plato's "Symposium."* Chicago: University of Chicago Press, 2003.

——. *On Tyranny, Including the Strauss-Kojève Correspondence.* Ed. Victor Gourevitch and Michael S. Roth. Chicago: University of Chicago Press, 2000.

——. "Plato." In *An Introduction to Political Philosophy: Ten Essays by Leo Strauss,* ed. Hilail Gildin. Detroit: Wayne State University Press, 1989.

——. "Progress or Return? The Contemporary Crisis in Western Civilization." In *An Introduction to Political Philosophy: Ten Essays by Leo Strauss,* ed. Hilail Gildin. Detroit: Wayne State University Press, 1989.

——. *Spinoza's Critique of Religion.* Trans. E. M. Sinclair. New York: Schocken Books, 1965.

——. *Thoughts on Machiavelli.* Chicago: University of Chicago Press, 1958.

——. *What Is Political Philosophy? and Other Studies.* Chicago: University of Chicago Press, 1959.

Tatalovich, Raymond, and Thomas S. Engeman. *The Presidency and Political Science: Two Hundred Years of Constitutional Debate.* Baltimore: Johns Hopkins University Press, 2003.

Thurow, Glen E. *Abraham Lincoln and the American Political Religion.* Albany: SUNY Press, 1976.

Tocqueville, Alexis de. *Democracy in America.* Trans. George Lawrence. Garden City, N.Y.: Anchor, 1969.

Todorov, Tzvetan. *The Conquest of America: The Question of the Other.* Trans. Richard Howard. New York: HarperPerennial, 1982.

Troeltsch, Ernst. *Protestantism and Progress: The Significance of Protestantism for the Rise of the Modern World.* Philadelphia: Fortress Press, 1986.

Trueblood, Elton. *Abraham Lincoln: Theologian of American Anguish.* New York: Harper and Row, 1973.

Viereck, Peter. "The Philosophical 'New Conservatism.'" In *The Radical Right,* ed. Daniel Bell. New York: Anchor Books, 1964.

——. "The Revolt against the Elite." In *The Radial Right,* ed. Daniel Bell. New York: Anchor Books, 1964.

Voegelin, Eric. *Israel and Revelation.* Ed. Maurice Hogan. Vol. 1, *Order* and History. Vol. 14 of *The Collected Works of Eric Voegelin.* Columbia: University of Missouri Press, 2001.

——. *The New Science of Politics.* Chicago: University of Chicago Press, 1952.

——. "The Political Religions." In *Modernity without Restraint: The Political Religions, the New Science of Politics, and Science, Politics, and Gnosticism,* ed. Manfred Henningsen. Vol. 5 of *The Collected Works of Eric Voegelin.* Columbia: University of Missouri Press, 2000.

Walzer, Michael. *Exodus and Revolution.* New York: Basic Books, 1985.

Weaver, Richard M. *The Ethics of Rhetoric.* Davis, Calif.: Hermagoras Press, 1985.

——. *In Defense of Tradition: Collected Shorter Writings of Richard M. Weaver, 1929–1963.* Indianapolis: Liberty Fund, 2000.

West, Thomas G. "The Transformation of Protestant Theology as a Condition of the American Revolution." In *Protestantism and the American Founding,* ed. Thomas S. Engeman and Michael P. Zuckert. Notre Dame: University of Notre Dame Press, 2004.

——. *Vindicating the Founders: Race, Sex, Class, and Justice in the Origins of America.* Lanham, Md.: Rowman and Littlefield, 1997.

Wilhelmsen, Frederick D., ed. *Christianity and Political Philosophy.* Athens: University of Georgia Press, 1978.

Will, George F. "The Slow Undoing: The Assault on, and Underestimation of, Nationality." In *The Neocon Reader,* ed. Irwin Stelzer. New York: Grove Press, 2004.

Wills, Garry. *Explaining America: "The Federalist."* New York: Penguin, 2001.

——. *Lincoln at Gettysburg: The Words That Remade America.* New York: Simon and Schuster, 1992.

Wilson, Francis G. "The Political Science of Willmoore Kendall." *Modern Age* 16 (Winter 1972): 38–47.

Wilson, Woodrow. "Abraham Lincoln: A Man of the People." In *Woodrow Wilson: Essential Writings and Speeches of the Scholar-President,* ed. Mario DiNunzio. New York: New York University Press, 2006.

——. "The Ideals of America." In vol. 12 of *The Papers of Woodrow Wilson, 1900–1901,* ed. Arthur S. Link. Princeton: Princeton University Press, 1972.

——. "The Reconstruction of the Southern States." In *Reconstruction in Retrospect: Views from the Turn of the Century,* ed. Richard N.

Current. Baton Rouge: Louisiana State University Press, 1969.

———. "Second Inaugural Address." In *The Inaugural Addresses of the Presidents, from George Washington to George W. Bush,* ed. John Gabriel Hunt. New York: Gramercy Books, 1997.

Winthrop, John. "A Modell of Christian Charity." In *God's New Israel: Religious Interpretations of American Destiny,* ed. Conrad Cherry. Chapel Hill: University of North Carolina Press, 1998.

Wish, Harvey. Introduction to *Reconstruction in the South, 1865- 1877: Firsthand Accounts of the American South after the Civil War, by Southerners and Northerners.* New York: Noonday Press, 1965.

Wolfowitz, Paul. "Statesmanship in the New Century." In *Present Dangers: Crisis and Opportunity in American Foreign and Defense Policy,* ed. Robert Kagan and William Kristol. San Francisco: Encounter Books, 2000.

Wood, Gordon S. *The Radicalism of the American Revolution.* New York: Vintage, 1991.

Ye-Or, Bat. *The Dhimmi: Jews and Christians under Islam.* Floram, N.J.: Fairleigh Dickinson University Press, 1985.

Yoder, John Howard. *The Politics of Jesus.* Grand Rapids: Eerdmans, 1994.

Zakaria, Fareed. *The Future of Freedom: Illiberal Democracy at Home and Abroad.* New York: W. W. Norton, 2003.

Zuckert, Catherine, and Michael P. Zuckert. *The Truth about Leo Strauss: Political Philosophy and American Democracy.* Chicago: University of Chicago Press, 2006.

Zuckert, Michael P. "Lincoln and the Problem of Civil Religion." In *Lincoln's American Dream: Clashing Political Perspectives,* ed. Kenneth L. Deutsch and Joseph R. Fornieri. Washington, D.C.: Potomac Books, 2005.

———. "Natural Rights and Protestant Politics." In *Protestantism and the American Founding,* ed. Thomas S. Engeman and Michael P. Zuckert. Notre Dame: University of Notre Dame Press, 2004.

———. "Natural Rights and Protestant Politics: A Restatement." In *Protestantism and the American Founding,* ed. Thomas S. Engeman and Michael P. Zuckert. Notre Dame: University of Notre Dame Press, 2004.

Index